Entrepreneurship and Innovation Policy and the Economy 1

T0345929

Entrepreneurship and Innovation Policy and the Economy 1

Edited by
Josh Lerner and Scott Stern

The University of Chicago Press
Chicago and London

NBER Entrepreneurship and Innovation Policy and the Economy, Number 1, 2022

Published annually by The University of Chicago Press.
www.journals.uchicago.edu/EIPE

© 2022 by the National Bureau of Economic Research.

Subscriptions: Individual subscription rates are $63 print + electronic and $30 e only ($15 for students). Institutional print + electronic and e-only rates are tiered according to an institution's type and research output: $102 to $215 (print + electronic), $89 to $187 (e-only). For additional information, including back-issue sales, classroom use, rates for single copies, and prices for institutional full-run access, please visit www.journals.uchicago.edu /TPE/. Free or deeply discounted access is available in most developing nations through the Chicago Emerging Nations Initiative (www.journals.uchicago.edu/ceni/).

Please direct subscription inquiries to Subscription Fulfillment, 1427 E. 60th Street, Chicago, IL 60637-2902. Telephone: (773) 753-3347 or toll free in the United States and Canada (877) 705-1878. Fax: (773) 753-0811 or toll-free (877) 705-1879. E-mail: subscriptions @press.uchicago.edu.

Standing orders: To place a standing order for this book series, please address your request to The University of Chicago Press, Chicago Distribution Center, Attn. Standing Orders/Customer Service, 11030 S. Langley Avenue, Chicago, IL 60628. Telephone toll free in the U.S. and Canada: 1-800-621-2736; or 1-773-702-7000. Fax toll free in the U.S. and Canada: 1-800-621-8476; or 1-773-702-7212.

Single-copy orders: In the U.S., Canada, and the rest of the world, order from your local bookseller or direct from The University of Chicago Press, Chicago Distribution Center, 11030 S. Langley Avenue, Chicago, IL 60628. Telephone toll free in the U.S. and Canada: 1-800-621-2736; or 1-773-702-7000. Fax toll free in the U.S. and Canada: 1-800-621-8476; or 1-773-702-7212. In the U.K. and Europe, order from your local bookseller or direct from The University of Chicago Press, c/o John Wiley Ltd. Distribution Center, 1 Oldlands Way, Bognor Regis, West Sussex PO22 9SA, UK. Telephone 01243 779777 or Fax 01243 820250. E-mail: cs-books@wiley.co.uk.

The University of Chicago Press offers bulk discounts on individual titles to Corporate, Premium and Gift accounts. For information, please write to Sales Department—Special Sales, The University of Chicago Press, 1427 E. 60th Street, Chicago, IL 60637 USA or telephone 1-773-702-7723.

This book was printed and bound in the United States of America.

ISSN: 0892-8649
E-ISSN: 1537-2650
ISBN-13: 978-0-226-82175-7 (pb.:alk.paper)
ISBN-13: 978-0-226-82176-4 (e-book)

Relation of the Directors to the Work and Publications of the NBER

1. The object of the NBER is to ascertain and present to the economics profession, and to the public more generally, important economic facts and their interpretation in a scientific manner without policy recommendations. The Board of Directors is charged with the responsibility of ensuring that the work of the NBER is carried on in strict conformity with this object.

2. The President shall establish an internal review process to ensure that book manuscripts proposed for publication DO NOT contain policy recommendations. This shall apply both to the proceedings of conferences and to manuscripts by a single author or by one or more coauthors but shall not apply to authors of comments at NBER conferences who are not NBER affiliates.

3. No book manuscript reporting research shall be published by the NBER until the President has sent to each member of the Board a notice that a manuscript is recommended for publication and that in the President's opinion it is suitable for publication in accordance with the above principles of the NBER. Such notification will include a table of contents and an abstract or summary of the manuscript's content, a list of contributors if applicable, and a response form for use by Directors who desire a copy of the manuscript for review. Each manuscript shall contain a summary drawing attention to the nature and treatment of the problem studied and the main conclusions reached.

4. No volume shall be published until forty-five days have elapsed from the above notification of intention to publish it. During this period a copy shall be sent to any Director requesting it, and if any Director objects to publication on the grounds that the manuscript contains policy recommendations, the objection will be presented to the author(s) or editor(s). In case of dispute, all members of the Board shall be notified,

and the President shall appoint an ad hoc committee of the Board to decide the matter; thirty days additional shall be granted for this purpose.

5. The President shall present annually to the Board a report describing the internal manuscript review process, any objections made by Directors before publication or by anyone after publication, any disputes about such matters, and how they were handled.

6. Publications of the NBER issued for informational purposes concerning the work of the Bureau, or issued to inform the public of the activities at the Bureau, including but not limited to the NBER Digest and Reporter, shall be consistent with the object stated in paragraph 1. They shall contain a specific disclaimer noting that they have not passed through the review procedures required in this resolution. The Executive Committee of the Board is charged with the review of all such publications from time to time.

7. NBER working papers and manuscripts distributed on the Bureau's web site are not deemed to be publications for the purpose of this resolution, but they shall be consistent with the object stated in paragraph 1. Working papers shall contain a specific disclaimer noting that they have not passed through the review procedures required in this resolution. The NBER's web site shall contain a similar disclaimer. The President shall establish an internal review process to ensure that the working papers and the web site do not contain policy recommendations, and shall report annually to the Board on this process and any concerns raised in connection with it.

8. Unless otherwise determined by the Board or exempted by the terms of paragraphs 6 and 7, a copy of this resolution shall be printed in each NBER publication as described in paragraph 2 above.

Contents

Series Introduction 1
James Poterba

Introduction 3
Josh Lerner and Scott Stern

Entrepreneurship during the COVID-19 Pandemic: Evidence from the Business Formation Statistics 9
John C. Haltiwanger

Closing the Innovation Gap in Pink and Black 43
Lisa D. Cook, Janet Gerson, and Jennifer Kuan

Mapping the Regions, Organizations, and Individuals That Drive Inclusion in the Innovation Economy 67
Mercedes Delgado and Fiona Murray

Funding Risky Research 103
Chiara Franzoni, Paula Stephan, and Reinhilde Veugelers

Crisis Innovation Policy from World War II to COVID-19 135
Daniel P. Gross and Bhaven N. Sampat

Series Introduction

James Poterba, *NBER,* United States of America

Economic growth depends critically on entrepreneurship, which drives the creation of new enterprises and the generation and commercialization of new ideas by start-ups as well as established businesses. New businesses account for an outsize share of new job creation. Two of the distinguishing features of the US economy are its robust rate of business creation, particularly in technology-intensive sectors, and its well-developed capital market institutions that support new ventures. A wide range of public policies, ranging from tax incentives for small businesses and their investors to provisions facilitating the transfer of intellectual property from government-funded research to businesses that can commercialize it, also promote entrepreneurial activity. Although the level of entrepreneurial activity has long been a policy focus, recently there has been increased emphasis on who becomes an entrepreneur, with attention to expanding pathways to entrepreneurial sectors as a means of supporting broadly shared prosperity.

Economic analysis can identify key trade-offs and quantify the impact of policy-driven incentives on various outcomes. The determinants and consequences of entrepreneurship are the subject of active research in many subfields of economics, including corporate finance, industrial organization, labor, macro, organizational economics, productivity, and public finance. Past research has investigated the impact of a host of public programs on the level and direction of entrepreneurship and on the pace of economic growth. This research has also explored which segments of the population benefit from these programs, and how they in turn affect the composition of the entrepreneurial pool.

Entrepreneurship and Innovation Policy and the Economy, volume 1, 2022.

To advance the role of economics in analyzing the entrepreneurial ecosystem, the National Bureau of Economic Research (NBER), with the support of the Ewing Marion Kauffman Foundation, has launched a new initiative to draw leading researchers in economics into the study of current issues in both entrepreneurship and innovation policy. The researchers, established scholars and as well as newcomers to the entrepreneurship field, must abide by the NBER's prohibition on policy recommendations. They are encouraged, however, to draw on cutting-edge research to distill findings that can bear on the policy process. These scholars share their findings with members of the policy and research communities at a capstone research meeting in Washington, DC. Their research papers are collected in *Entrepreneurship and Innovation Policy and the Economy (EIPE)*, a new annual publication of the University of Chicago Press. *EIPE* builds on the NBER's very successful *Innovation Policy and the Economy* series, which was published from 2001 until 2020.

I am very grateful to Josh Lerner of the Harvard Business School and Scott Stern of the MIT Sloan School of Management for launching this new initiative and serving as the editors of this inaugural *EIPE* issue. For the second and subsequent issues of *EIPE*, Benjamin Jones of the Kellogg School of Management at Northwestern University will join Lerner as coeditor. All three are leading scholars in the fields of entrepreneurship and innovation with great judgment about the important topics in this area and high standards in research quality. I also wish to thank Derek Ozkal of the Ewing Marion Kauffman Foundation for his enthusiastic support for the *EIPE* initiative, Helena Fitz-Patrick at NBER for her outstanding management of the publication process, and the members of the NBER Conference Department, especially Brett Maranjian and Rob Shannon, for handling meeting planning with extraordinary efficiency and good cheer.

I am confident that this new series will contribute a great deal to our understanding of the entrepreneurial ecosystem and to the role of public policy in supporting it.

Introduction

Josh Lerner, *Harvard Business School and NBER,* United States of America
Scott Stern, *Massachusetts Institute of Technology and NBER,* United States of America

This volume is the first annual volume of the National Bureau of Economic Research (NBER) *Entrepreneurship and Innovation Policy and the Economy (EIPE)* series. Entrepreneurship and innovation are widely recognized as key drivers of long-term economic growth, yet the development of rigorous economics research evaluating the causes and consequences of entrepreneurship and innovation (and the relationship between innovation and entrepreneurship) is more recent. Building on the 20-year legacy of the NBER *Innovation Policy and the Economy* series, *EIPE* broadens the focus of this NBER annual conference and volume to reflect more directly the significant growth in academic and policy interest in entrepreneurship and entrepreneurship policy.

The EIPE meeting seeks to provide an accessible forum to bring the work of leading academic researchers to an audience of policy makers and those interested in the interaction between public policy and innovation. Our goals are

- to provide an ongoing forum for the presentation of research on the impact of public policy on the process of entrepreneurship and innovation,

- to stimulate such research by exposing potentially interested researchers to the issues that policy makers consider important, and

- to increase the awareness of policy makers (and the public policy community more generally) concerning contemporary research in economics and the other social sciences that usefully informs the evaluation of current or prospective proposals relating to entrepreneurship and innovation policy.

Entrepreneurship and Innovation Policy and the Economy, volume 1, 2022.
© 2022 National Bureau of Economic Research. All rights reserved. Published by The University of Chicago Press for the National Bureau of Economic Research. https://doi.org/10.1086/718956

We would like to thank the Ewing Marion Kauffman Foundation for generous support of this volume. The foundation has been a critical source of support for the NBER's research activities on entrepreneurship and innovation for nearly 2 decades. We would also like to thank the NBER Conference Department, especially Rob Shannon, and Helena Fitz-Patrick of the NBER Publications Department.

This volume contains revised versions of the papers presented in the group's meeting held virtually in April 2021. As the first volume in this new series, the individual chapters highlight important ways in which both the production and impact of entrepreneurship and innovation is changing and the role of policy in that process. Two of the chapters in the volume draw on recent research directly related to the COVID-19 pandemic. The first paper focuses on the (perhaps surprising) persistent surge in new business formation that commenced in the wake of the pandemic, and the final paper considers the broader lessons for "crisis" innovation and entrepreneurship policy gained by a comparison between the current era and lessons from World War II. The second and third chapters in the volume focus squarely on inclusion within the process of innovation and entrepreneurship. These highlight differences in participation in innovation and entrepreneurship by women and Black Americans, and the significant variation in the degree of inclusion across locations, industries, and even individual universities and firms. The fourth chapter in the volume draws on both qualitative historical episodes (such as the history of mRNA vaccines), as well as more systematic empirical research into the institution of research funding to assess what types of research funding systems encourage novel research, and the consequence of funding systems that discourage novelty. Throughout, our aim has been to draw out the lessons of recent research in economics and related fields for policy analysis and future research into entrepreneurship and innovation.

The first chapter, by John Haltiwanger, offers an assessment of the impact of the ongoing pandemic (and associated policy response) on the rate and nature of entrepreneurship. At the onset of the pandemic, there was considerable concern not only about the survivability of existing businesses but what impact the pandemic (and public health response to the health crisis) would have on the rate and nature of new business formation. Concern about the rate of entrepreneurship was particularly salient given (a) the long-term secular decline in the quantity of new business formation since the 1980s (with only a modest uptick over the years preceding the pandemic), and (b) the fact that the major Federal economic relief and support legislation focused primarily on supporting existing businesses rather than encouraging the creation of new businesses. Leveraging the timely and granular nature of the Business Formation Statistics (BFS, a new data series developed at the US Census Bureau over the past several years), Halti-wanger documents a striking uptick (rather than an anticipated decline) in new business formation in the wake of the pandemic. Specifically, after a sharp but short decline at the beginning of the pandemic, the BFS registers a sizeable uptick starting in June 2020 and continuing through the first half of 2021. Moreover, this surge in new business formation seems to be occurring in both employer and nonemployer firms and is concentrated in sectors such as nonstore retail, potentially reflecting a process of reallocation of economic activity induced by the pandemic (and policy responses). In addition to providing novel evidence about the potential positive shift in overall business dynamism, these insights highlight the value of timely and granular data for formulating and assessing entrepreneurship policy.

The next two papers in the volume address the impact of historical and institutional barriers to inclusion within innovation and entrepreneurship for both women and African Americans. In the first of these papers, Lisa Cook, Janet Gerson, and Jennifer Kuan undertake a broad overview of the broad economy-wide loss in innovative capacity and productivity arising from inequality in the process of innovation and entrepreneurship, and the impact of interventions and policies attempting to address these inequalities. The paper focuses on three distinct stages of the "innovation gap": the science, technology, engineering, and mathematics pipeline; employment within the invention process; and commercialization. Using data from a variety of sources, the authors are able to document striking patterns across each stage. For example, although there has been progress over time in the inclusion of women and African Americans in the share of doctorates in science and engineering fields, a sizeable gap persists: women still account for just over 40% and African Americans account for less than 6% in these fields. A higher level of inequality exists in the process of invention and commercialization. As but one example, only 0.2% of all venture capital funding is allocated to firms founded by African American women. Cook, Gerson, and Kuan consider the role of both public and private interventions and policies aimed at each of these stages (and the evidence for impact of these approaches) and highlight that inclusion in the process of innovation and entrepreneurship can not only enhance equality but also be a direct driver of innovative capacity and ultimately economic growth.

Mercedes Delgado and Fiona Murray complement this analysis by characterizing and analyzing the gender gap in patented innovation. Specifically, this paper not only examines the overall level of inclusion by women in the innovation process but also specifically documents substantial variation across locations, industries, and even individual firms. To do so, the authors use a probabilistic name-matching algorithm across patents. Across the entire population of patents, this metric of inclusion is low: for example, in 2015, only 10% of all inventors are women. Importantly, even after accounting for differences in technological specialization across regions or organizations, there is significant variation in the gender gap across locations, universities, and firms. For example, New York boasts a much higher rate of inclusion of female inventors than Dallas. By providing a measurement framework for assessing the gender gap in innovation in a systematic but granular way, Delgado and Murray offer insight for policy makers seeking to compare alternative policies or initiatives aimed at enhancing inclusion within the innovation economy.

The fourth chapter of the volume focuses squarely on the potential impact of innovation-funding policies on shaping the novelty of research. Motivated by the uneven path by which the research that ultimately resulted in the development of mRNA vaccines was funded, Chiara Franzoni, Paula Stephan, and Reinhilde Veugelers offer a synthesis of an emerging body of evidence that a significant fraction of publicly funded research may be prone to substantial bias against breakthrough research. The authors suggest that this is not due to the biases of any one individual but reflects more systematic consequence of the research system. Pressure to demonstrate findings in a short time window, little tolerance for failure, and a prioritization on short-term bibliometric impact all have effects. Each of these factors is then reflected at each stage of the research process: by research agencies that fund projects on a case-by-case (rather than portfolio) basis, by a review process that places a penalty on novel proposals that take more time to assess, and ultimately by researchers themselves who choose to apply for less novel (but more fundable) projects. The authors conclude by suggesting a range of potential approaches, from deemphasizing near-term bibliometrics to adopting staged funding approaches, that may result in a reduction in the bias against novelty in the research funding process.

The question of how to allocate and organize research funding has become particularly timely with the need for timely and scalable innovation impact in the wake of the COVID-19 pandemic. In the final paper in this year's volume, Daniel Gross and Bhaven Sampat take a historical perspective on "crisis innovation" policy. Drawing on historical lessons from World War II and ongoing analysis of innovation policy during COVID-19, the paper considers the unique challenges that arise when a crisis necessitates that innovation be unusually rapid in nature and able to be deployed at scale. The authors synthesize their ongoing work into the specific ways in which innovation policy was implemented during World War II. They emphasize the importance of strategic prioritization, attraction of talent, providing appropriate incentives to researchers both external and internal to the Federal government, and achieving a high level of coordination and investment in production and diffusion. Some of these elements also featured prominently in Operation Warp Speed during COVID-19, such as a focus on using external contracting and precommitments to accelerate the process of innovation and diffusion in vaccines. At the same time, there are important differences: a much greater fraction of innovation during the current crisis seems to have emerged from a "bottoms-up" process through the efforts of researchers around the globe. Although it is too early to assess the long-term impact of the innovation response to COVID-19, Gross and Sampat emphasize that maintaining a long-term capacity to engage in crisis innovation is a necessary element for being able to implement effective innovation policy when the next crisis emerges.

Together, these five papers offer synthetic treatments of a range of timely areas in entrepreneurship and innovation policy that are the subject of active research. Although it is clear there are no easy answers, this new series aims to connect the best of recent economic research to the major issues facing entrepreneurship and innovation policy makers today.

Endnote

Author email addresses: Stern (sstern@mit.edu), Lerner (jlerner@hbs.edu). For acknowledgments, sources of research support, and disclosure of the authors' material financial relationships, if any, please see https://www.nber.org/books-and-chapters/entrepreneurship -and-innovation-policy-and-economy-volume-1/introduction-entrepreneurship-and-inno vation-policy-and-economy-volume-1

Entrepreneurship during the COVID-19 Pandemic: Evidence from the Business Formation Statistics

John C. Haltiwanger, *University of Maryland and NBER,* United States of America

Abstract

Applications for new businesses from the US Census Bureau's monthly and weekly Business Formation Statistics fell substantially in the early stages of the pandemic but then surged in the second half of 2020. This surge has continued through May 2021. The pace of applications since mid-2020 is the highest on record (earliest data available is 2004). The large increase in applications is for both likely new employers and nonemployers. These patterns contrast sharply with those in the Great Recession, when applications for likely new employer businesses and in turn actual start-ups of employer businesses declined sharply and persistently. The surge in new business applications has been uneven across sectors. Ten three-digit North American Industry Classification System industries account for 75% of the surge. Dominant industries include Nonstore Retail (alone accounting for 33% of the surge), Professional, Scientific and Technical Services, Truck Transportation, and Accommodation and Food Services. Given that existing small businesses in Retail Trade and Accommodation and Food Services have suffered especially large declines in the pandemic, these patterns are consistent with restructuring induced by the pandemic.

JEL Codes: L26, E32

Keywords: entrepreneurship, pandemic

The COVID-19-induced recession (henceforth COVID-19 Recession) began with an extraordinarily large contraction in economic activity. The net employment contraction between February and April 2020 exceeded 20 million for total nonfarm employment. Since then, employment has recovered substantially, but as of April 2021, it is still more than 8 million

Entrepreneurship and Innovation Policy and the Economy, volume 1, 2022.

below the level in February 2020.[1] The massive contraction and recovery have been very uneven. Existing small businesses have been hit especially hard, particularly in sectors such as Accommodation and Food Services, Health Services, and Other Services where remote work and remote interactions between businesses and consumers are difficult. Even in sectors that have experienced a net increase in jobs from February 2020 to early 2021, such as Finance and Insurance, existing small businesses have exhibited indicators of negative net growth, business sentiment, and recovery through early 2021.[2]

This characterization of existing small businesses being hit very hard with only limited recovery contrasts with the patterns of new business applications (BAs) from the Business Formation Statistics (BFS). After an initial sharp decline from late March through May, new BAs started to surge by June 2020. This surge has continued through May 2021. Overall, calendar year 2020 is the highest year on record for new BAs since 2004 (the first year the BFS is available).[3] The surge in new BAs in 2020 and 2021 includes a surge in applications for both likely employer and likely nonemployer businesses. These patterns contrast not only with the experiences of existing small businesses in 2020 but also with BAs in the Great Recession. In the Great Recession, new applications for likely employers as well as actual employer business start-ups declined sharply.

The surge in new applications in 2020 and 2021 for likely employer businesses is surprising especially given historical experience and the evidence and expectations early in the pandemic. The decline in new applications for likely employer businesses early in the pandemic exhibited a similar pattern to the sharp downturn after the collapse of Lehman Brothers in Fall 2008.[4] Even some aspects of the rapid fiscal policy response did not appear to bode well for starting new employer businesses in the pandemic. A key component of the CARES Act of March 2020 is the Payroll Protection Program (PPP), designed to protect jobs of existing small businesses. Given the unprecedented nature of the shutdown of the economy in the pandemic, it is not surprising that there was strong support to protect jobs in this manner. However, from the perspective of economic theory (see, e.g., Acemoglu et al. [(2018]), subsidizing incumbents can potentially suppress business entry. Viewed from this perspective, the surge in new BAs in 2020 that has continued into 2021 is even more surprising. The analysis in this paper provides insights and guidance into the underlying likely sources of these surprising patterns.

In considering these issues, it is critical to distinguish between new applications for likely employer and likely nonemployer businesses. In the

Great Recession, applications for likely new nonemployer businesses increased consistent with a countercyclical component of self-employment. In the pandemic, the surge in new BAs has been especially large for likely nonemployer businesses, with the surge four times larger than the increase in the Great Recession.

The BFS is derived from administrative data from the Internal Revenue Service (IRS) on Employer Identification Number (EIN) applications. All employer businesses in the United States are required to have an EIN to file payroll taxes. New nonemployer businesses also file for an EIN if forming a partnership or an incorporated business. Even new sole proprietor nonemployers often file for an EIN to facilitate their business activity (e.g., working with other businesses or opening a business bank account). The EIN application form includes the name and address of the applicant and business, business start date, type of business entity, principal industry, and planned date of initial wage payments (if applicable). The filing date and business location information are used to aggregate individual applications to weekly and monthly frequency. The IRS transmits these applications to the US Census Bureau on a weekly flow basis in virtually real time.[5]

The detailed information on the application permits decomposing new BAs into likely employers and likely nonemployers. Businesses that have a high propensity of becoming an employer business—based upon, for example, the application indicating planned wages—are designated as high-propensity business applications (HBA). Consistent with Bayard et al. (2018), evidence presented in this paper shows that there is a tight relationship between HBA and actual new employer start-ups over the subsequent 8 quarters. The difference between BA and HBA is referred to as likely nonemployers (NHBA) in this paper and the analysis below shows that fluctuations in NHBA closely track fluctuations in nonemployers. The public domain BFS also includes series by geography (state) and industry. The geographic and industry variation permits analysis of the dispersion in entrepreneurial activity across sectors and locations.

This surge in new BAs in the pandemic is of interest given the important role that employer start-ups play in job creation, innovation, and productivity growth (Haltiwanger, Jarmin, and Miranda 2013; Acemoglu et al. 2018; Alon et al. 2018; Guzman and Stern 2020). More generally, new employer start-ups are an important point of the ongoing creative destruction dynamics in the US economy (e.g., Davis and Haltiwanger 1999). The surge in likely nonemployer new applications is also of interest given increasingly important role that gig workers are playing in the US economy (e.g., Abraham et al. 2021).

The potentially changing nature of the relationship between applications and transitions in the pandemic period necessitates appropriate caution in interpreting the patterns of nascent entrepreneurship from the BFS during the pandemic period. Still, the historically tight relationships indicate that these have been highly predictive indicators of entrepreneurship in the past. In addition, the patterns of new applications by sector and industry during the pandemic presented below are consistent with the shifts toward remote activity interactions between businesses and workers (i.e., telework) and businesses and consumers (i.e., online retail and restaurant purchases with accompanying delivery to customers residential locations). These patterns suggest that the surge in new applications reflects ongoing restructuring in the economy induced by the pandemic. There are open questions about how much of this will persist and, to the extent there is persistence, whether the pandemic is accelerating prepandemic trends.

The paper proceeds as follows. Section II provides a description of the BFS to help interpret the striking patterns of this novel data. Section III presents the main results, providing insights on the basic patterns, the contrast between the patterns in the COVID-19 Recession and the Great Recession, and the sectoral and geographic differences in applications during the pandemic. Analysis of the relationship between new BAs and indicators of business and worker turnover is presented in Section IV. Section V includes a discussion of whether programs like the PPP have affected the observed surge in new BAs. Concluding remarks, including discussion of next steps for research, are provided in Section VI.

I. Description of Business Formation Statistics

The public domain BFS series are available weekly from 2006:w1 through the present and monthly from 2004:m7 through the present.[6] The weekly series include total applications (BA), high-propensity applications (HBA), applications with planned wages (WBA), and applications for corporations (CBA) at the national and state level (all not seasonally adjusted). The monthly series include all the same application series and some formation series. For the latter, actual new employer business formations from these applications over the next 4 and 8 quarters (BF4Q and BF8Q) as well as projections for new business formations (PBF4Q and PBF8Q) are released at the national, sectoral, and state level. The series are available both seasonally adjusted and unadjusted (only the seasonally adjusted monthly series are used in the current paper). The BFS data are very timely: weekly data are released for a given reference week on the Thursday after the reference week and monthly data are released within 2 weeks of the end of the reference month. The NHBA series used in this paper is constructed directly from the difference between BA and HBA.

Applications designated likely employers (HBA) include applications that have at least one of the following indicators on the application: (1) are from corporations, (2) indicate hiring an employee, (3) indicate a first wages paid/planned date, and (4) in certain industries, namely Manufacturing, Food and Accommodation Services, Health Care, and part of Retail. Overall, HBA have less than 50% likelihood of becoming employer businesses within 8 quarters after application, but fluctuations in HBA closely track actual employer start-ups. Applications denoted as likely nonemployers (NHBA) have a low probability of becoming employer businesses, only 3.8%.[7] However, as shown below, fluctuations in NHBA closely track fluctuations in nonemployers.

The empirical model used to predict transitions for the series PBF4Q and PBF8Q is described in detail in Bayard et al. (2018). Briefly, the projections are based on a linear probability model (LPM), which relates observed transitions of BAs to employer businesses in the Longitudinal Business Database (LBD) to a set of predictors from the EIN application form. The variables include indicators of the business start date, type of entity, industry, limited liability status, reason for applying, and wage date. The model also controls for location (state), week of application submission within the year, presence of prior EIN, and whether the application indicates a trade name or a distinct business address. The covariates of the empirical model also include interactions between industry, wage date, type of entity, and reason for applying. Figure 6 of Bayard et al. (2018) shows that projected transitions track actual transitions closely, both within and out of sample. In the analysis in this paper, the focus is on the spliced business formations using the actual formations up through 2018 and the projected transitions thereafter. During the period that the actual and projected transitions are available (from 2004 to 2018), these series closely track each other.

II. Evidence on Entrepreneurship in the Pandemic

This section starts with some basic facts about BA series before proceeding to analyses from cyclical, sectoral, and spatial perspectives.

A. Basic Facts

The patterns of new business applications (BA, HBA, and NHBA) from 2004:m7 through 2021:m4 are shown in panel *A* of figure 1. Panel *B*

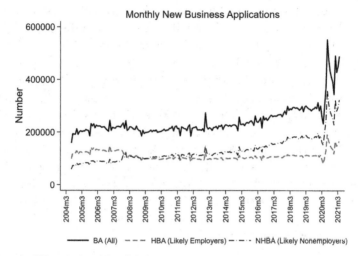

A. BFS applications 2004:m7–2021:4

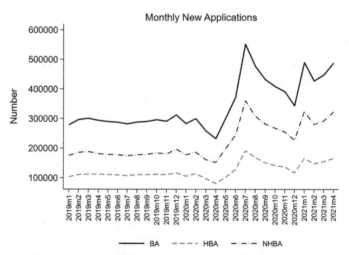

B. BFS applications 2019:m1–2021:m4

Fig. 1. BFS monthly applications. *A*, BFS applications 2004:m7–2021:m4. *B*, BFS applications 2019:m1–2021:m4. Color version available as an online enhancement.

Note: BA = All business applications, HBA = high-propensity applications (likely employers); NHBA = BA – HBA (likely nonemployers).

Source: Business Formation Statistics.

repeats panel *A* but narrows the time frame to 2019:m1–2021:m4 to permit greater focus on the pandemic. The upward trend in NHBA and the downward trend in HBA from 2004:m7 through 2020:m2 are evident.[8] At the outset of the pandemic there is a sharp decline in BA, HBA, and NHBA in March through May 2020. However, by June 2020 the number of applications of all types exceeds any month from January 2019 through February 2020. The surge in applications of all types peaks in July 2020 but the numbers in August 2020 to March 2021 exceed the number of applications in all prior months back to 2004:m7 for BA and NHBA and in all prior months back to 2007:m12 for HBA.

HBA tracks actual (through 2018) and projected transitions to new employer start-ups as shown in figure 2. Indices are depicted in figure 2 given differences in levels, and the projected transition series is for transitions to employer business over the next 8 quarters. The transition rate is lower than 50% (see Bayard et al. 2018) even for HBA, highlighting that HBA should be interpreted as an indicator of nascent entrepreneurship in terms of potential new employer start-ups. However, because the correlation in the monthly indices series is 0.88 it is apparent that variation in this indicator of nascent entrepreneurship closely tracks variation in new

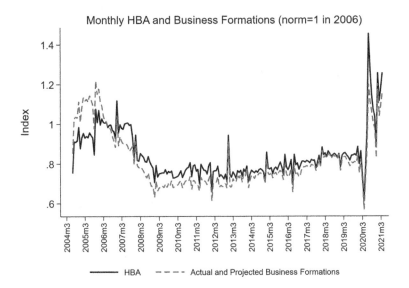

Fig. 2. Monthly applications for likely employers and new employer start-ups. Color version available as an online enhancement.

Notes: HBA = high-propensity applications. Actual and projected transitions = SBF8Q. Actual transitions through 2018.

Source: Business Formation Statistics.

employer start-ups.[9] It is, of course, of great interest to identify the determinants of the applications that successfully make the transition to an actual employer start-up. Bayard et al. (2018) highlight that there is enormous spatial variation in both application and the transition rates. Active research is underway to identify the sources of such variation.

The BFS does not provide indicators of actual or projected new nonemployers. However, a comparison of NHBA with published nonemployer statistics indicates a tight relationship. Figure 3 presents indices of the actual total number of nonemployers and the predicted number of nonemployers.[10] The correlation between the actual and projected series is almost one.

B.   Cyclical

The weekly data enable a detailed comparison of the dynamics of new BAs in the COVID-19 Recession and the Great Recession. For both recessions, a simple event study characterization of the dynamics is instructive where the patterns of BAs prior to and after a reference week 0 are

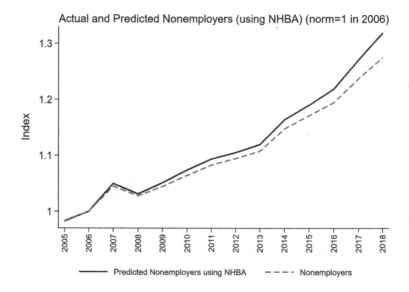

Fig. 3.   The relationship between NHBA and nonemployers. Color version available as an online enhancement.

Notes: NHBA = likely nonemployers. Predicted nonemployers using NHBA uses exit rates from nonemployers from Davis et al. (2009) and entry rates based on NHBA.

Source: Business Formation Statistics and Nonemployer Statistics from US Census Bureau.

examined (see Dinlersoz et al. 2021 for a related empirical analysis).[11]
For the COVID-19 Recession, week (0) is defined as week 10 of 2020
(the week ending March 13, 2020). Given that the weekly data are not
seasonally adjusted, it is instructive to compute the cumulative difference (backward and forward) relative to week 10 of 2020 with the cumulative difference relative to week 10 of a base period, which we choose to
be week 10 of 2018. For the Great Recession, the reference week 0 for the
crisis that is considered is week 37 of 2008 (the week just prior to the Lehman Brothers collapse). The cumulative differences computed for the
Great Recession use 2006 as the base period (with week 0 of the base period being week 37 of 2006). The cumulative differences are reported
63 weeks after the reference week 0 for both the Great Recession and
the COVID-19 Recession. For the latter, this reflects cumulative differences through May 29, 2021.

The patterns for the COVID-19 Recession are depicted in the upper
panel of figure 4. Prior to the crisis (i.e., prior to week 10 in 2020), applications for likely employers in the first 10 weeks of 2020 were similar to
those for the base period of 2018. As such there is not much cumulative
difference going backward. After week 0 of the crisis, applications fell
initially in 2020 relative to base period of 2018 but then have risen substantially. Through May 2021, new applications for likely employers were
almost 500,000 greater over a similar period from March 2018 through
May 2019. For likely nonemployers, the first part of 2020 had slightly
higher applications than the comparable first part of 2018. Applications
for nonemployers also declined initially early in the crisis but then quickly
rebounded. Through May 2021, new applications for likely nonemployers
were more than 1.3 million greater than a similar period from March 2018
through May 2019.

The lower panel depicts the same exercise for the Great Recession. The
patterns are dramatically different. For likely employer applications, applications in the 10 weeks prior to the reference week in 2006 are higher
than those in 2008. This is evident from figure 1. After the Lehman Brothers collapse, applications for likely employers fell substantially for the 63
subsequent weeks compared with the reference period. These patterns
for likely employers in the Great Recession are also evident for actual
new employer start-ups as shown in figure 2.

The decline in actual employer start-ups in the Great Recession has
been examined at length elsewhere (see Davis and Haltiwanger [2019]
and references therein). The analysis here highlights the decline in actual entrepreneurship is anticipated by the observed decline in nascent

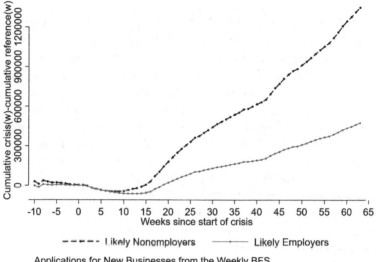

Applications for New Businesses from the Weekly BFS

A. COVID-19

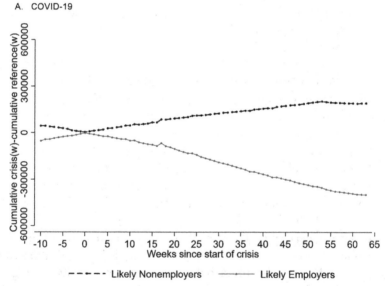

Applications for New Businesses from the Weekly BFS

B. Great Recession

Fig. 4. Comparison in patterns of business applications between COVID-19 and Great Recession. *A*, COVID-19. *B*, Great Recession. Color version available as an online enhancement.

Notes: Week 0 for COVID-19 Recession in crisis period is week ending March 7, 2020 (referred to as week 10 in BFS weekly calendar). Week 0 for reference period for COVID-19 Recession analysis is the equivalent week 10 in 2018. Week 0 for Great Recession in crisis period is week ending September 13, 2008 (referred to as week 37 in BFS weekly calendar). Week 0 for reference period for Great Recession analysis is the equivalent week 37 in 2006.

Source: Business Formation Statistics Weekly through May 15, 2021.

entrepreneurship in the BFS. One interesting feature of the decline in both nascent and actual entrepreneurship for employer businesses over this period is that the decline began before the start of the Great Recession (December 2007) and as such prior to the Lehman Brothers collapse in September 2008. Although the trend decline in the pace of actual entrepreneurship precedes 2006, the sharp cyclical downturn in employer start-ups that is often linked to the Great Recession begins in 2006 prior the start of the Great Recession. Davis and Haltiwanger (2019) highlight that the sharp decline in actual entrepreneurship that began in 2006 is associated with the sharp decline in housing prices that also began in 2006. An interesting area for future research is to investigate the differing impact of changing financial conditions on nascent versus actual entrepreneurship.

Turning back to figure 4, for nonemployers the 10 weeks in 2008 prior to the Lehman collapse had similar patterns to the comparable period in 2006. After Lehman's collapse, applications for nonemployers increased relative to the comparable period in 2006. Although this is qualitatively similar to the COVID-19 Recession, the latter is four times larger than the increase in the Great Recession. Moreover, by 52 weeks after the crisis week 0 in the Great Recession, the cumulative difference had stopped increasing. In contrast, for the COVID-19 Recession, the cumulative difference continued to surge for weeks 52–63.

Why are the patterns for applications for likely employers and likely nonemployers so different between the Great Recession and the COVID-19 Recession? This is an open and active area of current research; however, some factors already appear to be important. First, financial conditions are dramatically different across these episodes. The financial crisis that is at the root of the Great Recession included a decline in housing prices, a decline in net worth for households, and substantial challenges for bank balance sheets. Small business lending collapsed over this period. Some of this reflected likely reflected demand-side factors, but Davis and Haltiwanger (2019) identify a credit supply channel that adversely affected young businesses. In contrast, financial markets have been robust in the COVID-19 Recession with housing prices rising and financial intermediaries much healthier in this period.

Secondly, the COVID-19 Recession has induced a change in the structure of the US economy toward more remote activity and this provides incentives for new businesses to explore such potential opportunities. The restructuring component of the surge in BAs can be investigated by examining the changing sectoral composition of new BAs. This is the topic of the next section.

C. Sectoral

The surge in new BAs in the pandemic has been uneven across industries. The top panel of figure 5 shows the monthly patterns of applications for likely new employers for selected sectors for the 2004:m7–2021:m4 period, and the bottom panel shows the patterns for the 2019:m1–2021:m4 period. The surge in new applications for likely employers in the pandemic is dominated by Retail Trade but other sectors with substantial increases include Food and Accommodations and Health Services.[12] New applications for likely nonemployers for selected sectors are reported in figure 6. The surge in 2020 is dominated by Retail Trade accompanied by Professional, Scientific and Technical Services; Construction; and Trucking and Warehousing.

A special release in October 2020 of the weekly BFS covering 2019:w1–2020:w40 provides more industrial detail for overall applications. Figure 7 presents the three-digit North American Industry Classification System (NAICS) sectors with the largest change in the number of new applications over the first 40 weeks of 2020 compared with the first 40 weeks of 2019. The largest change in share is for Nonstore Retailers, which increased its number of applications by about 200,000 over this period. In 2019, Nonstore Retailers accounted for only 9% of overall applications. Thirty-three percent of the increase in applications from 2019 to 2020 is accounted for by this industry alone. The top 10 industries listed in figure 7 account for 75% of the increase in applications over the first 40 weeks of 2020 compared with 2019.

Figures 5–7 highlight the uneven nature of the surge in applications across industries. Figure 8 presents the between-sector dispersion in year-over-year growth rates of the monthly growth rates of HBA and NHBA. The top panel shows that dispersion in new application growth rates across sectors for HBA rose in the Great Recession, declined in its aftermath, and exhibited an upward trend through 2019. The dispersion fell in the early stages of the pandemic but has risen steadily since May 2020.

Between-sector dispersion in NHBA did not change much in the Great Recession, but like dispersion for HBA has exhibited a positive trend from 2012 to 2019. After falling early in the pandemic, between-sector dispersion in NHBA growth rates has risen sharply since March 2020. Dispersion peaked in August 2020 and has fallen since then but remains above levels pre-2020.

All this highlights that the pandemic surge in BAs is associated with intensified restructuring on several dimensions. For one, entry by itself

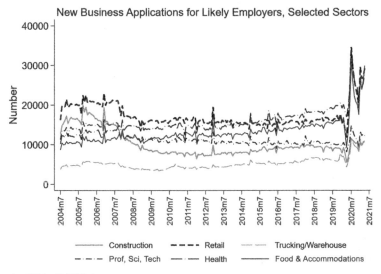

A. 2004:m7–2021:4

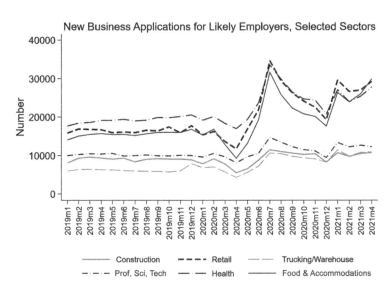

B. 2019:m1–2021:4

Fig. 5. New business applications for likely employers (HBA), selected sectors. *A*, 2004:
m7–2021:4. *B*, 2019:m1–2021:4. Color version available as an online enhancement.
Source: Business Formation Statistics.

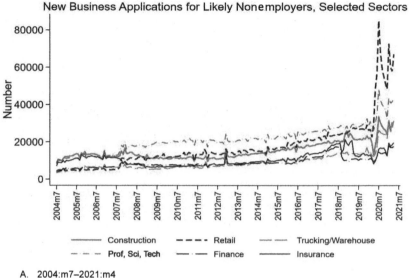

A. 2004:m7–2021:m4

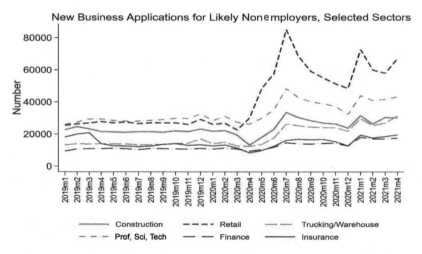

B. 2019:m1–2021:m4

Fig. 6. New business applications for likely nonemployers (NHBA), selected sectors. *A*, 2004:m7–2021:m4. *B*, 2019:m1–2021:m4. Color version available as an online enhancement.

Source: Business Formation Statistics.

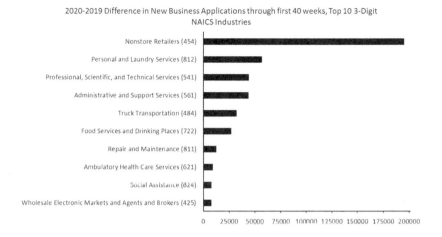

2020-2019 Difference in New Business Applications through first 40 weeks, Top 10 3-Digit NAICS Industries

Fig. 7. Changing sectoral composition of applications between 2019 and 2020. Color version available as an online enhancement.

Note: North American Industry Classification System (NAICS) three-digit code in parentheses.

Source: Census Bureau, Business Formation Statistics.

an important component of restructuring in terms of business turnover. Second, the uneven patterns across sectors that change rapidly over a short period of time suggests that the restructuring has an important between-sector component. The sectors with especially high BA rates provide guidance about the nature of this restructuring. The dramatic rise in sectors such as Nonstore Retail is consistent with the shift toward remote interactions between businesses and consumers. The rise in applications in sectors such as Retail Trade and Food and Accommodations are notable given the employment losses in those sectors as well as the especially adverse effects of the pandemic on existing small businesses in these sectors. From February 2020 to April 2021, employment losses in these two sectors are 400,000 and 2.2 million, respectively.[13]

Putting these BFS patterns into perspective, the SBPS from the Census Bureau highlights that existing small businesses have been pivoting their business operations during the pandemic in several ways (Buffington et al. 2021). Remote work activity has increased dramatically especially in sectors such as information. Moreover, online activity connecting existing small businesses to customers has increased substantially. The surge in new applications mirrors this shift in business activity. However, strikingly the SBPS shows that even by January 2021, existing small businesses in all sectors exhibit negative indicators in terms of growth, business

A. 2005:m7–2021:m4

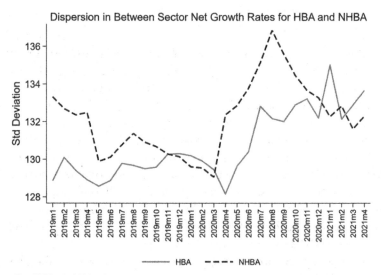

B. 2019:m1–2021:m4

Fig. 8. Dispersion in between-sector net growth rates for likely employers (HBA) and nonemployers (NHBA). *A*, 2005:m7–2021:m4. *B*, 2019:m1–2021:m4. Color version available as an online enhancement.

Note: Standard deviation of Y/Y monthly growth rates across two-digit North American Industry Classification System sectors.

Source: Business Formation Statistics.

sentiment, and expectations. The surge in applications in the BFS concentrated in specific sectors suggests the restructuring involves a shift away from existing small businesses toward new businesses.

D. Spatial

The surge in new BAs in the pandemic has also been uneven across locations. The top panel of figure 9 shows the monthly patterns of applications for likely new employers for selected states for the 2004:m7–2021:m4 period; the bottom panel shows the patterns for the 2019:m1–2021:m4 period. For this state-level analysis, index numbers equal to one on average in 2006 to adjust for the size of the state at specific point in time (2006). The surge in new applications for likely employers in the pandemic is especially large in Georgia, Florida, and Texas compared with California, New York, and New Jersey. New applications for likely nonemployers for the same selected states are reported in figure 10. The surge in 2020 for likely nonemployers is again especially large in Georgia, Florida, and Texas compared with California, New York, and New Jersey.

Figures 9 and 10 highlight the uneven nature of surge in applications across states.[14] Figure 11 presents the between-state dispersion in year-over-year growth rates of the monthly growth rates of HBA and NHBA. The top panel shows that dispersion in new application growth rates across states changed little in the Great Recession and has been reasonably stable through 2019. The dispersion rose substantially in May through July and has declined since then. However, it remains at a level higher than prepandemic.

Between-state dispersion in NHBA also did not change much in the Great Recession and has been reasonably stable through 2016 but exhibited a decline and then recovery in the 2017–18 period. Between-state dispersion in NHBA in the pandemic follows the patterns for HBA closely, rising sharply from May through July 2020 and then declining through March 2021 but at a level higher than prepandemic.

Comparing the patterns of between-sector and between-state dispersion (figs. 8 and 11, respectively), the increasing dispersion in between-sector growth rates is more persistent than the increase in dispersion in between-state growth rates. Although more research is needed on understanding these differences, these patterns suggest a more profound restructuring between sectors than between states. Interestingly, Buffington et al. (2021) find that the uneven impact of the pandemic on existing small businesses is more persistent between sectors than between states.

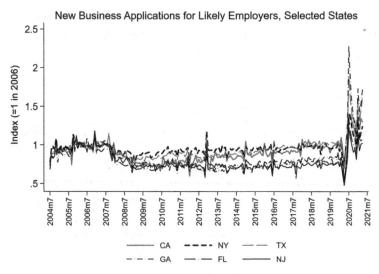

A. 2004:m7–2021:m4

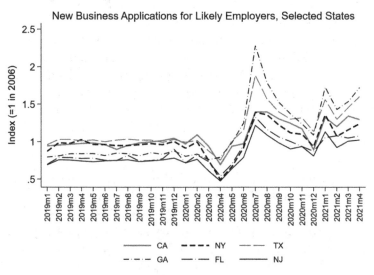

B. 2019:m1–2021:m4

Fig. 9. New business applications for likely employers (HBA), selected states. *A*, 2004: m7–2021:m4. *B*, 2019:m1–2021:m4. Color version available as an online enhancement. Source: Business Formation Statistics.

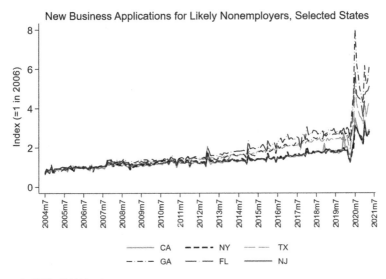

A. 2004:m7-2021:m4

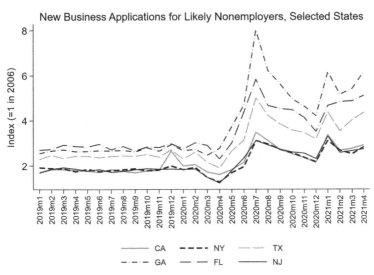

B. 2019:m1-2021:m4

Fig. 10. New business applications for likely nonemployers (NHBA), selected states. *A*, 2004:m7–2021:m4. *B*, 2019:m1–2021:m4. Color version available as an online enhancement.
Source: Business Formation Statistics.

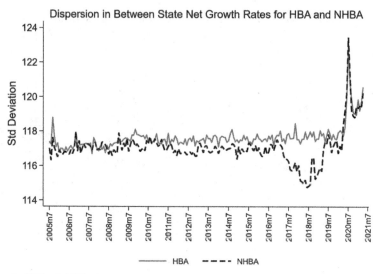

A. 2005:m7–2021:m4

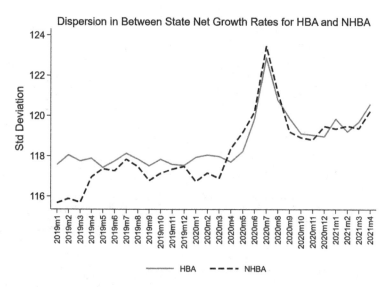

B. 2019:m1–2021:m4

Fig. 11. Dispersion in between-state net growth rates for likely employers (HBA) and nonemployers (NHBA). *A*, 2005:m7–2021:m4. *B*, 2019:m1–2021:m4. Color version available as an online enhancement.

Note: Standard deviation of Y/Y monthly growth rates across two-digit North American Industry Classification System sectors.

Source: Business Formation Statistics.

What we do not know from the public domain BFS is how the restructuring across sectors and states are related. For example, in the locations where existing small businesses in specific sectors have been hit the hardest, are new applications surging? Alternatively, it may be that it is in the locations where existing small businesses in specific sectors have fared the best that new applications are surging. In other words, is the observed restructuring within sector/location cells or between sector/location cells? Future research using the micro data underlying the BFS can be used to investigate these issues.

III.   New Business Applications, Business and Worker Turnover

Figure 2 makes clear the tight relationship between new BAs for likely employers (HBA) in each month and new employer business start-ups in the subsequent 8 quarters. As discussed above, new employer start-ups play a disproportionate role in job creation, innovation, and productivity growth. This contribution is a noisy and complex one as start-ups are part of an ongoing creative destruction dynamic in the economy. Although it is beyond the scope of this paper to explore this latter connection fully, in this section the relationship between new BAs for likely employers and indicators of business and worker turnover is explored.

For this purpose, the monthly applications for likely employers are aggregated to the quarterly frequency to enable analysis of indicators from the Business Employment Dynamics (BED). The latter provides quarterly estimates of business births and deaths (at the establishment level). Estimates of hires, separations, and job openings from Job Openings and Labor Turnover Survey (JOLTS) are also used. Although JOLTS is available at the monthly level, for the analysis in this section these measures are also aggregated to the quarterly frequency to facilitate a joint analysis of the indicators from the BFS, BED, and JOLTS.

Simple bivariate vector autoregression (VAR) is used to quantify joint dynamics. Technical details of the specifications are described in the appendix. The analysis of these dynamics is restricted to the quarterly data from 2004:3 to 2019:4. This restriction in this dynamic VAR analysis is for a number of related reasons. First, as is evident from figure 1, there are dramatic fluctuations in the BAs during the COVID-19 pandemic that are unprecedented in magnitude. Second, new BAs are inherently forward-looking because the BFS shows that it can take more than 1 year for HBA applications to yield actual new employer business start-ups.[15] Given the potentially substantial lags, the surge in BAs in the second half of 2020 is unlikely to have its full effect on other indicators until several quarters in the future. Given the nature of the analysis, appropriate caution is needed in making inferences about the implications of the surge in applications during the pandemic for business and worker turnover. Still, the analysis in this section provides guidance about the potential future impact of the pandemic surge in applications based on historical patterns.

Figure 12 reports cumulative impulse response functions of a quarterly innovation in HBA to establishment openings and closings.[16] An innovation in HBA yields a substantial and significant increase in business births over the next 16 quarters (see panel A). This evidence is consistent with figure 2. The novel insight from figure 12 is that an innovation in HBA also yields a substantial and significant increase in business deaths over the next 16 quarters (panel B). In unreported results (available upon request), there is no evidence of reverse causality.[17] That is, there is no evidence that an innovation in business births or deaths yields subsequent significant changes in new BAs.

Figure 13 illustrates that distinct but related dynamics are present for hires and separations. An HBA yields substantial and significant increases in hires and separations rates over the next 16 quarters.[18] Figure 14A shows that the impact on hires is greater than the impact on separations as the net employment growth impact (hires minus separations from JOLTS) is positive. There is also a substantial and significant impact on job openings over the next 16 quarters (fig. 14B).[19]

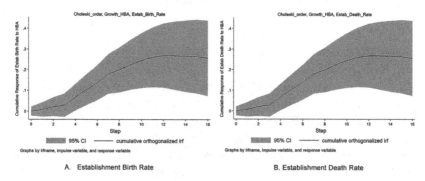

A. Establishment Birth Rate   B. Establishment Death Rate

Fig. 12. Cumulative impulse response of establishment birth and death rates to HBA growth innovation. A, Establishment birth rate. B, Establishment death rate. Graphs by irfname, impulse variable, and response variable.

Notes: HBA = likely employers. Bivariate VARS (panel A with Growth in HBA and Establishment Birth Rate and panel B with Growth in HBA and Establishment Death Rate) lags equal to 8. Steps refer to quarters.

Source: Business Formation Statistics (aggregated to quarterly frequency) and Business Employment Dynamics 2004:3–2019:4.

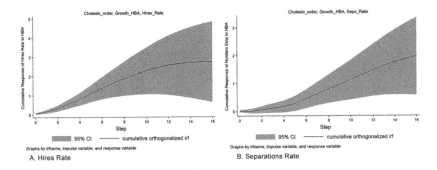

A. Hires Rate   B. Separations Rate

Fig. 13. Cumulative impulse response of hires and separations rates to HBA growth innovation. *A*, Hires rate. *B*, Separations rate.

Notes: HBA = likely employers; JOLTS = Job Openings and Labor Turnover Survey. Bivariate VARS (panel *A* with Growth in HBA and Hires Rate and panel *B* with Growth in HBA and Separation Rate) lags equal to 8. Steps refer to quarters.

Source: Business Formation Statistics and JOLTS aggregated to quarterly frequency 2004:3–2019:4.

The results in this subsection are suggestive and call for further research. Figures 12 through 14 do not provide guidance on the mechanisms underlying these patterns but highlight the close connection between new BAs and business and worker turnover. For example, the surge in business deaths following an innovation in new applications may reflect creative destruction forces at work or alternatively but relatedly the propensity

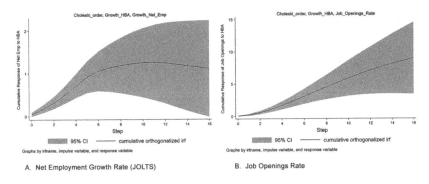

A. Net Employment Growth Rate (JOLTS)   B. Job Openings Rate

Fig. 14. Cumulative impulse response of net employment growth and job openings rates to HBA growth innovation. *A*, Net employment growth rate (JOLTS). *B*, Job openings rate.

Notes: HBA = likely employers; JOLTS = Job Openings and Labor Turnover Survey. Bivariate vector autoregressions (panel *A* with Growth in HBA and Net Employment Growth Rate (Hires Rate – Separations Rate) and panel *B* with Growth in HBA and Job Openings Rate) lags equal to 8. Steps refer to quarters.

Source: Business Formation Statistics and JOLTS aggregated to quarterly frequency 2004:3–2019:4.

of many new businesses to exit. More generally it may be that new BAs react quickly to current or expected changes in economic conditions that are harbingers of indicators of business and worker turnover. Further evidence and discussion of these issues is provided in Asturias et al. (2021). This latter research provides evidence that an innovation in the growth in HBA yields a substantial and persistent increase in nonfarm payroll employment growth. This latter finding is consistent with the implied larger impact of HBA on hires versus separations discussed above.

IV.   COVID-19 Economic Stimulus Policies and Entrepreneurship

Given the importance of the PPP for existing small businesses (75% of existing small businesses in the SBPS report receiving PPP assistance), a natural question to ask is whether the PPP affected new BAs.[20] This is a complex question that requires more research in part because the PPP and other fiscal stimulative programs may have affected new business formation indirectly via the impact on the overall economic outlook. Alternatively, economic theory implies (Acemoglu et al. 2018) that support for incumbent businesses can have a negative impact on business formation.

The key to thinking about this question is that the PPP program is designed to provide support to existing businesses. Applicants for PPP must have been in business by February 2020, with the loan application requiring documentation of business activity prepandemic. This implies that employer businesses that received a PPP loan already had an EIN in February 2020, well before the surge in new BAs. Most of the PPP loans went to employer businesses.[21] Holding the state of aggregate economy fixed, this support for existing small businesses is, if anything, likely to have dampened the incentives for starting new employer businesses. Viewed from this perspective, the surge in applications for likely employer businesses is arguably not because of, but despite, the PPP program.

Of course, the state of the economy has been anything but fixed. In considering these issues, the discussion of the cyclical patterns of new BAs and business formation in Subsection III.C is relevant. Davis and Haltiwanger (2019) highlight that all economic downturns since the early 1980s have exhibited a decline in employer business start-ups relative to trend. From this perspective, the pandemic would have been expected to lead to a decline in applications for new employers. However, given that self-employment has a countercyclical component, the pandemic would have been expected to yield an increase in nonemployer activity and in turn applications for likely nonemployers. To the extent the CARES Act dampened the adverse effect of the pandemic on the economy, the cyclical impact on new business formation would have been expected to have been dampened. Moreover, as discussed above, the PPP component of the CARES Act by subsidizing incumbents may have dampened new applications for likely employers. Other components of the CARES Act (e.g., direct payments to households) may have helped boost the incentives to start new businesses.[22]

This discussion helps highlight why the surge in applications for both likely employers and nonemployers is at least ex ante surprising. As it has become clear that the pandemic is leading to both short-run and potentially longer-run restructuring of the US economy, this surge is less surprising.

V. Concluding Remarks

The surge in applications for new businesses in the pandemic has been large and distinct. The total number of applications in 2020 is the highest by far compared with all years for which the data have been available. The increase from 2019 to 2020 in total applications exceeds 20%, which is double the growth rate in any other year. The increase is in applications for both likely employers and nonemployers. All of the increase in 2020 is accounted for by a surge in applications in the second half of 2020. This surge in applications has continued through May 2021. Based on historical patterns, this surge in applications should result in a surge in new employer and nonemployer businesses. The increase in new employer businesses should be within 4–8 quarters of the date of the applications, based upon historical patterns.

The surge in new BAs has been uneven across sectors. Ten three-digit industries out of about 100 three-digit industries account for 75% of the surge. Dominant industries include Nonstore Retail, alone accounting for 33% of the surge; Personal Services; Professional, Scientific and Technical Services; Administrative and Support Services; Truck Transportation; and Accommodation and Food Services. Given that existing small businesses in Retail Trade and Accommodation and Food Services have suffered especially large declines in the pandemic, these patterns are consistent with restructuring induced by the pandemic. As the economy recovers from the pandemic, an open question is the extent to which the increases in remote/telework activity observed during the pandemic will persist. The extent to which these changes "stick" is likely to vary across types of businesses and locations. The shift toward e-commerce is likely to stick as this reflects a prepandemic trend. Viewed from this perspective, the pandemic may be accelerating ongoing trends and the surge in BAs is part of this process.

Does this surge in new BAs imply there will be a surge in job creation, innovation, and productivity growth over the next few years? Obviously, this is an open question, but in considering these possibilities several factors are important to consider. First, basic facts about new businesses (see Haltiwanger et al. 2013; Decker et al. 2014) highlight that most new employer businesses fail within the first 5 years after entry and conditional on survival, most do not grow. A relatively small fraction of young businesses grow very rapidly and it is these high-growth firms that are especially important for job creation that persists, innovation, and productivity growth. The analysis in this paper shows that prepandemic a surge in new BAs has yielded substantial and significant increases in indicators of both business and worker turnover over the subsequent 4 years. It remains to be seen whether similar patterns will apply in the next few years.

The surge in applications for likely nonemployers is also of interest as an indicator of the changing structure of the economy. The number of nonemployer businesses has been on an upward trend over the past 15 years or so with rapid acceleration in the post-2010 period. As discussed in Abraham et al. (2021), this reflects an increase in the gig economy including especially the ridesharing industries. The evidence presented in Abraham et al. (2021), and references therein, highlight that much of the nonemployer activity reflects supplemental and stopgap activity.

The surge in applications for likely nonemployers thus may reflect at least in part an acceleration of prepandemic trends. However, several factors suggest the surge is more complicated. For one, the surge in applications for likely nonemployers are for those applying for EINs. Most of the nonemployers in the ridesharing industry are sole proprietors that are not required to have an EIN. In addition, the surge in applications for likely nonemployers are in sectors that reflect promoting remote activity, such as Nonstore Retailers. Just as for new employer start-ups, an open question is whether new nonemployers also will "stick." A closely related question is whether the new nonemployers business activity will mostly be stopgap or supplemental as in the past. Alternatively, are we seeing an increase in the share of individuals for whom nonemployer activity is the primary or only source of work activity?

Finally, the surge in new BAs raises a variety of important measurement questions and challenges. For one, the high-frequency traditional statistical series such as the Bureau of Labor Statistics (BLS) monthly payroll report rely on imputing aggregate growth based on survey respondents that provide reports in consecutive months.[23] An adjustment is made for the impact of births and deaths using a birth-death model. Benchmark revisions are made annually based on comprehensive administrative data. An open question is whether this surge in applications will imply large benchmark adjustments as the birth-death model is based on historical relationships that do not hold in the pandemic. Second, interpreting the impact of the surge in applications is hampered by limitations in other key related series. To understand the implications of business entry variation over time, industry, and location, evidence on business exit is also needed. As highlighted by Crane et al. (2021), official statistical agency reports on business closures emerge only slowly given the relatively slow processing of key administrative data at Census (e.g., payroll tax reports) and BLS (e.g., ES-202 employment reports as part of the Quarterly Census of Employment and Wages program). Business closure data from these sources for all of 2020 will begin to become available in published statistics in late 2021. Relatedly, reports on the outcomes of existing young and small businesses by sector and location depend on this same administrative data. This implies that understanding where the observed fluctuations in the BFS fit into these outcomes will take some time to sort out. Novel high-frequency surveys like the SBPS help fill in the gaps but have some limitations. As noted by Buffington et al. (2021), the SBPS is more informative about continuing small businesses than business closures (as survey nonresponse is inherently higher for businesses that have ceased operations). More research is needed to help develop these important measures of business deaths.

Appendix

I. Projected Nonemployers

Figure 3 depicts projected nonemployers from NHBA using the following transition equation:

$$NES_t = (1 - ExitRate_t)NES_{t-1} + NHBA_t.$$

The exit rate is estimated from Davis et al. (2009). Appropriate caution is needed in using this measurement approach because NES (Nonemployer Statistics) includes sole proprietor nonemployers not captured in NHBA. The index number approach in figure 3 alleviates implied level differences, but the lack of information on entry of sole proprietor non-employers still suggests caution.

II. VAR Specifications

For Section IV, the VAR relationships are specified as follows:

$$Z_t = A(L)Z_t + v_t, \tag{A1}$$

where Z_t is a vector of observable variables, L is the lag operator, and v_t is a vector of reduced form innovations. The analysis in Section IV focuses on simple bivariate VAR specifications with, for example, the growth rate of HBA as one variable and business and worker turnover indicators as the other variable. Insights from the VAR emerge from inverting the autoregressive (AR) representation in equation (A1) to the MA representation given by

$$Z_t = M(L)v_t = S(L)\eta_t, \tag{A2}$$

where $M(L)$ are the MA coefficients from inverting the AR representation and η_t represents the innovations to each of the orthogonalized "structural" innovations after making some identifying assumptions.[24] Specifically, a Cholesky recursive structure is used for this identification. In the results reported in Section IV, HBA is chosen as first in the causal ordering. However, unreported results show the patterns in figures 12–14 are largely robust to changing the causal ordering. Although this might be surprising, it is important to remember that this is imposing restrictions on the covariance structure of the structural innovations relative to the reduced form residuals. The latter reflect the period t residual after controlling for lags of the variables in Z_t.

The business and worker turnover measures used are as follows: establishment birth rate in figure 12A from the BED, establishment death rate in figure 12A from the BED, hires rate in figure 13A from JOLTS, separations rate in figure 13B from JOLTS, net employment growth rate (hires minus separations rate from JOLTS) in figure 14A, and job openings rate in figure 14B from JOLTS. All rates are measured as percent of employment. The HBA growth rate is the quarterly log first difference multiplied by 100.

For these specifications, the lag length is 8. Unreported results show robustness to alternative lag lengths. Although results are robust on several dimensions, appropriate caution is required in interpreting the VAR results because they are simple bivariate specifications. The results provide insights into the dynamic covariance structure between HBA and indicators of business and worker turnover. More research is needed to understand the mechanisms underlying the reported results.

Supporting evidence using closely related VAR analysis is presented in Asturias et al. (2021). The latter investigates the relationship between HBA growth rate innovations and Principle Federal Economic Indicators (PFEIs). Using data at the monthly frequency (because most PFEIs are monthly) and using bivariate VAR specifications, they find that an innovation to HBA growth yields a substantial increase in the growth rate of nonfarm payroll employment that peaks at about 12 months but persists for more than 24 months. Putting the pieces together, the findings in the current paper highlight that an innovation in HBA growth yields substantial persistent increases in business and worker turnover. The Asturias et al. (2021) results show there is also a substantial persistent increase in net employment growth. Thus, a surge in HBA is associated by an increase in both net and gross flows.

III. PPP and New Business Applications: Further Discussion

The primary group of PPP recipients that may have been induced to apply for an EIN by the program directly are sole proprietor nonemployers that did not have an EIN prior to applying for a PPP loan. Using Small Business Administration (SBA) data on all loans, about 600,000 of the 5.2 million PPP loans by August 2020 went to sole proprietor nonemployers. This is an upper bound on the number of PPP loan recipients that also applied for a new EIN after February 2020.[25] This upper bound is relatively small compared with almost 4 million new BAs from May 2020 to January 2021.

An EIN was not required for the PPP application, but it is possible that some of this group may have applied for an EIN as part of this process. This may have occurred before or after receiving a first-round loan. For example, sole proprietor nonemployers using a Social Security Number (SSN) as the Taxpayer Identification Number (TIN) for their loan application may have applied for an EIN after receiving a loan, as having a business checking account facilitates managing the PPP financial reporting. Relatedly, it has been reported that some draw 2 PPP loan applications have experienced delays in processing for those applications with a TIN mismatch between round 1 draw 1 loan and round 2 draw 2 application. This mismatch could occur for those sole proprietors, nonemployers that used their SSN in round 1 and an EIN in round 2. The upper bound on such mismatches is low relative to the total number of EIN applications from May 2020 to January 2021.

It is also worth emphasizing that the surge in new BAs is not just in overall applications but also in applications for likely new employers (HBA and WBA). Employer businesses getting PPP loans must have had an EIN prepandemic, so this pandemic surge in HBA and WBA cannot be accounted for by the PPP program. The surge in HBA and WBA applications (see figs. 1 and A1) is roughly proportional to the surge in overall applications. If the PPP program had a large impact on EIN applications by existing nonemployers without an EIN, one would expect that BA would have risen much more sharply than HBA or WBA. This approximate proportionality holds in the recent second surge in January 2021 implying that the second round of PPP is not the primary driving factor for this second surge.

Figures 1 and A1 do show that BA rose more rapidly than HBA and WBA in the July 2020 and January 2021 surges. However, these surges are primarily accounted for by new applications in NAICS 454 (Nonstore Retail) as seen in figure 7. Nonstore Retailers has traditionally been a

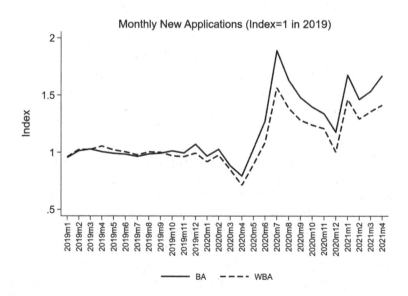

Fig. A1. Indices of business applications (BA) and those with planned wages (WBA), 2019:m1–2021:m4. Color version available as an online enhancement.

Source: Business Formation Statistics.

nonemployer intensive industry. In 2018, 92% of Nonstore Retail businesses were nonemployers. It is not obvious why PPP should have generated a surge in nonemployer applications in Nonstore Retail.

Endnotes

Author email address: John Haltiwanger (haltiwan@econ.umd.edu). Thanks to Lucia Foster, Josh Lerner, Scott Stern, and participants at the 2021 NBER Conference on Entrepreneurship and Innovation Policy and the Economy for helpful comments on an earlier draft and to Chris Roudiez for excellent research assistance. This paper, without implication, draws on collaborative research with numerous colleagues I have worked with in the development and analysis of the Business Formation Statistics (BFS). The research and development papers for the BFS with these colleagues are cited extensively in the text and included in the references. This paper uses only public domain data from the BFS and other sources. The views expressed in the paper are those of the author alone. For acknowledgments, sources of research support, and disclosure of the author's material financial relationships, if any, please see https://www.nber.org/books-and-chapters/entrepreneurship-and-innovation-policy-and-economy-volume-1/entrepreneurship-during-covid-19-pandemic-evidence-business-formation-statistics.

1. Statistics from http://www.bls.gov for Current Establishment Survey total nonfarm employment.

2. See Buffington et al. (2021) for details about this characterization of the impact on existing small businesses. The evidence briefly summarized here is from the Census Small Business Pulse Survey (SBPS) discussed at length in this paper. By examining self-employment patterns from the CPS, Fairlie (2020) presents evidence that existing small businesses were hit hard. Abraham et al. (2021) raise questions about how well the CPS captures self-employment relative to the administrative data. The concerns they raise apply primarily the unincorporated self-employment statistics from the CPS. Haltiwanger and Rendell (2021) find that although new applications for likely employers closely tracks actual new employer start-ups from the Business Dynamics Statistics (BDS) (consistent with the evidence shown here), the flow into unincorporated self-employment businesses does not match the patterns from the BFS or the BDS in terms of new employer start-ups.

3. The surge in new BAs in the BFS is matched by other sources such as the Startup Cartography Project (SCP) as reported in Fazio et al. (2021). The latter covers only eight states but offers rich and novel findings into how these patterns vary across narrow geographic areas. See further discussion in Sec. III.

4. New applications for likely employers and actual employers started to decline prior to the Great Recession at least partly due to the decline in financial conditions (e.g., the collapse in housing prices) that preceded the Great Recession. See Fort et al. (2014) and Davis and Haltiwanger (2019) for more analysis of the decline in employer start-ups in the Great Recession. See Dinlersoz et al. (2021) for an in-depth comparison of BAs in the Great Recession relative to the COVID-19 Recession.

5. Bayard et al. (2018) describe in detail how certain types of applications are automatically excluded from the BFS because they are tax entities not engaging as employer or nonemployer self-employment activity. For example, applications for trusts and estates are excluded. It is also worth noting that the application process itself is largely online and automated so that disruptions in IRS activity early in the pandemic have apparently had little or no impact on the tracking and reporting of applications.

6. As of the writing of this paper, the weekly series is available through 2021:w21 (through May 29, 2021), and the monthly series is available through 2021:m4.

7. See Bayard et al. (2018) for the rates of employer business formation associated with different application characteristics.

8. In fact, HBA is greater than NHBA from 2004 to 2008, when NHBA begins to be larger than HBA.

9. This is the correlation through 2018 using only actual start-ups.

10. The predicted number of nonemployers uses the actual number of nonemployers in 2006, exit rates from nonemployers (from Davis et al. 2009), and projecting entry into nonemployers from NHBA; see appendix for details. Use appropriate caution for interpreting this crude calculation. NHBA only includes applications for new EINs that are likely nonemployers. Nonemployers include sole proprietors without EINs. The index approach helps overcome these limitations.

11. Dinlersoz et al. (2021) conduct a closely related but more sophisticated econometrics exercise using state-level weekly data. The findings reported here are consistent with their findings. This closely related work using a regression framework enables establishing that the variation presented here reflects not only economically significant but also statistically significant differences. The findings reported here include applications through April 2021, and Dinlersoz et al. (2021) report patterns through the end of 2020. Also, Dinlersoz et al. (2021) use DHS (Davis, Haltiwanger and Schuh 1996) growth rates to accommodate the state-level variation they exploit; the analysis reported here uses national totals.

12. Appropriate caution is required in interpreting the results for Accommodations and Food Services as well as Health Services given that applications in both sectors are automatically classified into HBA. As explained in Bayard et al. (2018), applications in those sectors have a higher-than-average propensity of becoming employers.

13. Statistics from http://www.bls.gov, CES employment by sector.

14. Fazio et al. (2021) present evidence across eight states that is broadly consistent with that presented here in terms of an uneven surge in applications across geographic areas. A novel and interesting finding in this work from the SCP is that the surge in new firm formation has been especially in zip codes including a high proportion of African American residents and in particular higher median income African American neighborhoods. Investigating the cross-sectional and time series patterns of entrepreneurship by race and ethnicity at both the individual and neighborhood level should be a high priority for future research.

15. This can be seen by the finding that SBF8Q exceeds SBF4Q.

16. The mean establishment birth and death rates are about 3% per quarter with a standard deviation of about 0.2.

17. That is, an innovation in the business births or deaths variable yields no substantial subsequent change in HBA applications. These statements hold regardless of the Cholesky ordering used in the VAR analysis. See the appendix for more detail. The orthogonalized MA representation of the impulse response functions can be given a causal interpretation. Often the causal inferences depend on the Cholesky ordering, but not in this case.

18. The mean hires and separations rates are about 10.7% and 10.5% per quarter, respectively. The corresponding standard deviations are about 0.9% and 0.8%, respectively. For the net employment growth rate (from hires minus separations), the mean is 0.2 per quarter with a standard deviation of 0.5. The job openings rate has a mean of about 10% per quarter with a standard deviation of 2.5.

19. Unreported results available upon request show little evidence of reverse causality for hires, separations, net employment growth, or job openings.

20. See also Buffington et al. (2021) for a discussion of this issue.

21. About one-seventh of the recipients of PPP were nonemployers as of February 2020. Many of these likely also had an EIN. An EIN is required for nonemployer corporations and partnerships. Also, many sole proprietor nonemployers have an EIN, as this facilitates doing business with other businesses and an EIN is required for having a business bank account. It is possible that some of the relatively small fraction of nonemployer, sole proprietor PPP loan recipients were induced to apply for an EIN as part of the PPP program. See the appendix for further discussion.

22. Fazio et al. (2021) offer some evidence in support of this hypothesis.

23. This limitation is shared by many high-frequency economic indicator surveys.

24. By definition, the MA coefficients for the current period 0 in terms of the reduced form residuals is the identity matrix, $M(0) = I$. Of greater interest is to specify the MA representation in terms of orthogonalized innovations. This requires identifying assumptions. A common set of identifying assumptions is to use the Cholesky decomposition,

which imposes short-run restrictions on the relationship between the contemporaneous reduced form residuals and the orthogonalized innovations. Let $S(0) = S_0$ and let the relationship be $\eta_t = S_0 v_t$ and $S(L) = M(L)S_0$. Under Cholesky, S_0 is lower triangular so that identification is through assuming a recursive structure. In a two-variable VAR under Cholesky, all of the covariance between the reduced form residuals is attributed to the orthogonalized innovation for the variable specified first in the VAR.

25. For SBA data on all loans see https://www.sba.gov/funding-programs/loans/coronavirus-relief-options/paycheck-protection-program/ppp-data#section-header-2.

References

Abraham, Katharine G., John C. Haltiwanger, Kristin Sandusky, and James R. Spletzer. 2021. "Measuring the Gig Economy: Current Knowledge and Open Issues." In *Measuring and Accounting for Innovation in the 21st Century*, ed. Carol Corrado, Jonathan Haskel, Javier Miranda, and Daniel Sichel, 257–98. Chicago: University of Chicago Press.

Acemoglu, Daron, Ufuk Akcigit, Nicholas Bloom, and William R. Kerr. 2018. "Innovation, Reallocation and Growth." *American Economic Review* 108:3450–91.

Alon, Titan, David Berger, Robert Dent, and Benjamin Pugsley. 2018. "Older and Slower: The Startup Deficit's Lasting Effects on Aggregate Productivity Growth." *Journal of Monetary Economics* 93:68–85.

Asturias, Jose, Emin Dinlersoz, John Haltiwanger, and Rebecca Hutchinson. 2021. "Business Applications as Economic Indicators." Working Paper CES WP-21-09, Center for Economic Studies, US Census Bureau, Washington, DC.

Bayard, Kimberly, Emin Dinlersoz, Timothy Dunne, John Haltiwanger, Javier Miranda, and John Stevens. 2018. "Early-Stage Business Formation: An Analysis of Applications for Employer Identification Numbers." Working Paper no. 24364, NBER, Cambridge, MA.

Buffington, Catherine, Daniel Chapman, Emin Dinlersoz, Lucia Foster, and John Haltiwanger. 2021. "High Frequency Business Dynamics in the United States during the COVID-19 Pandemic." Working Papers no. 21–06, Center for Economic Studies, US Census Bureau.

Crane, Leland D., Ryan A. Decker, Aaron Flaaen, Adrian Hamins-Puertolas, and Christopher Kurz. 2021. "Business Exit during the COVID-19 Pandemic: Non-Traditional Measures in Historical Context." Finance and Economics Discussion Series 2020-089r1, Board of Governors of the Federal Reserve System, Washington, DC. https://doi.org/10.17016/FEDS.2020.089r1.

Davis, Steven, and John Haltiwanger. 1999. "Gross Job Flows." In *Handbook of Labor Economics*, vol. 3 and 4, ed. Orley Ashenfelter and David Card, 2711–805. New York: North-Holland.

———. 2019. "Dynamism Diminished: The Role of Housing Markets and Credit Conditions." Working Paper no. 25466 (January), NBER, Cambridge, MA.

Davis, Steven, John Haltiwanger, C. J. Krizan, Ron Jarmin, Javier Miranda, Al Nucci, and Kristin Sandusky. 2009. "Measuring the Dynamics of Young and Small Businesses: Integrating the Employer and Non-Employer Businesses." In *Producer Dynamics: New Evidence from Micro Data*, ed. Timothy Dunne, J. Bradford Jensen, and Mark J. Roberts, 329–66. Chicago: NBER/University of Chicago Press.

Davis, Steven J., John C. Haltiwanger, and Scott Schuh. 1996. *Job Creation and Destruction*. Cambridge, MA: MIT Press.

Decker, Ryan, John Haltiwanger, Ron Jarmin, and Javier Miranda. 2014. "The Role of Entrepreneurship in US Job Creation and Economic Dynamism." *Journal of Economic Perspectives* 28 (3): 3–24.

Dinlersoz, Emin, Timothy Dunne, John Haltiwanger, and Veronika Penciakova. 2021. "Business Formation: A Tale of Two Recessions." *AEA Papers and Proceedings* 111:253–57.

Fairlie, Robert. 2020. "The Impact of COVID-19 on Small Business Owners: Evidence from the First 3 Months after Widespread Social-Distancing Restrictions." *Journal of Economics and Management Strategy.* https://doi.org/10.1111/jems.12400.

Fazio, Catherine, Jorge Guzman, Yupeng Liu, and Scott Stern. 2021. "How Is COVID Changing the Geography of Entrepreneurship? Evidence from the Startup Cartography Project." Working Paper no. 28787, NBER, Cambridge, MA.

Fort, Teresa, John Haltiwanger, Ron Jarmin, and Javier Miranda. 2014. "How Firms Respond to Business Cycles: The Role of Firm Age and Firm Size." *IMF Economic Review* 61:520–59.

Guzman, Jorge, and Scott Stern. 2020. "The State of American Entrepreneurship: New Estimates of the Quantity and Quality of Entrepreneurship for 32 US States, 1988–2014." *American Economic Journal: Economic Policy* 12 (4): 212–43.

Haltiwanger, John, Ron S. Jarmin, and Javier Miranda. 2013. "Who Creates Jobs? Small versus Large versus Young." *Review of Economics and Statistics* 95 (2): 347–61.

Haltiwanger, John, and Lea Rendell. 2021. "Tracking Entrepreneurship in the US: Survey vs. Administrative Data." Photocopy, University of Maryland.

Closing the Innovation Gap in Pink and Black

Lisa D. Cook, *Michigan State University* and *NBER,* United States of America

Janet Gerson, *University of Michigan,* United States of America

Jennifer Kuan, *California State University, Monterey Bay,* United States of America

Abstract

Recent research shows the negative impact of discrimination not only on the targets of discrimination but also on the economy as a whole. Racial and gender inequality can limit the entire economy's productive capacity and innovation outcomes. Using new data from the National Science Foundation's Survey of Earned Doctorates on the scientific workforce from 1980 to 2019, as well as patenting and commercialization data, we examine racial and gender disparities at each stage of the innovation process: education and training, the practice of invention, and commercialization. Although improving along certain dimensions over time, we find persistent racial and gender disparities consistent with the current literature. To reverse the negative effects on productive capacity and long-run economic growth, we also discuss the literature on mitigating discriminatory practices at each juncture, which could have significant distributional effects as access to good jobs expands.

JEL Codes: I24, I26, J7, O32, O34

Keywords: technology, innovation, commercialization, racial discrimination, gender discrimination

I. Introduction

The role of innovation in driving economic growth is nowhere more central than in endogenous growth theory, which posits that increasing the arrival rate of ideas is essential to increasing economic growth (Romer 1990).[1] However, a growing body of evidence shows that discrimination,

Entrepreneurship and Innovation Policy and the Economy, volume 1, 2022.

especially systemic racism and sexism, hinders innovation at every stage of the process, from education and training, to the practice of invention, to the commercialization of those inventions (Cook and Kong-charoen 2010; Cook 2014, 2019). In principle, this discrimination not only diminishes outcomes for African Americans and women but also affects the rate and direction of innovation for the economy as a whole. In a study of PhDs, Cook and Yang (2018) estimate that gross domestic product per capita could be 0.6%–4.4% higher if women and African Americans were able to participate more fully in the innovation economy. Similarly, Hsieh et al. (2019) estimate a reduction in productivity of 20%–40% over the past 50 years as a result of the misallocation of talent due to discrimination, and Peterson and Mann (2020) estimate the cost of systemic racism to be $16 trillion and more than 6 million jobs over the past 20 years. In sum, there is a growing body of evidence that racism has limited our productive capacity.

In light of this scholarship, we examine discriminatory behavior and outcomes at each stage of the innovation process: education and training, the practice of invention, and commercialization of invention. We also discuss the literature on ways to mitigate discrimination and increase inclusiveness, which could have significant distributional effects as access to good jobs expands.

In general, jobs in the innovation economy are attractive relative to jobs in the broader economy. In 2017, the unemployment rate for scientists and engineers was 2.7% compared with 3.1% for college graduates and 4.9% for the United States overall, and included 7–25 million workers in jobs related to the innovation process (NSF 2020). These innovation-related jobs have grown 3% annually from 1960 to 2013 compared with 2% for the broader workforce, and have paid substantially more, with a median income in 2017 of $85,390 compared with $37,690 for all workers (NSF 2020).

Several data sets undergird the study of the innovation economy.[2] The National Science Foundation (NSF) collects data on the science and engineering (S&E) workforce, which it defines as workers in S&E occupations, workers holding S&E degrees, and workers who use technical expertise on the job. NSF surveys S&E students, graduates, and workers, including its Survey of Earned Doctorates and the National Center for Education Statistics Integrated Postsecondary Education Data System Completions Survey. In addition to NSF survey data, patenting and commercialization data are available from the US Patent and Trademark Office (USPTO). Race, ethnicity, and gender are not recorded in patent data, but a plethora of methods to identify inventor race and gender have been successfully applied (Cook and Kongcharoen 2010; Cook 2014).

II. Phase I: Education and Training

Women and African Americans have increasingly succeeded in accessing the first phase of the innovative process: getting doctorates in the sciences and performing basic research that undergirds the stock, flow, and direction of knowledge. In 1970, only 9% of all doctorates in S&E fields were awarded to women; by 2018, that share was nearly 47%. In 1970, only 1% of all S&E doctorates went to African Americans; by 2019, that share was roughly 5.5%. For context, African Americans represent more than 13% of the population (US Census Bureau 2019). Figures 1 and 2 show these data for 1980–2019.[3]

However, despite gains, a divide remains for both groups. Examples of persistent barriers to women and African Americans pursuing degrees in science, technology, engineering, and math (STEM) fields abound. Jennifer Selvidge, a former honors student in materials engineering at the Massachusetts Institute of Technology (MIT), related experiences she had as an undergraduate that are common to many women and African

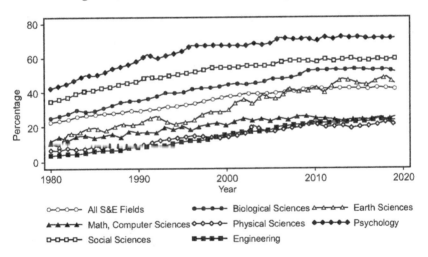

Fig. 1. Share of science and engineering (S&E) doctorates received by women by field, 1980–2019. Color version available as an online enhancement.

Note: Earth Sciences include Atmospheric and Ocean Sciences; Biological Sciences include Agricultural Sciences.

Source: National Science Foundation's National Center for Science and Engineering Statistics, Survey of Earned Doctorates.

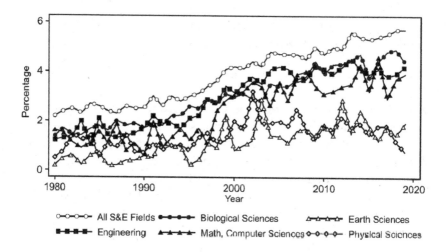

Fig. 2. Share of science and engineering (S&E) doctorates received by African Americans by field, 1980–2019. Color version available as an online enhancement.

Note: Earth Sciences include Atmospheric and Ocean Sciences; Biological Sciences include Agricultural Sciences. Data only include US citizens and permanent residents.

Source: National Science Foundation's National Center for Science and Engineering Statistics, Survey of Earned Doctorates.

Americans. She reported being told "hundreds of times" that, as a woman, she did not deserve to be there and that metallurgy was a "man's field," (Selvidge 2014). She witnessed sexual harassment by teaching assistants and male professors attempting to publicly humiliate the vastly outnumbered female faculty. In addition to observing people of color being actively advised to change majors and leave the department, she was subject to a teaching assistant who claimed that "black Americans are genetically inferior due to slavery era breeding practices" (Selvidge 2014, 3).

A. Interventions: Mentoring

Targeted mentoring programs have been shown to have significant and long-lasting effects on inclusion in STEM careers, where income, race, and gender gaps in acquiring education have been due to a lack of mentoring and exposure to science and innovation careers rather than differences in ability. Initiatives to increase the number and share of women and underrepresented minorities in STEM majors and fields can be effective (Haseltine and Chodos 2017). Mentoring programs can supply the essential exposure needed to expand participation. Oliver et al. (2021) study a specific example of this exposure effect, showing that minority teaching assistants in chemistry labs significantly improve minority student retention and performance.

The American Economic Association (AEA) launched a summer boot camp in the 1970s to increase racial and ethnic diversity in the economics profession. Students attend courses taught by faculty from a broad range of racial and other demographic backgrounds, and mentoring is a key component of the program. Becker, Rouse, and Chen (2016) estimate that program participants were more than 40 percentage points more likely to apply to and attend a PhD program in economics, 26 percentage points more likely to complete a PhD, and about 15 percentage points more likely to work in an economics-related academic job. All told, the AEA summer program may directly account for 17%–21% of the PhDs awarded to minorities in economics over the past 20 years.

The Makers + Mentors Network (formerly US2020) connects underserved and underrepresented youth with local STEM professionals in mentorship programs. Makers + Mentors Network operates in 21 communities across the country, serving more than 150,000 students and 20,000 mentors annually, with a goal of engaging 1 million STEM professionals as mentors for students in kindergarten through graduate school (see makersandmentors.org). The program also places AmeriCorps VISTA members in its community efforts, and a planned Maker Fellows program partners with community colleges and historically Black colleges and universities. Hands-on learning experiences, and after-school and summer programs, strengthen students' foundation for learning at key moments in their education and career.

B. Interventions: Exposure

Young children can benefit from exposure to invention and innovation. Recent empirical support for the role of early exposure in creating more inventors can be found in a study of the inventor life cycle (Bell et al. 2019). High school programs, such as the InventTeam® initiative at the Lemelson-MIT Program, are found to have a positive impact (Couch, Estabrooks, and Skukauskaite 2018). Spark Lab at the Lemelson Center for the Study of Invention and Innovation at the Smithsonian Institution and at a handful of affiliate museums is an example of a successful early education program. The activity space allows children to create an invention and helps them think about making the invention useful. To be sure, in the face of systemic racism, sexism, and other forms of discrimination, interventions promoting mentoring and exposure may be insufficient to augment the participation of women and underrepresented minorities. We discuss this further below.

III. Phase II: The Practice of Invention

The second stage of the innovation process is the practice of invention (e.g., in corporate or academic laboratories). Here, women and African Americans have also faced pervasive barriers. For example, throughout history women and African Americans have had to battle the perception that they were mentally inferior and technically incompetent and were not welcome in the White, male culture of corporate research and development (R&D) labs. They were also barred from participating or limited in their participation in scientific fairs and barred from joining professional scientific and engineering societies until the mid-twentieth century, thus depriving them of the social capital and connections required to advance their careers and develop their inventions (Oldenziel 1999; Sinclair 2004; Cook 2011). Patent data can provide crucial measures and indicators of discriminatory access.

A. Access to Patenting

Legal access to the US patent system offered opportunities, albeit limited, for women and African Americans. There was no language in the original Patent Act of 1790 limiting patentees based on gender, race, age, or religion. Therefore, decades before emancipation and universal suffrage, women and (free) African Americans could, and did, invent and earn US patents.[4] Still, women and African Americans did not have equal protection under patent laws. Although free African Americans were allowed to obtain patents, the USPTO refused to grant patents to enslaved African Americans. Moreover, laws in many states assigned all marital property rights to husbands, thus prohibiting married women from owning or controlling patents in their own names. These draconian social norms and policies deterred many women and African Americans from becoming inventors.[5]

Even without discriminatory laws, discriminatory practice leads to inequality in patenting outcomes to this day. Jensen, Kovács, and Sorenson (2018) find that, all else being equal, patent applications with female lead inventors are rejected more often than those with male lead inventors. Addressing this unequal gender-based access to patenting is important, because patents are an input to commercialization, as discussed below. The 2018 SUCCESS Act—and companion IDEA Act currently being considered—are a response to research on diversity in innovation (especially Cook and Kongcharoen 2010) and seek to collect demographic data on patent applicants to increase participation by underrepresented groups.

Patent enforcement is also a factor in the differential ability of women and minorities to profit from the fruits of their invention. Lonnie Johnson, inventor of the Super SoakerTM water gun, who is African American, had to doggedly pursue Hasbro to receive the $72.9 million owed to him for his patented and trademarked invention. Although his lawsuit was ultimately successful, most African American firms are small and do not have the legal and financial resources to aggressively protect their intellectual property.[6] This is in addition to a substantial literature on gender and racial pay gaps.

Patent data, however imperfect, provide a measure of inventive activity and of unequal access for women and African Americans.[7] USPTO data from 1970 to 2006 show patent output of 235 patents per million for all US inventors; for women, the number is 40 patents per million, and for African Americans, it is 6 patents per million (Cook 2007, 2014; Cook and Kongcharoen 2010). These figures understate the effect of unequal representation because patent teams comprising men and women generate higher-value patents than single-sex teams (Cook and Kongcharoen 2010). The misallocation of resources suggested by these findings could lead to suboptimal levels and rates of innovation and economic growth, which are exacerbated by intergenerational effects of inventorship. Bell et al. (2019) find that children from high-income families who grow up around other inventors are more likely to patent, whereas children from low-income families with limited exposure to emerging technology are less likely to patent.

B.   Access to Resources

Patent data provide clues to some of the mechanisms behind the underrepresentation of women and African Americans in invention, especially access to workplaces that provide the necessary resources for invention and innovation. Employees who produce inventions on the job are contractually obligated to assign their patents to their employers (usually for $1) once they are issued by the patent office (Fisk 2009; Mirowski 2011). Thus, a patent assignment typically implies an employee invention with commercial value, and gender and race gaps can be measured in patent assignments as well. The likelihood of female inventors assigning a patent was 51% lower than male inventors, and African American inventors were 46% less likely than other US inventors to assign a patent (Cook and Kongcharoen 2010).[8]

In addition, private firms are better at commercializing inventions than government employers, where African American scientists and engineers are concentrated. Commercialization is more difficult in the government sector because of historical practices prior to the Government Patent Policy Act (Bayh-Dole Act), which encourages the development of government patents. These practices include strict ethics policies and risk aversion among government laboratory employees and contractors, especially with respect to entrepreneurship, production, and ownership.[9] But even among government employees who invent, African Americans are less likely to move to a corporation than their White coinventors (Cook 2003).

NSF data on employment provide more direct evidence that women and African Americans have unequal access to corporate employment and invention resources. The share of women working in an S&E field rose from 31% to 37% between 1993 and 2010. Over the same period, women in S&E occupations rose from 23% to 28% (NSF 2014). By 2019 women made up 29% of the S&E workers, and the percentage of African Americans working in S&E had increased to 5% (NSF 2021). But both female and African American scientists and engineers are more likely to work in non-S&E occupations than in S&E occupations.

Figures 3A and 3B report selected occupations for women and African Americans with doctorates. Note that 70% of psychologists were women in 2019 but just 14% of engineers. In 2010, 25% of the workforce in computer and mathematical sciences were women, and in engineering 13% were women; in 2019 these shares were 29% and 14%, respectively (NSF 2014, 2021).

Examining specific occupations within a field, more than 57% of all the people in S&E-related occupations are women, with women making up nearly 70% of health-related workers, more than half of S&E precollege teachers, and one-fifth of S&E technologists and technicians.[10] Female scientists and engineers constitute more than half of scientists and engineers in non-S&E occupations. Women often start their careers working in the innovation economy but then leave for various reasons, including the need to provide child care, the lack of family leave policies, and poor workplace climate (Pepitone 2011; NSF 2021).

A similar pattern emerges for African American scientists and engineers, who make up just 5% of workers employed in S&E occupations. Among S&E occupations, African American scientists and engineers are

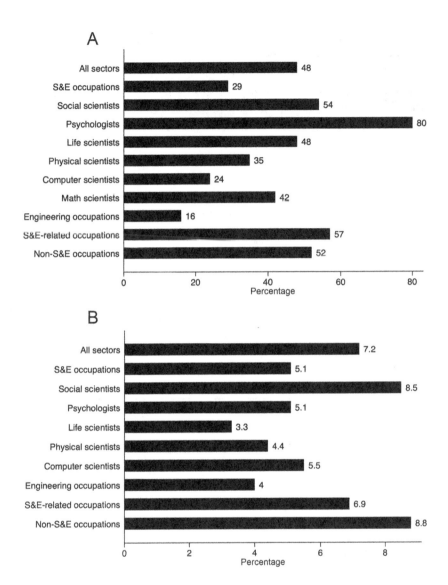

Fig. 3. (*A*) Employed women scientists and engineers (S&E), percentage of selected occupations, 2019. (*B*) Employed African American scientists and engineers, percentage of selected occupations, 2019. Color version available as an online enhancement.

Note: Data were not available for the math scientists occupation.

Source: National Science Foundation *Women, Minorities, and Persons with Disabilities in Science and Engineering* report 2021.

more concentrated among social and related scientists and computer and math scientists than they are in other S&E occupations. Among S&E-related occupations, African American scientists and engineers, like female scientists and engineers, are more concentrated in health-related occupations and in precollege teaching than in other S&E occupations. More African American scientists and engineers are in non-S&E occupations than are in S&E and S&E-related occupations.

Although women and African American scientists and engineers are growing as a share of the innovation labor force, unemployment rates vary significantly by racial and ethnic group (see figs. 4 and 5). The African American unemployment rate, at just under 4%, is higher than for Hispanics and Asians, and higher than the average for all scientists and engineers.

Figure 6 shows where scientists and engineers are employed by sector. Most scientists and engineers are employed in business or industry, but underrepresented minorities are more heavily employed in education and government. This has implications for economic growth; although scientists in government laboratories work hard at patenting, they have binding constraints on their ability to commercialize their inventions relative to their private-sector peers.

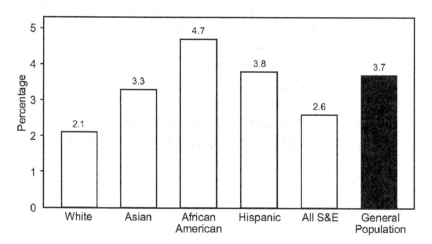

Fig. 4.   Unemployment rates among scientists and engineers (S&E), 2019. Color version available as an online enhancement.

Note: Unemployment rate calculated as the percentage of the labor force not working and looking for work. Total US labor force unemployment rate covers the labor force ages 16 and over.

Source: National Science Foundation *Women, Minorities, and Persons with Disabilities in Science and Engineering* report.

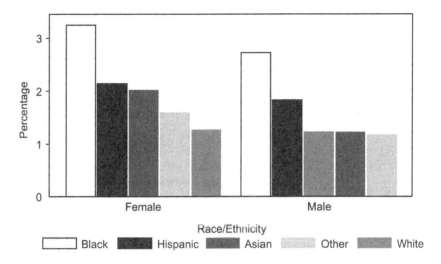

Fig. 5. Unemployment rate in 2019 in science and engineering fields by gender and race. Color version available as an online enhancement.

Source: Survey of doctorate recipients, 2019.

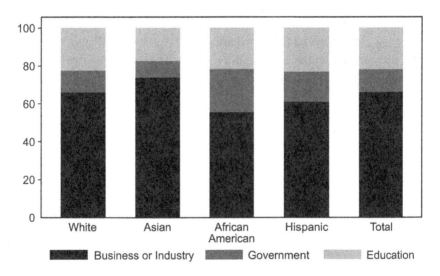

Fig. 6. Employment sector of scientists and engineers, by race and ethnicity, 2019. Color version available as an online enhancement.

Source: National Science Foundation *Women, Minorities, and Persons with Disabilities in Science and Engineering* report 2021.

C. *Interventions: Workplace Policies*

This equilibrium underemployment of women and minorities is crucial to address if efforts to expand their recruitment into education and training are to succeed. The "Lost Einsteins" (Bell et al. 2019) will be an even greater loss if they have been educated but sidelined, which NSF employment data suggest is currently the case for many women and minority scientists.

At present, the literature in economics on interventions related to problems of discrimination in the patent office and innovative firms is scant. Instead, data are analyzed to estimate the magnitude of the problem. The patent and employment data discussed above relate to the extensive margin in innovative activity; that is, whether women and minorities are able to access the patent office or private employment. However, the weak retention of women and minorities in private firms suggests that the intensive margin may also play a significant role in unequal outcomes—how women and minorities are treated once they are inside private firms can cause them to leave, resulting in an equilibrium with relatively few women and minorities engaging in inventive activity.

Edray Goins's experience is illustrative. Dr. Goins was one of the few African American mathematicians with tenure at a major research university. In 2018, after more than a decade on the faculty of Purdue University, he left, choosing a full professorship at Pomona College, a liberal arts college, instead. He explained that this practically unheard-of move was due to a feeling of isolation, along with instance after instance of subtle hostilities and unspoken disrespect, such as reports from graduate students that they'd been warned by a White professor not to work with him (Harmon 2019). Many similar anecdotes from the sciences and beyond were shared on Twitter and other social media platforms under the hashtags #BlackandSTEM, #blackintech, and #BlackInTheIvory, particularly following the murder of George Floyd.

Income data are indicative of unequal treatment within firms. Although the median salary for men in the innovation economy in 2010 was $80,000, it was only $53,000 for women, or 66% of the median male salary (NSF 2014).[11] In 2019, the median salary for scientists and engineers was $95,000 for men, yet it was only $70,000 for women, or 74% of the median male salary (NSF 2021). Some of the gap is attributable to the different occupations people perform across gender, with more men in S&E occupations, which tend to be higher paid. Female scientists and engineers have lower median salaries than men in most S&E occupational groups.

Within S&E occupations, the female-to-male median salary narrows to 80% and ranges from 67% for workers ages 50–75 to 84% for workers ages 30–39. The female-to-male median salary is 80% in S&E-related occupations and 68% for non-S&E occupations. "Biological, agricultural, and other life science" is the only occupation in which the median female salary exceeds the male median salary, with a female-to-male median salary of 1.05.[12]

The salary gap between African Americans and Whites is less than that between men and women. In 2010, the median salary for Whites was $72,000, and for African Americans it was $56,000, or 78% of the median salary for Whites.[13] In 2019, this gap remained largely the same, at 79%. For S&E occupations, the gap narrows to 88%. However, among S&E occupations, the gap is widest among physical scientists (79%). There is practically parity in engineering, with psychologists' and social scientists' median salary for African Americans higher than the median salary for Whites, with a ratio of 1.03 and 1.06, respectively.[14]

Comparing across women, African American S&E salaries were 87% of White women in all occupations, and African American non-S&E salaries were 84% of White women in all occupations. However, there is practically salary parity in S&E occupations and in S&E-related occupations. The largest gaps within S&E occupations are among engineering occupations (85%), but among social scientists and psychologists, the ratio of the median salary of African American women to White women is 1.24 and 1.12, respectively.[15]

These race and gender wage gaps are concerning in their own right, generating cross-sectional wealth inequities. However, where they may also indicate hostile work environments that lead to equilibrium underrepresentation in private firm employment, long-term distributional consequences may also arise. The earnings gap between workers in the innovation economy and the overall economy is substantial, with workers in the innovation economy earning more than double the average American worker in 2019.[16] Thus, when women and minorities leave private firms, they experience lower earnings, either working outside the innovation economy or in government and education, where salaries are lower than those in business or industry. This further deepens the income inequality among S&E workers.

IV. Phase III: Commercialization of Invention

The third and final stage in the innovation process is the commercialization of invention. Commercialization requires drawing on financial and social capital to introduce the invention into the economy. In addition to the activity of large firms, in which S&E employees invent and commercialize an invention as discussed above, inventors also start their own firms. This latter avenue also presents disproportionate obstacles for women and African Americans.

The gap in the commercialization process was in the public eye in 2012 when Ellen Pao sued her employer, the noted venture capital firm Kleiner Perkins Caufield and Byers, for gender bias in promotion. She argued that her performance, like that of other women and people of color, was negatively affected because the firm's partners did not sponsor her investments or include her in key activities and decisions of the firm. She has also described her experience as CEO of a social media technology company, Reddit, where she faced gender-related harassment and threats of violence (Pao 2017).

Female and African American inventors once intentionally obscured their identities to counter discrimination and to profit from their inventions. For example, Garrett Morgan, an African American inventor based in Cleveland at the turn of the twentieth century, correctly surmised that White consumers would be skeptical of buying products from an African American inventor. Therefore, Morgan hired White and Native American actors to portray him to sell his gas mask (Cook 2012). Many of the iconic lamp designs associated with Louis Comfort Tiffany were in fact created by Clara Driscoll and other "Tiffany Girls." Their identities were not revealed so the value of the designs could be maximized (Eidelberg, Gray, and Hofer 2007). Discrimination also forced women and African Americans into bad deals or to forgo commercialization entirely.

Contemporary inventors can generate income from an invention in at least three ways: (1) engage in entrepreneurship and start a new firm (or business unit) to develop, manufacture, and sell the invention; (2) assign (sell) the patented invention for a lump sum; and (3) license the patented invention to another manufacturer and collect royalties until the patent expires. Data on entrepreneurship, firm ownership, patent assignments, and wealth accumulation from innovative assets suggest that innovation gaps exist and persist for women and African American inventors compared with their White male counterparts.

Start-up data help elucidate how the commercialization of new inventions through entrepreneurship can unlock enormous wealth. Therefore, the differential ability of women and African Americans to accumulate proceeds from innovation and entrepreneurship is striking and helps explain wealth inequality in the United States more broadly.

Equity ownership of technology start-ups is the stage of the innovative process where the largest pecuniary gains are found. Those who own equity stakes, including angel and venture capital investors, founders, and employees with stock options, stand to profit greatly from initial public offerings, mergers and acquisitions, stock splits, and other liquidity events.

Details of this process show why unequal access to patenting and resources for invention and commercialization is problematic for economic growth. The practice among venture capital firms of restricting their attention to start-ups with patents pending (Cook and Kongcharoen 2010) exclude women and minorities whose patent applications are disproportionately rejected. And with fewer women and minorities participating in innovative activity, patent quality declines, according to a growing literature on the better outcomes of more-diverse teams (Rock and Grant 2016). When a founding team includes a woman, it outperforms all-male peers by 63%, but female CEOs receive only 2.7% of all venture funding, and women of color get virtually none: 0.2% (Weisul 2016).

In general, it is difficult to find women and African Americans among the ranks of entrepreneurs, top management teams, and boards in the innovation economy. Women and African Americans are often found in legal and marketing departments but are largely missing in technical positions and on boards. In 2014, *Fortune* ranked several large tech firms based on recently released demographic data. With respect to female executives, Indiegogo was ranked highest, with women in 43% of leadership roles. Cisco and Pinterest were ranked lowest, with 19% women in executive roles. Women constituted just 18.7% of directors of boards of S&P 500 firms in 2014, which was up from 16.3% in 2011 (Huddleston 2014). In 2015, just 11% of venture capitalists were women, and 2% were African American (NVCA 2016).

What interventions can be undertaken to improve the inclusiveness of commercialization? Legal and policy remedies may offer some mitigation, and practitioners offer suggestions for private ordering solutions.

A. Public Ordering Solutions

Legal remedies are currently being tested in several cases of discriminatory behavior by private firms. The US Department of Labor is suing Oracle for $400 million for pay discrimination against women and racial minorities and is continuing to investigate Google's gender gap in salaries. In the spring of 2017, it reported systemic discrimination of women at Google (Lam 2017). Pinterest has similarly been sued for pay discrimination (Schwab 2020). In addition, workers from minoritized groups in the innovation economy have begun to speak more openly about their experiences that identify these firms as allowing or cultivating suboptimal or openly hostile workplaces. A number of these workers have spoken out on social media platforms.

Another approach is legislation, such as California's Women on Boards law, which requires all publicly held corporations whose principal executive offices are located in California to have at least one female director on their boards. In principle, this approach could be extended to include targets for underrepresented racial and ethnic minorities and to apply nationally. Data collection and reporting are another approach to combating racism and sexism in the workplace generally, which could be particularly appropriate for the innovation economy (Frye 2019). Requiring public reporting of employer pay and promotion data by race and gender would provide greater transparency of employer pay practices (and could include detailed data on domestic and foreign composition). Employers could also be required to report steps taken to address pay and promotion discrimination based on race, gender, ethnicity, and other factors in Securities and Exchange Commission filings. Such steps could include eliminating forced arbitration in sexual harassment cases, implementing anti–African American and antisexist bias training for all levels of staff (especially leadership, managers, and supervisors), increasing funding for enforcement to ensure compliance with equal pay protections, and undertaking targeted efforts to examine the prevalence of race and gender bias in pay discrimination cases.

Moreover, measures at federal agencies could also reduce discrimination. The National Academies of Science, Engineering, and Medicine just completed an extensive review of the premier programs within the US government to explicitly promote commercialization of innovation, the Small Business Innovation Research (SBIR) and Small Business Technology Transfer (STTR) programs, which are housed within the Small Business Administration (SBA) (NASEM 2020). Although the report focused on the Department of Energy SBIR and STTR programs, the lessons and suggestions directed at the Department of Energy, the SBA, and Congress are largely applicable to any agency. The salient major suggestions relate to diversifying the applicant pool by expanding reviewer pools, optimizing matches between applicants and R&D partners, and implementing virtual mentoring programs to connect SBIR/STTR applicants to national laboratories. Suggestions from the report would be pertinent for the recruitment, application, and review processes.

The report suggests that the lack of diversity of the applicant pool for flagship innovation programs is partly explained by the lack of diversity among the people who review applications for the programs. Currently the people who serve as reviewers of applications for premier innovation programs are primarily White men, selected for their demonstrated expertise as leaders, research managers, and technical managers at national labs or research universities—positions in which women and minorities are woefully underrepresented. In engineering departments, for example, only 16% of professors are women, 2.3% are African American, and 3.6% are Hispanic. A more diverse reviewer pool might help to identify more diverse and more innovative projects. To minimize the service burden that underrepresented minorities would have to bear as reviewers, agencies, departments, and national labs could provide incentives in the form of compensation, promotion credits, and so on, in the same way as has been executed at the National Institutes of Health.

The report also speculated that potential female and underrepresented minority applicants might lack information about prospective R&D partners. Women and underrepresented minorities are less likely to be in the same professional networks as their White male counterparts and so lack information and connections to research partners that are critical for successful applications. Making this information more publicly available could disproportionately help women and minorities. For example, data on research partners for previous awards in a public and searchable database could be particularly helpful to applicants outside these networks. This would be a low-cost measure that government agencies could undertake that could have substantial impact.

Finally, the report suggested that proximity to national labs that provide R&D expertise confers an advantage on applicants. As a result, potential applicants from underrepresented regions with little or no access to the connections and mentoring essential to find suitable R&D partners are disadvantaged. These geographic distances can be a substantial barrier. The report suggests virtual mentoring programs for women and underrepresented minorities to connect applicants with national labs, thus reducing the barrier caused by geographic distances. A model for this program would be the longstanding Mentor-Protégé Program, which fosters long-term business relationships between small disadvantaged firms and prime contractors. The SBA and various other agencies have this program. In addition, presentations, fairs, and other gatherings to promote the SBIR/STTR program could be extended to locations where there are already inventors from underrepresented minority groups, such as Atlanta and Austin.

B.   Private Ordering Solutions

In 2014, less than 7% of US venture capital investment was in businesses founded by women, and a mere 0.2% was in businesses founded by African American women (NVCA 2016), even though start-ups with diverse executive teams yield a return two times greater than entirely White teams. A CNBC report faults racial bias of nondiverse venture capital investors. Recent Bloomberg interviews with African American CEOs in Silicon Valley revealed a routine assumption that they were not in charge of their companies: there were constant challenges to their credentials, subtle and overt discrimination, and the regular suggestion that they hire a White business partner to put investors at ease (Anand and McBride 2020). African Americans also lack mentors and social networks, weakening the pipeline of potential entrepreneurs, executives, board members, and funders.[17]

Freada Kapor Klein, a venture capitalist and longtime advocate for diversity in technology companies, points out that although many technology companies claim they are addressing a lack of diversity in their workforce, they can do more (Harrison 2019). Among her suggestions are continued investment in diversity in hiring at all levels, retention initiatives, and making sure all employees value and prioritize a workforce that is diverse and inclusive. Recognizing unequal outcomes is the first step. Policies and business plans that address these inequalities are essential for shared prosperity.[18] If shareholders and investors are committed to reducing these inequities, they will need to set specific diversity targets and hold management accountable for meeting them.

Separately, CNBC pledged to do its part with access to information, highlighting founders, innovators, and investors who help the business world move toward a more diverse and more inclusive future. Information is the key behind increasing firm collection of data on the gender, racial, and ethnic composition of their workforce and sharing it with policy makers and researchers.

V.   Discussion and Final Thoughts

Innovation is an essential input to economic growth. The innovation process begins with education, which macroeconomists have studied as human capital formation, but must be followed by two additional steps, invention and commercialization. By placing existing scholarship on education into the wider context of innovation, bottlenecks in the process can be identified. For example, the impact of policies that create more Einsteins, such as those suggested by van Reenen (2021), may be inefficiently limited by discrimination, which sidelines these new Einsteins.

This sidelining moves distributional issues to the foreground. Whereas distribution and efficiency are typically regarded as separate policy goals, in the innovation setting, unequal access to opportunity creates inefficiencies in the quality, quantity, and direction of innovation. The institutional details and mechanisms of discrimination, which normally elude mainstream economic scholarship, are on full display in the innovation process. Discrimination within the patent office, wage gaps, and the low rates of minority female S&E PhDs in S&E jobs all demand greater scrutiny and investigation. Economists must work across disciplines, including institutional and business economists as well as related disciplines outside economics, if a more complete picture is to be obtained.

As a policy goal, distribution has grown increasingly salient. Income tax data show that income inequality is higher now than in the Gilded Age and has grown recently: from 1993 to 2011, real income grew 10 times more for the top 1% than for the bottom 99%: 57.5% compared with 5.8% (Saez 2016). This inequality has led to profound political polarization and social unrest and led to greater attention to distribution as a policy goal. The innovation sector raises fundamental questions related to inequality, with its relatively high incomes, considerable wealth, and substantial and growing political influence. If women and African Americans are disproportionately excluded from the sector, even when they have the skills demanded of skill-biased technological change, they will be unfairly and inefficiently deprived of their share of opportunity, wealth, and influence. Indeed, innovation inequality—and the resulting income and wealth inequality—fly in the face of the American ideals of equal opportunity, shared responsibility to achieve shared prosperity, and more and better technological advances to raise living standards for all.

In short, addressing innovation inequality is likely to require solutions that are not just efficient but also just, such as policies that promote equal access and investment in human capital and that challenge the racism and sexism now rampant in the technology sector. Economics can play a critical role by moving beyond the narrow analysis of the efficiency cost of discrimination and engaging with the design of systemic solutions. The faulty rhetoric of sexism is exemplified by a Google engineer, James Damore, who wrote a memo that leaked and went viral in the summer and fall of 2017. This memo, directed at diversity initiatives at Google, argued that women were underrepresented in technology careers because of "innate dispositional differences" between the genders (Wakabayashi 2017). In fact, women's contributions follow a pattern consistent with economic theories of discrimination, in which women and minorities must clear a higher bar to participate. One consequence of discrimination is that their contributions are higher than average quality. For example, Grace Hopper was a pioneer of computing who invented the COBOL language. And African American women, mathematicians Mary Jackson, Katherine Johnson, and Dorothy Vaughn, made key contributions to human space flight at the National Aeronautics and Space Administration. Featured in the book and film *Hidden Figures*, these female and minority scientists would otherwise have gone unacknowledged. Google dismissed Damore for "perpetuating gender stereotypes" (Bergen and Huet 2017). A few weeks later a former Google software engineer, Kelly Ellis, and two other women sued Google, alleging discrimination in both the pay and promotion of women. Addressing these inequalities in a systemic way will be central to closing the innovation gap.

Endnotes

Author email addresses: Cook (lisacook@msu.edu), Gerson (jgerson@umich.edu), Kuan (jkuan@csumb.edu). The authors thank participants in the April 2021 NBER EIPE meeting for helpful discussion, and Scott Stern and Josh Lerner for helpful comments. We are grateful to Steven Wu-Chaves for able research assistance. Earlier versions of this research were generously supported by the National Science Foundation, Grant #1064157, and the Lemelson Center for the Study of Invention and Innovation at the Smithsonian Institution. Part of this research was completed while Lisa D. Cook was visiting at the Opportunity and Inclusive Growth Institute at the Federal Reserve Bank of Minneapolis, the US Patent and Trademark Office, and the Institute for Research on Innovation and Science at the University of Michigan, and their support is appreciated. All mistakes are our own. For acknowledgments, sources of research support, and disclosure of the authors' material financial relationships, if any, please see https://www.nber.org/books-and-chapters /entrepreneurship-and-innovation-policy-and-economy-volume-1/closing-innovation -gap-pink-and-black.

1. The paper draws heavily on Cook (2019, 2020a, 2020b).

2. For the purposes of this paper, the terms "innovation economy," "innovation sector," "science and engineering (S&E) economy," and "S&E workforce" are used interchangeably, as are the terms "innovation jobs" and "S&E occupations."

3. NSF (2001, 2021). The trends are similar for master's and bachelor's degrees and are comparable through 2018. This is significant because most commercialized inventions originate from those with bachelor's degrees and master's degrees.

4. For example, in 1809 inventor Mary Kies was the first woman to receive a US patent, for an improved method of weaving straw with silk thread to make hats. Similarly, Thomas L. Jennings was the first free person of color to receive a US patent, in 1821 for a dry cleaning process. On Kies, see USPTO (1999). On Jennings, see Sluby (2004). On the egalitarian nature of the US patent system, see Khan (2005).

5. On discriminatory patent laws and policies, see Gage (1883), Baker (1902), Pursell (1981), Lubar (1991), and Sluby (2004).

6. See *Black Enterprise*'s list of top 100 African American firms, which reports their size (Blodgett 2019).

7. For a variety of reasons, patent data are an imperfect proxy for measuring inventive activity. First, not all inventions are legally protected. Second, the mechanisms for legal protection vary widely, including patents, copyrights, trademarks, trade secrets, or some combination thereof. Finally, many patents are not economically viable. These include vanity patents, defensive patents (patents obtained but purposely not developed to prevent a competitor from inventing in a complementary area), and inventions whose commercialization may be cost prohibitive. On the methodological possibilities and limitations of using patent data, see Schmookler (1966), Griliches (1990), and Jaffe and Trajtenberg (2002).

8. Odds are calculated relative to assignment to an individual.

9. Beyond the greater barriers to commercialization in the government sector relative to other sectors, there is also an issue of selection. Government jobs are often more stable relative to the private sector, and government agencies have traditionally been risk averse.

10. These data refer to all degree holders—bachelor's, master's, and doctorate.

11. As is true for any salary data, differences vary across occupations, age groups, race, ethnicity, etc.

12. NSF (2021); authors' calculations.

13. Salary data for 2010 are from NSF (2014) and are for full-time workers with the highest degree in an S&E field. Salary data for 2019 are from NSF (2021).

14. NSF (2021); authors' calculations.

15. NSF (2021); authors' calculations.

16. NSF (2021), Federal Reserve Economic Data.

17. Sanders and Ashcraft (2019) includes a rich discussion of gender and implicit bias.

18. A more comprehensive strategy to address shortcomings related to diversity and inclusion in the tech sector appears in Klein et al. (2018).

References

Anand, Priya, and Sarah McBride. 2020. "For Black CEOs in Silicon Valley, Humiliation Is a Part of Doing Business." *Bloomberg*, June 16.

Baker, Henry. 1902. "The Negro as an Inventor." In *Twentieth Century Negro Literature*, ed. D. W. Culp, 399–413. Naperville, IL: Nichols.

Becker, Charles M., Cecilia Elena Rouse, and Mingyu Chen. 2016. "Can a Summer Make a Difference? The Impact of the American Economic Association Summer Program on Minority Student Outcomes." *Economics of Education Review* 53:46–71.

Bell, Alex, Raj Chetty, Xavier Jaravel, Neviana Petkova, and John van Reenen. 2019. "Who Becomes an Inventor in America? The Importance of Exposure to Innovation." *Quarterly Journal of Economics* 134 (2): 647–713.

Bergen, Mark, and Ellen Huet. 2017. "Google Fires Author of Divisive Memo on Gender Differences." *Bloomberg*, August 7. https://www.bloomberg.com/news/articles/2017-08-08/google-fires-employee-behind-controversial-diversity-memo.

Blodgett, Sequoia. 2019. "Largest Number of Black Software Engineers to Date Join this Tech Group." *Black Enterprise*, January 29. https://www.blackenterprise.com/black-software-engineers-join-group.

Cook, Lisa D. 2003. "The African American and Women Inventors and Patents Data Set." Stanford University, Palo Alto, CA. Last revised November 2008, extended to women inventors August 2009.

———. 2007. "Inventing Social Networks: Evidence from African American 'Great Inventors.'" Working paper, Michigan State University, East Lansing.

———. 2011. "Inventing Social Capital: Evidence from African American Inventors, 1843–1930." *Explorations in Economic History* 48 (4): 507–18.

———. 2012. "Overcoming Discrimination by Consumers during the Age of Segregation: The Example of Garrett Morgan." *Business History Review* 86 (2): 211–34.

———. 2014. "The Innovation Economy in Pink and Black." Working paper, Michigan State University, East Lansing.

———. 2019. "The Innovation Gap in Pink and Black." In *Does America Need More Innovators?* ed. Matthew Wisnioski, Eric S. Hintz, and Marie Stettler Kleine. Cambridge, MA: MIT Press.

———. 2020a. "Addressing Gender and Racial Disparities in the US Labor Market to Boost Wages and Power Innovation." In *Boosting Wages for US Workers in the New Economy*. Washington, DC: Washington Center for Equitable Growth.

———. 2020b. "Policies to Broaden Participation in the Innovation Process." Report, Brookings Institution, Washington, DC.

Cook, Lisa D., and Chaleampong Kongcharoen. 2010. "The Idea Gap in Pink and Black." Working Paper no. 16331 (September), NBER, Cambridge, MA. http://www.nber.org/papers/w16331.pdf.

Cook, Lisa D., and Yanyan Yang. 2018. "Missing Women and African Americans, Innovation, and Economic Growth." http://www.yanyanyang.com/uploads/5/6/5/2/56523543/aeapinkblack_cookyang.pdf.

Couch, Stephanie, Leigh B. Estabrooks, and Audra Skukauskaite. 2018. "Addressing the Gender Gap among Patent Holders through Invention Education Policies." *Technology and Innovation* 19 (4): 735–49.

Eidelberg, Martin, Nina Gray, and Margaret Hofer. 2007. *A New Light on Tiffany: Clara Driscoll and the Tiffany Girls*. New York: New-York Historical Society.

Fisk, Catherine L. 2009. *Working Knowledge: Employee Innovation and the Rise of Corporate Intellectual Property, 1800–1930*. Chapel Hill: University of North Carolina Press.

Frye, Jocelyn. 2019. "Racism and Sexism Combine to Shortchange Working Black Women." Center for American Progress, Washington, DC.

Gage, Matilda Joslyn. 1883. "Woman as an Inventor." *North American Review* 136 (318): 478–89.

Griliches, Zvi. 1990. "Patent Statistics as Economic Indicators: A Survey." *Journal of Economic Literature* 28:1661–707.

Harmon, Amy. 2019. "For a Black Mathematician, What It's Like to Be the 'Only One.'" *New York Times*, February 18. https://www.nytimes.com/2019/02/18/us/edray-goins-black-mathematicians.html.

Harrison, Sara. 2019. "Five Years of Tech Diversity Reports—and Little Progress." *Wired*, October 1.

Haseltine, Florence P., and Mark Chodos. 2017. "'Why' vs. 'What,' or 'The Bad Penny Opera': Gender and Bias in Science." *Technology and Innovation* 18 (4): 275–79.

Hsieh, Chang-Tai, Erik Hurst, Charles I. Jones, and Peter J. Klenow. 2019. "The Allocation of Talent and US Economic Growth." *Econometrica* 87 (5): 1439–74.

Huddleston, Tom, Jr. 2014. "Boardroom Breakthrough: Gender Diversity Is Flourishing among Board Nominees." *Fortune*, September 25. http://fortune.com/2014/09/25/boardroom-breakthrough-gender-diversity-is-flourishing-among-board-nominees.

Jaffe, Adam, and Manuel Trajtenberg, eds. 2002. *Patents, Citations, and Innovations: A Window on the Knowledge Economy.* Cambridge, MA: MIT Press.

Jensen, Kyle, Balázs Kovács, and Olav Sorenson. 2018. "Gender Differences in Obtaining and Maintaining Patent Rights." *Nature Biotechnology* 36:307–309.

Khan, B. Zorina. 2005. "The Democratization of Invention: Patents and Copyrights in American Economic Development, 1790–1920." New York: Cambridge University Press.

Klein, Freada Kapor, Allison Scott, Frieda McAlear, Alexis Martin, and Sonia Koshy. 2018. "The Leaky Tech Pipeline: A Comprehensive Framework for Understanding and Addressing the Lack of Diversity across the Tech Ecosystem." Tech Report, Kapor Center for Social Impact, Oakland, CA.

Lam, Bourree. 2017. "The Department of Labor Accuses Google of Gender Pay Discrimination." *Atlantic Monthly*, April 7. https://www.theatlantic.com/business/archive/2017/04/dol-google-pay-discrimination/522411.

Lubar, Steven. 1991. "The Transformation of Antebellum Patent Law." *Technology and Culture* 32 (4): 932–59.

Mirowski, Philip. 2011. *Science-Mart: Privatizing American Science.* Cambridge, MA: Harvard University Press.

NASEM (National Academies of Sciences, Engineering, and Medicine). 2020. *Review of the SBIR and STTR Programs at the Department of Energy.* Washington, DC: National Academies Press. https://doi.org/10.17226/25674.

NSF (National Science Foundation). 2001. *Doctorate Recipients from United States Universities: Summary Report 2000.* Arlington, VA: National Science Foundation. http://files.eric.ed.gov/fulltext/ED459639.pdf.

———. 2014. *Science and Engineering Indicators 2014, Chapter 3.* Arlington, VA: National Science Foundation. https://www.nsf.gov/statistics/seind14.

———. 2020. *Science and Engineering Indicators 2020, Science and Engineering Labor Force.* Arlington, VA: National Science Foundation. https://ncses.nsf.gov/pubs/nsb20198.

———. 2021. *Women, Minorities, and Persons with Disabilities in Science and Engineering.* Arlington VA: National Science Foundation. https://ncses.nsf.gov/pubs/nsf21321.

NVCA (National Venture Capital Association). 2016. "Building a More Inclusive Entrepreneurial System." https://nvca.org/wp-content/uploads/2016/07/Final-NVCA-Diversity-Report.pdf.

Oldenziel, Ruth. 1999. *Making Technology Masculine: Men, Women, and Modern Machines in America, 1870–1945.* Amsterdam: Amsterdam University Press.

Oliver, Daniel, Robert Fairlie, Glenn Millhauser, and Randa Roland. 2021. "Minority Student and Teaching Assistant Interactions in STEM." Working Paper no. 28719, NBER, Cambridge, MA. http://www.nber.org/papers/w28719.

Pao, Ellen K. 2017. *Reset: My Fight for Inclusion and Lasting Change.* New York: Spiegel & Grau.

Pepitone, Julianne. 2011. "Silicon Valley Fights to Keep Its Diversity Data Secret." CNN Money, November 9. https://money.cnn.com/2011/11/09/technology/diversity_silicon_valley/index.htm.

Peterson, Dana M., and Catherine L. Mann. 2020. "Closing the Racial Inequality Gaps." Citi Global Perspectives and Solutions, September. https://www.citivelocity.com/citigps/closing-the-racial-inequality-gaps.

Pursell, Carroll. 1981. "Women Inventors in America." *Technology and Culture* 22 (3): 545–49.

Rock, David, and Heidi Grant. 2016. "Why Diverse Teams Are Smarter." *Harvard Business Review*, November 4. https://hbr.org/2016/11/why-diverse-teams-are-smarter.

Romer, Paul. 1990. "Endogenous Technological Change." *Journal of Political Economy* 98 (5): S71–S101.

Saez, Emmanuel. 2016. "Striking It Richer: The Evolution of Top Incomes in the United States (Updated with 2015 preliminary estimates)." University of California, Berkeley, June 30. https://eml.berkeley.edu/~saez/saez-UStopincomes-2015.pdf.

Sanders, Lucinda M., and Catherine Ashcraft. 2019. "Confronting the Absence of Women in Technology Innovation." In *Does America Need More Innovators?* ed. Matthew Wisnioski, Eric S. Hintz, and Marie Stettler Kleine. Cambridge, MA: MIT Press.

Schmookler, Jacob. 1966. *Invention and Economic Growth*. Cambridge, MA: Harvard University Press.

Schwab, Katherine. 2020. "Discrimination Charges at Pinterest Reveal a Hidden Silicon Valley Hiring Problem." *Fast Company*, July 2.

Selvidge, Jennifer. 2014. "Pushing Women and People of Color Out of Science Before We Go In." *HuffPost*, September 18. https://www.huffpost.com/entry/pushing-women-and-people-_b_5840392.

Sinclair, Bruce, ed. 2004. *Technology and the African American Experience: Needs and Opportunities for Study*. Cambridge, MA: MIT Press.

Sluby, Patricia Carter. 2004. *The Inventive Spirit of African Americans: Patented Ingenuity*. Westport, CT: Praeger.

US Census Bureau. 2019. "2018 Population Estimates by Age, Sex, Race and Hispanic Origin." https://www.census.gov/newsroom/press-kits/2019/detailed-estimates.html.

USPTO (Patent and Trademark Office). 1999. "U.S. Patenting by Women, 1977 to 1996, Buttons to Biotech, 1996 Update Report with Supplemental Data through 1998." U.S. Department of Commerce, Patent and Trademark Office. https://www.uspto.gov/web/offices/ac/ido/oeip/taf/wom_98.pdf.

van Reenen, John. 2021. "Innovation and Human Capital Policy." Working Paper no. 28713, NBER, Cambridge, MA.

Wakabayashi, Daisuke. 2017. "Contentious Memo Strikes Nerve Inside Google and Out." *New York Times*, August 8. https://www.nytimes.com/2017/08/08/technology/google-engineer-fired-gender-memo.html.

Weisul, Kimberly. 2016. "Venture Capital Is Broken. These Women Are Trying to Fix It." *Inc.*, November 1.

Mapping the Regions, Organizations, and Individuals That Drive Inclusion in the Innovation Economy

Mercedes Delgado, *Copenhagen Business School, Denmark, and MIT Innovation Initiative,* United States of America

Fiona Murray, *Massachusetts Institute of Technology School of Management, MIT Innovation Initiative, and NBER,* United States of America

Abstract

Innovation is essential for economic growth, prosperity, and social progress. However, there is strong evidence of persistent inequality and exclusion of women in the US innovation economy. We develop a framework to map the inventor (patentee) gender gap and identify contexts and catalysts for inclusion. Our approach has three main goals. First, to build inventor inclusivity metrics that capture the presence of women in the flow of new inventors, allowing comparisons across regions, organizations, and individuals. Second, to identify the overall gap between the rate of female new science, technology, engineering, and mathematics graduates and the rate of female new inventors, emphasizing that the inventor gender gap is more than a supply problem. Third, to understand the variation in inventor inclusivity across top patenting regions, organizations, and individuals, providing a window into policy and regional and organizational catalysts for change.

JEL Codes: J16, O30

Keywords: innovation economy, inventor gender gap, inclusivity metrics, STEM talent, inclusive regions, firms, universities

I. Introduction

The current focus on gender inclusion in the innovation economy not only serves as a reminder of the importance of gender diversity for social

Entrepreneurship and Innovation Policy and the Economy, volume 1, 2022.

progress (e.g., the United Nations Sustainable Development Goal 5: Gender Equality) but also emphasizes the fact that missing female inventors reduce innovation and economic growth (e.g., Romer 1990; Cook 2019, 2020; Acemoglu, Akcigit, and Celik forthcoming). Still, there is strong evidence of persistent inequality and exclusion of women in our innovation economy.

A simple review of female representation across the innovation pipeline, from idea to impact, illustrates the ongoing challenge of accomplishing both equity and inclusion for women in science, technology, engineering, and mathematics (STEM) and beyond.

It is well documented that inequality exists for women in academic STEM training and related activities. Female PhD students and postdocs are less likely to participate in elite labs and be trained by top inventors (Sheltzer and Smith 2014; Delgado and Murray 2020). Women represent only 9%–31% of STEM faculty in US universities (depending upon discipline) and remain underrepresented in tenure track roles (Thursby and Thursby 2005; Wolfinger, Mason, and Goulden 2008; Freeman et al. 2009; Li and Koedel 2017) and in many leadership roles (Madsen 2012).[1]

There is also gender inequality in knowledge production and commercialization. Women, and underrepresented minorities as well as those from lower socioeconomic categories, are systematically missing from patenting (Cook and Kongcharoen 2010; Lax Martínez, Raffo, and Saito 2016; Milli et al. 2016; Jensen, Kovács, and Sorenson 2018; Bell et al. 2019; Cook 2020; USPTO 2020). Within academia, female faculty in the life sciences patent at 40% the rate of males (Ding, Murray, and Stuart 2006) and represent only a small percentage of the founders of life science enterprises (Stuart and Ding 2006). Women with similar education levels to men also are less likely to become innovation-driven entrepreneurs (Roberts, Murray, and Kim 2015), and they receive less than 10% of venture capital flows (Brush et al. 2018).

Prior work also has found gender inequality in innovation governance. Women represent a small fraction of scientific advisory boards (Ding, Murray, and Stuart 2013), and only 10% of chief technical officers (CTOs) and chief information officers (CIOs) in the technology sector in 2019 according to a study by the firm Korn Ferry.[2]

Resolving this lack of inclusion in the innovation economy will affect both economic and social performance. First, it is inefficient to use only part of the talent pool (Bell et al. 2019; Cook 2020): we have "missing Einsteins" or, more appropriately, missing Curies and Lovelaces, Knights and

Donovans. Second, diverse inventors and researchers are more likely to search the solution space more widely and to emphasize different problem domains, including those that could be particularly relevant for women (Koning, Samila, and Ferguson 2020; Hofstra et al. 2020). Third, more diverse teams might incorporate more distributed sources of information, with higher "collective intelligence" (Woolley et al. 2010) and better outcomes (Apesteguia, Azmat, and Iriberri 2012; Joshi 2014; Joshi and Knight 2015). Finally, more diverse senior leadership within firms may lead to better governance and higher performance, but the evidence for that is mixed (e.g., Adams and Ferreira 2009; Post and Byron 2015; McKinsey & Company 2020).

Against this reality of continued exclusion from the innovation economy, we focus on the inventor (patentee) gender gap in the US economy where women constitute only 10% of inventors in 2015 US-granted utility patents. Patenting is an especially important arena for inclusion because it cuts across a wide range of organizational settings, from the public to the private sector, and from individuals to teams. It is also a context in which arguments for low inventor inclusion—the lack of STEM talent and role models growing up and early in careers (Cook and Kongcharoen 2010; Bell et al. 2019; Cook 2020)—seem especially challenging and suggest that a deeper examination is warranted. The STEM pipeline data illustrate significant aggregate improvement in the presence of women (especially for PhDs), but this improvement is not reflected in overall inventor inclusion (Delgado and Murray 2020). Specifically, female participation in STEM PhD degrees is about 35% among 2010–15 US graduates, but women represent only 14% of new (first patent) inventors in 2015 (fig. 1). This gap provides the backdrop to our more fine-grained analysis, one that emphasizes variation across STEM and invention fields, across regions, and across organizations.

We are motivated by the notion that technological (i.e., field), organizational, and locational factors play an important role in the inventor gender gap. Women's participation in innovation varies widely by technology field and application domain (Koning et al. 2020). Women's inclusion in innovation also varies by type of organization—university versus firms (Whittington and Smith-Doer 2008)—and across organizations as a result of differing innovation and managerial practices (e.g., Eaton 1999; Stuart and Ding 2006; Castilla 2011). It also changes by region due to different cultures, economic specialization, and knowledge networks (Florida 2002; Rosenthal and Strange 2012; Sorenson and Dahl 2016; Delgado, Mariani, and Murray 2019). As a result, a comprehensive analysis

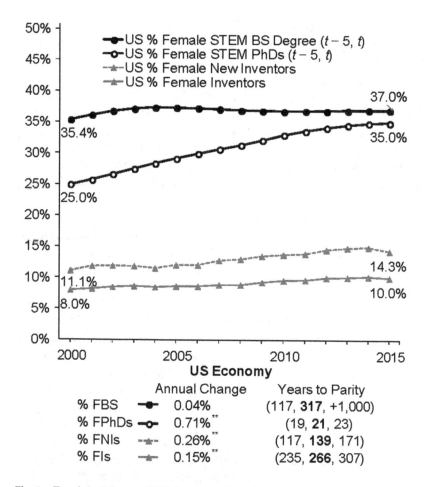

Fig. 1.   Trends in % female STEM degrees and female new inventors in the US economy. Color version available as an online enhancement.

Notes: Authors' calculations. Adapted from Delgado and Murray (2020). Inventors in patents granted in year t are compared with science, technology, engineering and math (STEM) PhDs and Bachelor of Science (BS) degrees granted in year t and the previous 5 years (from Integrated Postsecondary Education Data System). This time window takes into account that there is a delay between the patent filing and issued year and delay between graduation date and when graduates are at risk of patenting in an organization. The estimated Annual Change is the slope in the 2000–15 annual trends (** $p < .01$). Parity means that the score is 50%. Years to parity (and 95% CI estimates) are based on slope estimates.

of gender inclusion in innovation through the lens of patenting must consider how different regions, organizations, and individuals use their pipeline of STEM-trained women to a greater or lesser extent across technological fields in support of the wider innovation economy.

II. Methodology: Mapping Inventor Inclusivity across Regions, Organizations, and Individuals

We develop a novel empirical framework for mapping the inventor gender gap and identifying settings (regions, organizations, and individuals) that serve as catalysts for inclusion. This empirical approach has three main goals. First, to build metrics for female inventor inclusivity that capture participation in patenting by technological field (specifically the presence of women in the stock of inventors and in the flow of new inventors, as well as women's contribution to patenting taking into account team size). Second, to identify the gap between the rate of female new STEM graduates and the rate of female new inventors by field to quantify the nature of the invention gender gap. These two types of analysis allow for comparisons of gender participation in patenting across regions, organizations, and individuals while also accounting for different levels of female STEM talent and for the patent composition of these different contexts. Such comparisons serve our third main goal: to build an understanding of the variation in inventor inclusivity across top patenting contexts recognizing that by identifying and understanding those settings with high rates of female participation, we can drive and accelerate inclusion. We explain our empirical framework next.

A. Inventors and STEM Talent by Gender

We identify all US inventors (patentees located in the United States) in the utility patents of US origin granted to organizations during 2000–15 (USPTO 2017). Our first task is to assign the probable gender of each of the inventors on a patent using our name-gender match algorithm (Delgado and Murray 2020).[3] Then we can define inventor-level inclusion (% Female Inventors [FIs]) within a selected pool of inventors, rather than taking the more "token woman" approach of simply counting patents with "at least one woman." We are especially interested in the flow of new inventors (those with their first-ever utility patent granted in a given period): this allows us to capture the potential for cumulative advantage and long-term change in inventors' career dynamics that might be enabled by increasing the flow of new inventors into the economy at any given point in time (Merton 1968; Allison and Stewart 1974; Allison, Long, and Krauze 1982; David 1994; DiPrete and Eirich 2006). In that way, increases in women in STEM training might be clearly translated into the innovation economy.

To connect inventor data with STEM supply at an aggregate level, we use the Integrated Postsecondary Education Data System (IPEDS) data to measure the flow of STEM Bachelor's and PhD graduates by gender in the US economy (see appendix). We can also disaggregate this by region and by university to compare the presence of women in the training pipeline with the presence of female new inventors in patents. Although we are not able to match this STEM supply data at the firm level, this provides an important avenue for future work.

B.   Female Inventor Inclusivity Metrics

We compute three main Female Inventor Inclusivity scores for the regions, organizations and individuals in our sample. First, the % FIs of total inventors; that is, the number of FIs divided by all gender-matched inventors. This captures the presence of women in the pool of inventors. Second, the % Female New Inventors (FNIs) of total new inventors; that is, the number of new (first-ever utility patent) FIs divided by all gender-matched new inventors. As noted, this novel score of inclusivity captures the presence of women in the flow of inventors and is the focus of our analysis. Building on our work, the USPTO has recently started to report the % FNIs as a key metric for understanding inclusion (USPTO 2020). Third, the % Female Patents (FPs) of total patents (i.e., the number of patents by women divided by the number of gender-matched patents). This variable is based on the proportional allocation of each patent across its female and male coinventors and captures women's contribution to patenting.[4]

We note that the % Patents with a Female Inventor (i.e., the number of patents with at least one woman divided by all patents) has been the focus of many studies. This measure captures whether women are part of a team of inventors, but does not take into account that patents tend to have multiple coinventors. Inclusion and equity considerations are not necessarily met by having one woman on a large team of otherwise male inventors.

Importantly, we move beyond inclusivity scores and develop inclusivity indices to account for variation in patent composition across technology classes in different sets of patents (e.g., universities vs. firms). Both inclusivity scores and female talent availability vary across technological fields, as represented by patent technology classes (e.g., Computers & Communications vs. Drugs & Medical patents). Thus, we compute the inclusivity scores (% FNIs) by technology class using the six classes identified by Hall, Jaffe, and Trajtenberg (2001). We then build an "inclusivity index," a weighted average of the technology-class inclusivity subscores (see the appendix). This allows for better comparison of different sets of patents in multiple contexts: for example, one region to another, universities versus firms, or comparing one firm to another, such as IBM versus Medtronic patents. Our inclusivity index along with the inclusivity scores by technology class allow for a more fine-grained mapping of STEM talent into particular technological fields and provides for a more systematic understanding of the link between STEM talent supply and patent inclusion.

C. Mapping Context: Catalysts for Inclusion

We map variations in our inclusivity metrics—score and index—across top patenting regions, organizations, and individuals to uncover catalysts for inclusion. These three levels of analysis are each extremely salient as we explore ways to shape and improve inclusion in innovation. At the regional level, policies, culture, and innovation ecosystems can shape inclusive innovation (Florida 2002, 2010; Rosenthal and Strange 2012; Delgado et al. 2019). At the organization level, practices, climate, and culture influence inclusive outcomes (Ding et al. 2006, 2013; Settles et al. 2006; Bhaskarabhatla and Hegde 2014). At the individual level, there is evidence that key individuals—for example, faculty—influence graduate students' research and invention outcomes (Settles et al. 2006; Moss-Racusin et al. 2012; Sheltzer and Smith 2014; Pezzoni et al. 2016; NASEM 2018; Delgado and Murray 2020). Likewise, managers and CEOs can influence inclusion (Castilla 2011; Rocha and Van Praag 2020).

Part of our analysis is done with the full US sample. However, patenting is a highly skewed activity (O'Neale and Hendy 2012). This serves as a reminder that a small number of regions, organizations, and individuals may serve as critical catalysts and contexts for change in inclusion. We exploit this to understand the settings where inclusion is particularly high and to identify those where change may be catalyzed to great effect.

III. The Persistent Inventor Gender Gap in the Economy Is Not Just a STEM Skills Problem

Across each of our inclusivity scores, we observe the large inventor gender gap in the US economy (table 1). For 2015 US patents, only 10% of all inventors are women. Similar gaps in the % FIs have been identified in other countries (Lax Martínez et al. 2016; Hoisl and Mariani 2017). The % FNIs, although higher, is still only 14.3%. The contribution of women to patenting is also very low with a % FPs score of 7.8%. These scores contrast

Table 1
Female Inventor Inclusivity in the US Economy

Year	US Patents Granted	Female Inventors (FIs)	Male Inventors (MIs)	Female New Inventors (FNIs)	Male New Inventors (MNIs)	% FIs	% FNIs	% Female Patents	% Patents +1 FI
2015	127,300	18,740	168,134	6,300	37,688	10.0	14.3	7.8	18.9
2011–15	584,506	55,958	467,370	30,245	177,670	10.7	14.5	7.8	18.7
2000–15	1,394,632	106,243	939,836	73,511	486,129	10.2	13.1	7.2	17.1
PPA$_{00-15}$						.15**	.26**	.11**	.34**

Note: The analysis includes utility patents of US origin granted to organizations. For this set of patents, we use the inventors located in the United States (US Patent and Trademark Office). The definition of inventor is organization specific (i.e., an individual with patents in two organizations counts as two inventors). In the US sample, the organization refers to the first assignee listed in the patent. PPA is the estimated Percentage Point Annual Change (** $p <$ .01); the slope in the 2000–15 annual trends. See figure 1.

with the % Patents with a Female Inventor, which is 18.9% in 2015. This indicator is both overoptimistic and "tokenistic"; although the focus of many studies, it masks low female participation given that patents tend to have multiple coinventors (three on average).

The inventor gender gap is persistent: at the current rate of improvement (since 2000), it will take 139 years to reach parity in % FNIs and 266 years for female inventors (table 1 and fig. 1). This raises the question: Is the STEM pipeline limiting female new inventors?

Our data show that the low presence of female new inventors is not simply a STEM skills problem (fig. 1). Building on Delgado and Murray (2020), we quantify trends in the gender gap in STEM graduates (1995–2015) versus inventors in the 2000–15 period. To capture graduates at risk of patenting, we compare inventors in patents granted in a given year (e.g., 2000) to STEM Bachelors and PhDs granted that year and in the previous 5 years (1995–2000).[5] The % Female STEM Bachelors changed little during the period (35%–37%) and the gap between the % Female STEM Bachelors and % FNIs remained large: 37% versus 14% by 2015. In contrast, the presence of women in the pool of STEM PhDs increased significantly, from 25% to 35%.[6] The gap between the % Female STEM PhDs and % FNIs remained large and increased over our period: the % Female STEM PhDs was more than two times higher than the % FNIs by 2015 (35% vs. 14%). Our results show that female new inventor inclusion is not rising as fast as women in STEM: at current annual rates of change, parity in female PhDs will be achieved in 21 years versus 139 years for female new inventors.

These aggregate STEM and inventor statistics may hide field-specific differences: the presence of female inventors in the United States varies significantly by patent technology class (table 2). Let us consider the two largest classes by the count of women new inventors: Computers & Communications and Drugs & Medical patents granted 2000–15. Computers & Communications represents 36% of patents in the economy and 33% of all female new inventors and yet it has a low inclusivity score of 12.1% FNIs (of all new inventors). In contrast, Drugs & Medical accounts for only 13% of US patents but is the second-largest class for female new inventors (24%) and it has the highest inclusivity score of 25.5%.

Is the women STEM pipeline limiting female new inventors because of field-level mismatches? Although STEM fields cannot be mapped precisely into patenting classes, we can approximate the relationship between the pipeline in specific STEM fields and the patents in related technological fields. Focusing on the most inclusive field, we map the Biological & Biomedical Bachelors and PhDs to the Drugs & Medical inventor data and still find a

Table 2
Presence of Female New Inventors in the US Economy by Technology Class

	% Patents		% All Female New Inventors (FNI$_{Tech}$/FNIs)		% Female New Inventors Inclusivity Score	
	2000–15	2011–15	2000–15	2011–15	2000–15	2011–15
US Total	100	100	100	100	13.1	14.5
Chemical	11	9	14	13	17.7	18.9
Computers & Comm.	36	42	33	36	12.1	13.4
Drugs & Medical	13	15	24	25	25.5	26.4
Electrical & Elec.	18	16	10	9	8.7	9.6
Mechanical	11	9	7	6	7.0	7.9
Other	11	10	11	11	11.3	12.6

Note: Technology-class definitions are based on Hall, Jaffe, and Trajtenberg (2001).

significant gap. Drugs & Medical patents have the highest inventor inclusivity score: % FNIs is 25.5%. Yet this score is about 24 percentage points lower than expected because women's participation in Biological & Biomedical PhDs is 49% (1995–2015 graduates) and in Bachelors is 59% (table 3).

Table 3
Presence of Female STEM Graduates in the US Economy by Field

	% Female STEM Bachelors			% Female STEM PhDs		
	1995–2015	2006–15	2010–15	1995–2015	2006–15	2010–15
US STEM Degrees Flow	36.7	37.0	37.0	31.1	34.2	35.0
Agriculture[a]	47.1	50.6	51.8	36.8	44.3	46.6
Biological & Biomedical[b]	58.7	59.2	58.8	48.8	52.2	53.1
Computer & Comm.[c]	22.7	19.1	19.0	20.4	21.3	21.0
Engineering Tech.[d]	18.1	18.0	18.2	19.1	22.1	22.7
Math & Statistics[e]	44.7	43.5	43.1	27.8	29.3	28.8
Natural Resources[f]	45.0	47.4	48.2	39.4	44.8	46.3
Physical[g]	40.1	40.2	39.6	29.2	32.4	33.2

Note: Authors' calculations (Integrated Postsecondary Education Data System) based on all US institutions granting STEM (science, technology, engineering and math) degrees. The definition of STEM graduates used throughout this paper (see appendix) includes these National Center for Education Statistics fields.
[a]01-02.
[b]26.
[c]10-11.
[d]14-15 and 41.
[e]27.
[f]03.
[g]40.

Similarly, in Computers & Communications women represent 12.1% of new inventors versus 20% of PhDs and 23% of Bachelors.

Our findings strongly suggest that the inventor gender gap is not just about STEM education choices. So, where is female STEM talent best utilized across the economy?

IV. Potential Catalysts: Patenting Is Concentrated in Few Regions, Organizations, and Individuals

We want to examine whether there are parts of the innovation economy where patenting and inclusion are high so that we can identify catalysts for change: that is, contexts where best practices seem to lead to high levels of inclusion, and settings with high patent intensity where the use of these practices might have a significant positive impact. To do this, we measure the skewness of patenting activity in each of our three different contexts. Then we determine the degree to which, among the top patent producers, some of the regions, organizations and individuals are more inclusive than others. Our results could inform best practices for change.

A. Top Patenting Regions

The economic geography literature shows that patents are highly concentrated geographically by field (Audretsch and Feldman 1996; Feldman and Audretsch 1999; Delgado, Porter, and Stern 2014; Delgado 2020). We therefore use economic areas (EAs, defined by the US Bureau of Economic Analysis) as the geographic unit to identify the top patenting regions; they better capture a relevant market and the economic specialization of regions. There are 179 mutually exclusive EAs covering the entire continental United States (Johnson and Kort 2004).

We find that the top 10 patenting EAs account for 55% of patents and 51% of new inventors in the 2000–15 patents (table 4) versus 34% of all US jobs in 2015. Perhaps not surprisingly, the top patenting EA is San Jose–San Francisco–Oakland, CA (with 17% of all patents and 13% of all new inventors), followed by the New York City EA and then the Greater Boston EA. In many of these regions, and especially the top EA, performance is driven by significant patenting in information technology as well as in other sectors, including life sciences in the Boston EA (Forman, Goldfarb, and Greenstein 2016; Delgado 2020). This patenting performance is fueled by, among others, immigrant innovators (Saxenian 2002; Kerr 2008; Kerr

Table 4
Patenting and New Inventors Generated by Top Regions, Firms, and Universities

	Patents, 2000–15	%	New Inventors	%
US economy	1,394,632	100	607,732	100
10-Economic Areas (of 179)	763,992	55	311,381	51
30-Firms	346,033	25	115,952	19
All universities (201)	59,105	4	45,823	8
25-Universities	32,032	2	23,940	4

Note: Top 10 economic areas, top 30 firms and top 25 universities by granted patent count in 2011–15. See appendix.

et al. 2017). Yet we know very little about the presence of female inventors in top patenting regions (Delgado et al. 2019). It is therefore important to understand how large patenting organizations in and across these regions shape inclusive outcomes.

B.   Top Patenting Organizations

We examine the role of universities and firms in bringing new inventors into the innovation economy. Table 4 shows that the top 30 firms by patenting account for 25% of all patents and 19% of new inventors in the economy. Firms will shape overall levels of inclusion because the vast majority of STEM talent (Bachelors, Masters, and PhDs) will work at firms. In contrast, universities generate only 4% of all patents. Nonetheless, they are important organizations as they play a key role in shaping the skills and attitudes toward innovation of young PhD students (Pezzoni et al. 2016; Azoulay, Liu, and Stewart 2017; Delgado and Murray 2020), and early access to resources may lead to cumulative advantage (Merton 1968; Allison and Stewart 1974; Allison et al. 1982). We find that the top 25 universities shape the behavior of more than 50% of patenting activity by universities, accounting for 2% of US patents and contributing 4% of (highly trained) new inventors.

C.   Top Inventors within Organizations

Within organizations there are "superstars" in science and innovation who shape outputs and define the microclimate for research (Azoulay, Fons-Rosen, and Graff Zivin 2019; Delgado and Murray 2020), and superstar inventor-CEOs can drive firm patenting outcomes (Islam and Zein 2020). Building on Delgado and Murray (2020), we define top inventors (TIs) as

Table 5
Patents and New Inventors Generated by Top Inventors

	Inventors	%	Patents	%	Team Size	New Inventors	%
US Patents, 2000–15	1,130,834	100	1,394,632	100	2.7	607,732	100
Top Inventors (7+ patents)	114,071	10	873,878	63	2.9	241,317	40
30-Firms Patents, 2000–15	183,933	100	346,033	100	2.8	115,952	100
Top Inventors	34,167	19	289,038	84	3.0	75,948	65
25-University Patents, 2000–15	37,314	100	32,032	100	2.8	23,940	100
Top Inventors	2,243	6	18,956	59	3.0	10,664	45

Note: We define Top Inventors as those with 7+ patents granted within an organization during 2000–15 (90th percentile value in the US economy). In the US sample, the organization refers to the first assignee code in the patent. Team Size is the average number of inventors across patents.

those with seven or more patents granted within an organization during 2000–15 (the 90th percentile value across US inventors). Given their prolific activity and the team-based nature of patenting, these inventors likely play an outsized role in bringing new inventors into the innovation economy as part of their teams. We find that many patents (and many new inventors) in our sample of top patenting organizations are produced by a few top inventors (table 5): TIs within the top 30 firms represent 19% of their pool of inventors, generate 84% of their patents, and account for the inclusion of 65% of their new inventors. Academic TIs at the top 25 universities represent only 6% of inventors, generate 59% of patents, and account for 45% of their new inventors.

The outsize role of top inventors in inclusion suggests that it is important to examine whether there is variation in inclusivity among prolific inventors within their organizations and to highlight the practices that lead to high rates of inclusion (or to call out prolific inventors who have unusually low levels of inclusion).

V. Variation in Female Inventor Inclusivity across the Top Patenting Regions, Organizations, and Individuals

The high skewness of patenting suggests that to catalyze changes in inclusion we must understand the variation in patenting behaviors among the top 10 regions, 30 firms, and 25 universities (and among their top inventors). We examine this variation through our % FNIs metric across the most recent set of patents in our data (2011–15).

A. Female Inventor Inclusivity Variation across Top Patenting Regions

Figure 2 shows the % FNIs score across EAs compared with the US economy (14.5% in 2011–15 patents). The map illustrates the 90 EAs that together account for about 98% of the patents. There is large variation across regions, even across the top 10 patenting EAs: scores range from 11.2% for Dallas and Detroit EAs (below the US average) to 18.9% in New York EA (fig. 3).

Regional differences in inclusivity could be driven by regional specialization in different technology classes. Thus, we compare the two classes with the largest count of FNIs: Computers & Communications and Drugs & Medical (figs. 4 and 5, respectively). We find important variation conditioning on particular technology classes, and relevant differences across the two classes. These differences come against a backdrop in which Computers & Communications patenting is more geographically concentrated than Drugs & Medical (consistent with studies showing the high clustering

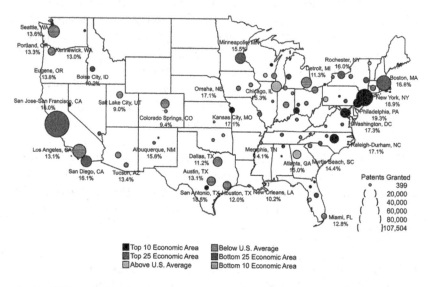

Fig. 2. % Female New Inventors across economic areas (EA), 2011–15. Color version available as an online enhancement.

Notes: The % Female New Inventors score refers to all (organization) patents by inventors located in the region (i.e., the number of women new inventors divided by the number of gender-matched new inventors in each EA). Circle size on map is proportional to total patents granted in 2011–15. Circles shaded without pattern have inclusivity above the US average (14.5%). The map shows the top 90 EAs (out of 179) by patent count. They account for about 98% of patents issued. Bottom 10 EAs have scores below or equal to 9.4%.

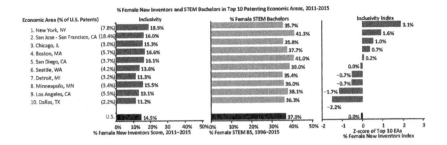

Fig. 3. % Female New Inventors and STEM Bachelors (BS) in top 10 economic areas (EA), 2011–15. Color version available as an online enhancement.

Notes: STEM = science, technology, engineering and math. The top 10 EAs ranked by 2000–15 patenting are San Jose–San Francisco–Oakland, CA; New York–Newark–Bridgeport, NY-NJ-CT-PA; Boston-Worcester-Manchester, MA-NH; Los Angeles–Long Beach–Riverside, CA; Seattle-Tacoma-Olympia, WA; Minneapolis–St. Paul-St. Cloud, MN-WI; Detroit-Warren-Flint, MI; Chicago–Naperville–Michigan City, IL-IN-WI; San Diego–Carlsbad–San Marcos, CA; and Dallas–Fort Worth, TX. New York EA has the highest score of 18.9% and the highest index (3.1%) across the top 10 patenting EAs. STEM Bachelors computed by gender based on the graduates trained by universities located in the region (2006–15).

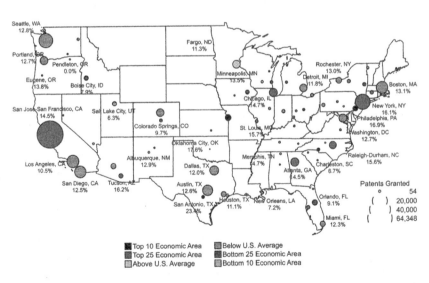

Fig. 4. % Female New Inventors across economic areas (EA), Computers & Communications, 2011–15. Color version available as an online enhancement.

Notes: % Female New Inventors scores for Computers & Communications patents in each EA. Circle size on map proportional to the patents granted in the technology in 2011–15. Circles shaded without pattern have inclusivity above the US average (13.4%). Bottom 10 EAs have scores below or equal to 6.7%.

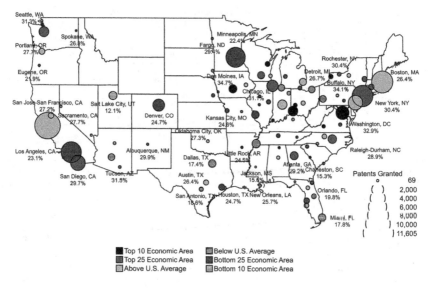

Fig. 5. % Female New Inventors across economic areas (EA), Drugs & Medical, 2011–15. Color version available as an online enhancement.

Notes: % Female New Inventors scores for Drugs & Medical patents in each EA. Circle size on map proportional to the patents granted in the technology in 2011–15. Circles shaded without pattern have inclusivity above the US average (26.4%). Bottom 10 EAs have scores 12.1% or lower.

of information technology activities, in particular in San Jose–San Francisco–Oakland, CA (Delgado 2020)). In terms of inclusion, some top patenting regions have high inclusivity (above the US score) in both technologies (New York, Chicago, and San Jose EAs), whereas others have low inclusivity in both (Dallas and Los Angeles EAs). Importantly, there is variation in inclusion across technologies within a region: for example, Seattle and San Diego have scores above the US average for Drugs & Medical but below for Computers & Communications. This variation within region could be driven by large patenting organizations that concentrate their inventive activities there (e.g., Amazon in Seattle) and by specialized regional clusters that could vary in their inclusion practices.

The different patent composition of regions and the variation in inclusion across technology classes within regions justify the need to compute the inclusivity index to compare the overall performance of the top regions (fig. 3). Five of the EAs perform better than the US economy in both the score and index. New York has the highest score (18.9%) and index (3.1%)

out of the 10 EAs. Other EAs underperform relative to the US economy (negative index): Dallas, Los Angeles, Minneapolis, and Detroit.

Although the rate of female new inventors is high in some regions, it remains much lower than the supply of women STEM talent trained within each region. To quantify this gap, we compute for each region the STEM Bachelors and PhD graduates (2006–15), by gender, trained by the universities located in each region (see appendix). The % Female STEM Bachelors score ranges from 35% (Detroit) to 41% (San Jose), much higher than the new inventor inclusivity scores (fig. 3). The ratio of % FNIs to % Female STEM Bachelors is highest at New York, yet it is only 0.5 (with lowest is being Dallas with a ratio of 0.3).[7] Likewise, the ratio of % FNIs to % Female STEM PhDs is also highest in New York at only 0.5. Overall these findings suggest that the supply of locally trained female STEM graduates is not the central issue in explaining the high inventor gender gap across top patenting regions.

The ability to retain talent and to engage women in innovation may vary across regions with different innovation ecosystems and sets of organizations. Thus, we ask next: What organizations (universities and firms) drive these regional differences?

B. Female Inventor Inclusivity Variation across Top Universities

With their increasing numbers of female STEM students, can leading research universities be catalysts for change and influence overall regional inclusivity? We know that women's inclusion in innovation tends to be higher at universities than at firms (e.g., Whittington and Smith-Doer 2008; Delgado and Murray 2020). We are interested in assessing the variation among universities (which ones are more inclusive than others) so as to identify and inform best practices for change across regions and across the US innovation economy.

As noted earlier, the top 25 US universities generate 2% of all patents but 4% of all the new inventors in the economy. The presence of female new inventors in their patents is higher than in the US economy overall: 22.6% versus 14.5% in 2011–15 patents (8 percentage point gap; see table 6).[8] Each of the top universities has an inclusivity score higher than the US average (fig. 6), but there is large variation across them, from 17.6% (Purdue) to 29.5% (University of Pennsylvania).

The higher inclusivity of universities could be driven by their technology composition. The patent composition of the US economy is very different from that of universities (Delgado and Murray 2020): Drugs &

Table 6
% Female New Inventors in the US Economy, Top 25 Universities, and Top 30 Firms

	Patents	% Female New Inventors	% Female New Inventors
	Granted Year	Score	Index
United States	2000–15	13.1	0
	2011–15	14.5	0
25-Universities	2000–15	21.2	3.8
	2011–15	22.6	4.0
All-Universities	2000–15	21.2	3.4
	2011–15	22.8	3.7
30-Firms	2000–15	13.8	1.6
	2011–15	14.9	1.3

Note: See equation (A1) for the Index definition (weighted average across tech subscores).

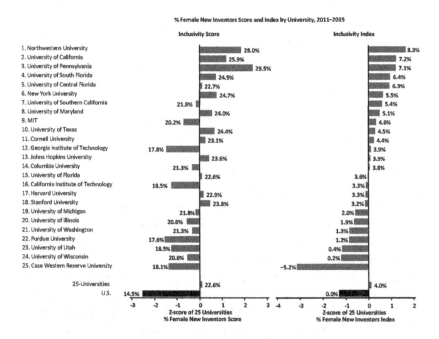

% Female New Inventors Score and Index by University, 2011–2015

Fig. 6. % Female New Inventors across 25-Universities: score and index, 2011–15. Color version available as an online enhancement.

Notes: The inclusivity index is a weighted average of the university's tech-class scores (see eq. [A3]). We also report the indicators for the pooled patents of the 25-Universities and the US economy.

Medical is the largest technology class in the 25 universities, with about 40% of 2011–15 patents (versus only 15% of US patents). Furthermore, individual universities vary in their patent composition. We compute the inclusivity index for the pool of 25 university patents and for each university to control for technology-class composition (see eqs. [A1] and [A3]). Some universities move up in the ranking based on the index: MIT has a higher percentage of patents in Mechanical (a field with fewer women) and moves up in the ranking from twentieth (score) to ninth (index). All universities (except one) have positive inclusivity indices, which confirms the greater inclusion of universities than the US economy. Importantly, there is large variation in the index, ranging from 8.3% at Northwestern University to −5.2% at Case Western Reserve University.[9] This suggests that other factors (beyond the technology field) influence university inclusivity.

Next we compare universities to their regions (fig. 7). We find that top universities are more inclusive than their regions: each has a % FNIs greater than their region. This gap ranges from 13 percentage points for Northwestern University (28% vs. 15.3% in Chicago EA) to 1 percentage point for University of Florida. On average, the university-versus-region gap is 7.3 percentage points in the % FNIs score (and 3.6% in the index). All universities (except Case Western Reserve) also have an index value greater than their regions.

% Female New Inventors Score, 2011-2015

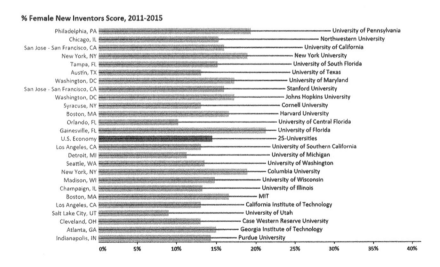

Fig. 7. Inclusivity of university versus region: % Female New Inventors (FNI), 2011–15. Color version available as an online enhancement.

Notes: Each university % FNI score is compared with that of its region (economic area).

This higher inclusivity of universities suggests that they have the potential to be regional catalysts for change. However, universities still have
far to go to reach parity in engaging female inventors in their patents. Therefore, we assess whether the limiting factor is the supply of women STEM
PhDs trained by each of these universities. We find that universities un-
derutilize their female STEM PhD pipeline (fig. 8). In fact, there is a large
female STEM PhD to female New Inventor gap across universities. In the
pool of 25 universities, the % Female STEM PhDs is 10 percentage points
higher than % FNIs (33% vs. 23%). There is a large STEM PhD inventor
gap for each university. This strongly suggests that the rate at which female
PhDs engage in university patenting is much lower than that of men (Delgado and Murray 2020).

C. Female Inventor Inclusivity Varies across Top Firms

Firms account for about 96% of US patents and thus strongly shape overall levels of inclusion. The top 30 firms account for 25% of patents and 19%
of all new inventors in the economy (table 4). The presence of female new
inventors in firms' patents is very similar to that in the US economy: 14.9%
versus 14.5% in 2011–15 patents, with 13 of the top firms having inclusion
scores above the US average. As with regions and universities, we find large
variations in the % FNIs across top patenting firms (fig. 9): from 27.5%

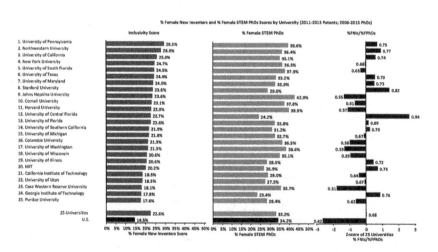

Fig. 8. % Female New Inventors and STEM PhDs by university (2011–15 patents, 2006–
15 PhDs). Color version available as an online enhancement.

Notes: STEM = science, technology, engineering and math. Flow of STEM PhD holders by
gender (Integrated Postsecondary Education Data System, 2006–15 graduates).

in Johnson & Johnson (with Drugs & Medical as the main tech class) to 8.1% in Broadcom (with Computers & Communications as the main class). Inclusivity scores do not allow us to properly compare inclusion across firms because firm patents tend to be highly concentrated in one (main) technology class (e.g., 74% of IBM patents are in Computers & Communications). Thus, the inclusivity index is essential to account for firm-level variation in technology specialization. For example, IBM moves up from seventh to third in the ranking, and Medtronic moves down from fifth to twentieth. The % FNIs index for the pooled 30-firms patents is 1.3%. Half of the firms do better than the US economy (positive index), ranging from AT&T with a 9.4% index to 0% in Hewlett-Packard. More troubling, given the magnitude of their patenting activity, the other half of firms are doing worse than the US economy (negative index), ranging from –0.2% in Boeing to –5.6% in Boston Scientific.

Finally, a firm's main technology class shapes the type of STEM skills that are likely to be relevant to the firm and thus the role of female STEM levels as a potential constraint to inclusion. We find that most of our firms

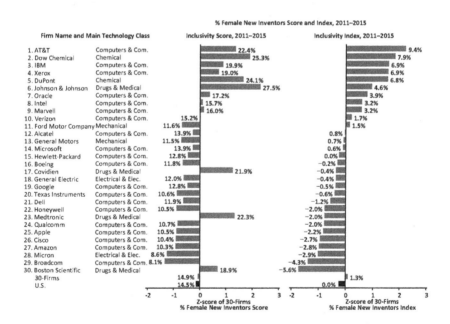

Fig. 9. % Female New Inventors across 30-Firms: score and index, 2011–15. Color version available as an online enhancement.

Note: Inclusivity indicators computed based on all the patents of the firm 2011–15 (all technologies). The figure shows the main technology of firm patents. Firms patent in multiple tech classes, but on average a single (main) tech concentrates 73% of firm patents.

have inclusivity scores lower than the US % Female STEM Graduates in their main technology: the % Female STEM Bachelors is 19% in Computers & Communications and 59% in Biological & Biomed fields, but the average inclusivity score is 14% and 23% across top firms whose main class are Computers & Communications and Drugs & Medical, respectively.

There are a few exceptions: AT&T, IBM (the largest patent producer), and Xerox have scores close to the STEM supply in Computers & Communications. This could be related to their practices to incentivize patenting across their employees (Bhaskarabhatla and Hegde 2014) or to other critical and effective organizational practices that can serve as catalysts of change for low-performing firms. More broadly, our findings suggest the urgent need for insights into the drivers of firm inclusivity, including the role of key individuals (top inventors) inside organizations.

D. Female Inventor Inclusivity Varies across Top Inventors within Organizations

To what extent might key individuals—top inventors—serve as catalysts for female inventor inclusion? Although patenting takes place within regions and organizations, the process of invention is driven by small teams of individuals. As noted earlier, in most organizational settings a few top inventors produce many patents (table 5). Their autonomy, reputation, and patenting intensity likely give them a key role in shaping the organizational culture for patenting and thus more specifically for female inventor inclusion. At universities, as faculty and principal investigators of labs, they have a role in training and mentoring new inventors among their graduate students (Pezzoni et al. 2016; Gaule and Piacentini 2018; Delgado and Murray 2020). This can have long-lasting effects on students' careers. At firms, top inventors (whom we might consider to be invention "superstars") may have less discretion in building their teams (although this is very poorly understood in the literature) but still have some autonomy in how they pursue their projects.

To examine the role of TIs within top patenting organizations, we divide the pooled 25-university and pooled 30-firm patents into four groups based on the absence or presence of a top inventor: Non-TI, TI, Female TI, and Male TI patents (table 7). Then we compare the inclusivity score across these four types of patents. Overall, top inventor patents have a higher inclusivity score than Non-TI patents in the university and firm settings. In the 25 universities, female TIs represent only 9% of all TIs, but their patents have much higher inclusivity scores than those of male TIs (7 percentage point gap). Similarly, in the 30 firms, female TIs are 8%

Table 7
% Female New Inventors in Top Inventors Patents

	# TIs	% Female New Inventors Score
25-Universities 2000–15:		
No-Top Inventor Patents		20.9
Top Inventors Patents:		22.4
FTIs	208	29.2
MTIs	2,035	22.0
30-Firms 2000–15:		
No-Top Inventor Patents		12.3
Top Inventors Patents:		15.7
FTIs	2,538	22.9
MTIs	28,717	15.5

Note: The indicators are based on the pooled patents by type: No TI, at least one TI (FTI or MTI) patents. New Inventors excludes those who become top inventors in 2000–15. Similar findings using the % FNIs Index. FTI = Female Top Inventors; MTIs = Male Top Inventors.

of all TIs and their patents have higher inclusivity than male TIs patents (also by 7 percentage point gap). We obtain similar findings using the inclusivity index.

These results suggest that top inventors indeed exert a strong influence over the inclusivity of their organizations (both within universities and firms). Furthermore, there is significant variation across TIs in their inclusivity practices—among all TIs but also specifically female versus male TIs. This calls for the need to understand the role of these key individuals in driving the inclusivity of their organizations. In other words, it is not sufficient to study organization-level drivers of inclusion; we also need to pay attention to the potential role of catalytic individuals whose inclusion of new inventors, and especially female new inventors, in their work has a strong impact on the US economy.

VI. Accelerating Change in Gender Inclusion in Innovation: Lessons and Next Steps

Accelerating change in gender inclusion in the innovation economy—in patenting and in the subsequent commercialization of inventions—is important for economic and social performance. Changes in the regional, organizational, and individual practices around patenting have the potential to advance the inclusion of inventors from a wide range of different backgrounds and experiences and therefore to increase the productivity of our economy. Nonetheless, increases in gender inclusion in patenting have been slow to materialize over the past 20 years, with only a 0.15 percentage point annual increase in female inventor inclusion and a 0.26 percentage point annual increase for female new inventor inclusion. At this rate of change it would take over a century to reach parity. Given the more rapid increase in women moving into STEM education (especially PhDs), our work moves beyond the traditional focus on the STEM education pipeline to explore whether, when, and where inventors (especially new inventors) are included in patenting.

We have shown that the participation of women in STEM Bachelors (% Female STEM Bachelors) and in STEM PhDs (% Female STEM PhDs) have remained much larger than the participation of female new inventors into patents (% FNIs). Furthermore, the % Female STEM PhDs has been increasing much faster than the % FNIs during our study period. The national-level gap of more than 20 percentage points between the % female new STEM graduates and female new inventors by 2015 warrants further investigation at the regional level and across organizations and individuals. This paper has examined this variation in the most recent set of patents in our data (2011–15).

At the regional level, the top 10 patenting EAs are responsible for more than 50% of patents. They vary widely in their female new inventors inclusion scores (11%–19%), with each of these rates being much lower than the rate of female STEM Bachelors and PhDs trained by universities within each region. The inclusion ranking shifts once we control for the composition of patents within a region using our inclusivity index—for example, accounting for whether a region is specialized in the Life Sciences or Computers & Communications. However, New York remains significantly more inclusive at the top of the ranking (3% index) than Dallas, which remains ranked tenth and underperforming relative to the economy (–2% index). The ratio of % FNIs to % Female STEM Bachelors is also highest in New York but is only 0.5. We find that if each top EA were to have its % FNIs score equal to the % Female STEM Bachelors in the given region, we would make significant inroads into inclusion in the innovation economy: the number of female new inventors in the US economy would have grown by 26% annually. That is, there would be almost 40,000 additional women new inventors during 2011–15, and the inclusivity score in the economy would increase from 14.5% to 28.3%.[10]

Our analysis recognizes that much of the regional-level variation in inclusivity is related to the behavior of firms and universities located within the regions. We find that across organizations, the top 25 US universities have significantly higher rates of inclusion of female new inventors than either the US economy as a whole or the top 30 firms (both by score and index). Among universities, and accounting for patent composition, all but one are more inclusive than the US economy and their region. This indicates their importance in seeding the inclusion of female new inventors. That said, universities also display significant variation in their rates of inclusivity, ranging from 18% to 30% in our score and from −5% to 8% in our index. Although universities can serve as catalysts for inclusion, each university has inclusivity scores lower than their % Female STEM PhDs. We find that if each top university were to have the % FNIs score equal to the % Female STEM PhDs, the number of female new inventors in the economy would have grown by 1% annually (i.e., 1,526 additional new inventors during 2011–15).[11]

Shifting our attention to firms, we examine female new inventors among the top 30 firms, responsible for more than 25% of US patents. Importantly, these firms vary widely in their inclusivity scores (8%–28%). Firms are specialized in particular technology fields, so it is especially important to use our inclusivity index to compare firms. According to our index, there is significant variation between inclusion at the top five firms (7–9 percentage points above US average) versus the bottom five (3–6 percentage points below US average).

In the absence of firm-level data on own-supply of STEM female employees, we use the US % Female STEM Bachelors by field as an imperfect proxy. Nonetheless, firms with the higher indices seem to better utilize the female STEM pipeline. In particular, AT&T and IBM have inclusivity scores similar to the % Female STEM Bachelors in fields related to their main technology (Computers & Communications). Once again, we find that if each top firm were to have the % FNIs score equal to the % Female STEM Bachelors (in fields related to their main technology class), the number of female new inventors in the US economy would have grown by 4% annually (i.e., 5,759 additional new inventors during 2011–15).[12]

By understanding the variation in the rate of participation of female new inventors across these organizations, we can identify specific settings with organizational (and individual) practices that seemingly lead to greater inclusion, thus laying the foundations for deeper analysis. Such analysis will allow us to pinpoint specific practices that then can be more widely adopted across the economy. These organizations and their inclusive individuals also will serve as role models and catalysts for change. Moreover, by focusing on those contexts—regions, firms, universities and even individuals—producing the vast majority of the inventions that are filed every year, we can identify potential leverage points for inclusion. If we can upgrade the behavior of the laggards among these prolific people and places, then we can make a significant difference in our economy.

Our work also underscores the importance of calculating the types of metrics and rankings for a range of regions, organizations, and individuals on an annual basis. For policy makers, this approach makes it possible to track improvements in inclusion in a granular way that may be of interest to the states and their subregions. It further holds the promise of capturing the causal impact of specific policy interventions and how they might differentially shape the inclusive nature of different types of organizations: new versus old, large versus small, those close to universities compared with those in more peripheral regions. For organizational leaders, our rankings, in particular our inclusion index, make it possible to perform annual benchmarking against peer organizations and against prior performance. Managers also might consider variations in inclusion rates from one business unit to another (and from one region to another). They could use the inclusion index to capture the effectiveness of specific organizational interventions at the business unit or division level. The same is true for universities where it is possible to rank and celebrate the most inclusive of faculty and to understand their practices more clearly. When combined with organization-specific data on the potential pool of innovators (i.e., those at risk of becoming inventors), our approach becomes particularly powerful as a way to examine pockets of best practice—as demonstrated by the link we make between STEM students within particular universities and their participation in invention and patenting.

Much work remains for innovation scholars who seek to understand the causes and consequences of inclusion in patenting within and across organizations, particularly when it comes to new inventors entering the innovation economy at different stages in their careers. At the organizational level, we should explore the role of culture and other organizational drivers of inclusion, motivated in part by the potential benefits from change and by the high rates of variation in inclusion among top patent producers elucidated in our work. Scholars should continue to seek out useful interventions and natural experiments that can shed light on inclusion. One obvious study would examine the ways in which the COVID-19 shock (and subsequent move to more remote working practices) differentially affected male versus female (new and existing) inventors. This could be a window into the wider issues of how geography and work practices shape diversity and inclusion. Another challenge is to understand the relationship between leadership composition and inclusion. Using our methods, it would be possible, for example, to examine the degree to which changes in senior leadership (e.g., the appointment of more diverse and inclusive leadership at the level of the chief technological officer, head of

R&D, or even CEO) changes inclusion. Other more targeted policy or program interventions within large innovation-oriented organizations also could be the subject of significant analysis and evaluation.

Our finding that new female inventors enter into the innovation economy from universities at higher rates than from other organizations suggests another line of research. It would be fruitful to study the pathways of inventors from their early PhD training in university laboratories through their inventive career across different organizations. It would be useful to understand whether male versus female new inventors graduating from PhD programs with experience as inventors make differential contributions to the innovation economy compared with one another and compared with other PhD students who do not patent while in graduate training. And, even before such new inventors leave the training grounds of their universities, we might seek to understand the drivers of variation in inclusion among top faculty inventors who often serve as PhD advisors and key role models (e.g., Delgado and Murray 2020).

Finally, turning to the regional level, our approach provides insights into understanding variation in inclusion across regions. It has been suggested that some regions are inherently more tolerant and creative (e.g., Florida 2002). Yet these characteristics have not been fully linked to diversity and inclusion in innovation. Relatedly, prior work shows that economies of agglomeration improve innovation and entrepreneurship, but we know very little about the female innovators' participation in industry clusters (e.g., Rosenthal and Strange 2012; Delgado et al. 2019). Our approach provides a platform for connecting lines of scholarly research emphasizing regional variation in culture, rules, norms, and socioeconomic networks to research that emphasizes innovation outcomes. The inclusive nature of innovation provides an important window into both the culture and practice of innovation, not only for female inventors but also for the diverse range of individuals whose talents are essential to our long-term economic future.

Appendix

I. Materials and Methods

A. STEM Degrees by Gender in the US Economy and by University

The Integrated Postsecondary Educational Data System (IPEDS) offers annual data on STEM bachelor's degrees and PhD completions by field and gender for US institutions of higher education. We use institution names to associate IPEDS institutions with our list of universities (Delgado and Murray 2020).

Our definition of STEM includes the following National Center for Education Statistics (NCES) fields that are more likely to patent: 01, 02, 03, 10, 11, 14, 15, 26, 27, 40, and 41. In the year-2000 classification these are named, respectively: Agriculture, agriculture operations, and related sciences (01); Agricultural sciences (02); Natural resources and conservation (03); Communications technologies/technicians and support services (10); Computer and information sciences and support services (11); Engineering (14); Engineering technologies/technicians (15); Biological and biomedical sciences (26); Mathematics and statistics (27); Physical sciences (40); and Science technologies (41).

B.   Method: Female Inventor Inclusivity Scores and Indices

To analyze women's inclusion in the US economy, we define metrics that characterize the presence of female versus male inventors (located in the United States) in utility patents. Our first task is to assign the probable gender of each of the inventors on a patent using our name-gender match algorithm (Delgado and Murray 2020). We then compute three main female inventor inclusivity (FII) scores for the organizations in our sample. First, the % FIs of total inventors (i.e., the number of FIs divided by all gender-matched inventors). Second, the % FNIs of total new inventors (i.e., the number of new [first patent granted] FIs divided by all gender-matched new inventors). Third, the % FPs of total patents (i.e., the number of patents by women divided by the number of gender-matched patents).

We compute the FII scores at multiple levels of analysis: for the entire pool of US patents, across regions (EAs) and fields, the top patenting universities (25-universities), the top patenting firms (30-firms), and their top inventors.

Note that our definition of inventor in the paper is organization specific; that is, an individual with patents in two organizations (e.g., two universities) during the particular time period counts as two distinct inventors. The inventor identification is sourced from the USPTO PatentsView's rawinventor data accessed in June 2017.

In the region-level analysis, we focus on EAs as the regional unit (Johnson and Kort 2004), and the definition of inventor is an inventor-organization-region in the particular set of patents (e.g., if an IBM inventor is located in two different EAs during the given period it will be allocated to each of the two EAs).[13]

The inclusivity scores and the supply of STEM women vary across patent technology classes (Delgado and Murray 2020). Thus, we develop inclusivity indices (for each of the three inclusivity scores) to account for variation in patent composition across technology classes in different sets of patents (e.g., universities vs. firms). Thus, we compute the inclusivity scores by technology class using the six classes identified by Hall et al. (2001). Then we build an "inclusivity index": a weighted average of the six technology-class inclusivity subscores. We compute the indices at multiple levels of analysis: the pool of the top universities ($u25$) and top firms ($f30$) in equations (A1) and (A2), each organization (firm or university o) in equation (A3), and each region r in equation (A4):

$$\text{Inclusivity Index}_{u25} = \sum_{tech} \text{Share Patents}_{u25}^{tech} \times (\text{Inclusivity Score}_{u25}^{tech} - \text{Inclusivity Score}_{US}^{tech}) \tag{A1}$$

$$\text{Inclusivity Index}_{f30} = \sum_{tech} \text{Share Patents}_{f30}^{tech} \times (\text{Inclusivity Score}_{f30}^{tech} - \text{Inclusivity Score}_{US}^{tech}) \tag{A2}$$

$$\text{Inclusivity Index}_{o} = \sum_{tech} \text{Share Patents}_{o}^{tech} \times (\text{Inclusivity Score}_{o}^{tech} - \text{Inclusivity Score}_{US}^{tech}) \tag{A3}$$

$$\text{Inclusivity Index}_{r} = \sum_{tech} \text{Share Patents}_{r}^{tech} \times (\text{Inclusivity Score}_{r}^{tech} - \text{Inclusivity Score}_{US}^{tech}) \tag{A4}$$

The index first normalizes each score relative to the US by technology class (e.g., difference between the 25-universities and the US score for patents granted in the same time period); and then weighs each normalized score based on the share of patents in the technology class (Share Patents^{tech}).

Equations (A1) and (A2) allow us to compare the inclusivity of types of organizations that may have different technology composition of their patents like the top 25 universities versus the top 30 firms and the US economy. For example, in 2011–15, the % FNIs index shows a 4 percentage points greater presence of women new inventors in top-25 university patents than the US economy. Equation (A3) allows us to compare across individual organizations that can vary in the technology-class composition of their patents (e.g., MIT has many patents in Mechanical, which is a field with fewer women). Finally, equation (A4) allows us to compare across regions that might specialize in different technology classes.

C. University Sample: University-Patent Assignee Bridge

To create our university sample, we build a bridge to map USPTO patent assignee codes into individual universities. We identify the set of 201 universities with at least 5 patents in the 2011–15 period and separate out the top 25 universities by patent count in the same period (25-Universities sample). The definition of the patents of a particular university is based on the first assignee listed in the patent. In our sample of top 25 universities, more than 90% of the patents granted (2000–15) have only one assignee. See Delgado and Murray (2020) for the detailed university-patent bridge.

D. Firm Sample: Firm-Patent Assignee Bridge

To create our top patenting firms sample, we identify the set of top 30 firms by granted patent count in the 2011–15 time period. Next, we build a bridge to map USPTO patent assignee codes into individual firms. The definition of patents attributed to a specific firm is based on the first assignee listed in the patent. In the USPTO data, some firms assign their patents to a single assignee entity (e.g., IBM) and thus are allocated a single assignee code, whereas others have multiple codes. Thus, we created a bridge to map patent assignee codes to firms. On average each firm is associated with 13 distinct assignee codes.

To build the firm-assignee bridge, we employed name-matching techniques to match patent assignee names to a list of parent and subsidiary names obtained from Securities and Exchange Commission sources. For each firm, we generate candidate matches by searching for patent assignee names that share words with the list of names or common abbreviations. These potential matches are then evaluated manually to determine whether they represent patent activity of the focal firm.

We further corroborate the preciseness of the bridge by crosschecking and integrating the list of assignee names and patents with Arora, Belenzon, and Sheer (2017). The latter data set has data on 25 out of our top 30 firms. Among these entities, the overlap is substantial: in the 2010–15 period, the two data sets agree on more than 90% of patents.

Endnotes

Author email addresses: Delgado (md.si@cbs.dk), Murray (fmurray@mit.edu). We are grateful for the comments by Maryann Feldman, Paula Stephan, Don Sull, Michael Cima, Adam Jaffe, Myriam Mariani, Scott Stern, Cathy Fazio, Shulamit Kahn, Gregory Hoverson, and Joan Wills, and by participants at the NBER Entrepreneurship, Innovation Policy, and the Economy Conference 2021; Geography of Innovation Conference 2020; DRUID PDW on Female Scientists 2019; Industry Studies Association Conference 2018; Innovation, Economic Complexity, and Economic Geography Workshop 2018; and research seminars at the OECD, Copenhagen Business School, USPTO, and Gran Sasso Science Institute (among others). Luca Gius, Rich Bryden, Peter Favaloro, and Melissa Staha have provided great assistance with the data analysis and visualization in the project. This project has been funded by a National Science Foundation, Science of Science and Innovation Policy Grant, 2018–21 (Grant # 1757344). For acknowledgments, sources of research support, and disclosure of the authors' material financial relationships, if any, please see https://www.nber.org/books-and-chapters /entrepreneurship-and-innovation-policy-and-economy-volume-1/mapping-regions -organizations-and-individuals-drive-inclusion-innovation-economy.

1. Prior studies offer a variety of explanations for the leaky academic pipeline, including motherhood and worse access to resources (e.g., Zuckerman, Cole, and Bruer 1991; Sonnert and Holton 1995; Fox 2005; Ding et al. 2006, 2013; Mairesse and Pezzoni 2015).

2. See *Business Wire* (2019), "Korn Ferry Analysis of Largest US Companies Shows Percentage of Women in C-Suite Roles Inches Up from Previous Year."

3. We estimate an inventor gender only when 80% or more of the individuals with that first name are of a single gender. Using this approach about 93% of the US inventors and 88% of university inventors were matched to one gender.

4. For example, if a patent has 1 woman and 3 men out of 4 inventors, then the contribution of women to this patent is 0.25 and the contribution of men is 0.75. When a patent has some inventors without gender estimate, their proportion of the patent is allocated to "unmatched" patents and not used to compute the % FPs score.

5. This lag takes into account that there is a delay between the patent filing and issued year and between graduation year and when graduates are at risk of patenting.

6. The count of female STEM PhDs now represents 8% of all female STEM bachelor's graduates (2010–15). Similarly, (male and female) STEM PhDs represent about 8% of the STEM labor force.

7. The correlation coefficient between the rate of female new inventors and STEM graduates is positive but small (0.2 for Bachelors and 0.3 for PhDs).

8. The top 25 universities have similar rates of inclusion of female new inventors as all universities (table 6).

9. Case Western Reserve's negative index is driven by its low inclusion (below the US scores) in multiple technology classes, and especially in Drugs & Medical patents. Many of these patents are assigned to the Cleveland Clinic Foundation.

10. The change in female new inventors (NIs) in each EA is computed under the assumption that the number of male NIs remained constant. A similar finding (21% annual growth in the number of female NIs in the economy) holds if the EAs inclusivity scores were to be equal to the % Female STEM PhDs (versus Bachelors).

11. The change in female NIs in each university is computed under the assumption that the number of male NIs remained constant.

12. The estimated change in female NIs in each firm is computed keeping the number of male NIs in the firm fixed. Figure 9 shows that 24 firms have as their main technology class Computers & Communications or Drugs & Medical, and we approximate their STEM pipeline using the US % female STEM Bachelors in Computers & Communications and Biological & Biomedical sciences, respectively. Two firms have Chemicals as main technology, and we approximate their STEM supply with the % female STEM Bachelors in Biological & Biomedical; and four firms have Electrical & Elec. or Mechanical as main technology, and we use % female Bachelors in Engineering as relevant STEM supply (table 3). The same finding (4% annual growth in the number of female NIs in the economy) holds if firm inclusivity scores were to be equal to the % Female STEM PhDs (vs. Bachelors).

13. Inventors may have multiple addresses within the same patent, and so we use a weighting function: patent-inventor-location is the unique observation; location can be any administrative unit (e.g., EAs). Note that even if an inventor has multiple addresses within a patent they often correspond to the same region (EA) in our analysis.

References

Acemoglu, D., U. Akcigit, and M. A. Celik. Forthcoming. "Radical and Incremental Innovation: The Roles of Firms, Managers and Innovators." *American Economic Journal: Macroeconomics*. https://www.aeaweb.org/articles?id=10.1257/mac.20170410.

Adams, R. B., and D. Ferreira. 2009. "Women in the Boardroom and Their Impact on Governance and Performance." *Journal of Financial Economics* 94 (2): 291–309.

Allison, P. D., J. S. Long, and T. K. Krauze. 1982. "Cumulative Advantage and Inequality in Science." *American Sociological Review* 47 (5): 615–25.

Allison, P. D., and J. A. Stewart. 1974. "Productivity Differences among Scientists: Evidence for Accumulative Advantage." *American Sociological Review* 39 (4): 596–606.

Apesteguia, J., G. Azmat, and N. Iriberri. 2012. "The Impact of Gender Composition on Team Performance and Decision Making: Evidence from the Field." *Management Science* 58 (1): 78–93.

Arora, A., S. Belenzon, and L. Sheer. 2017. "Back to Basics: Why Do Firms Invest in Research?" Working Paper no. 23187, NBER, Cambridge, MA.

Audretsch, D. B., and M. P. Feldman. 1996. "R&D Spillovers and the Geography of Innovation and Production." *American Economic Review* 86 (4): 253–73.

Azoulay, P., C. C. Liu, and T. E. Stuart. 2017. "Social Influence Given (Partially) Deliberate Matching: Career Imprints in the Creation of Academic Entrepreneurs." *American Journal of Sociology* 122 (4): 1223–71.

Azoulay, P., C. Fons-Rosen, and J. S. Graff Zivin. 2019. "Does Science Advance One Funeral at a Time?" *American Economic Review* 109 (8): 2889–920.

Bell, A., R. Chetty, X. Jaravel, N. Petkova, and J. van Reenen. 2019. "Who Becomes an Inventor in America? The Importance of Exposure to Innovation." *Quarterly Journal of Economics* 134:647–713.

Bhaskarabhatla, A., and D. Hegde. 2014. "An Organizational Perspective on Patenting and Open Innovation." *Organization Science* 25 (6): 1744–63.

Brush, C., P. Greene, L. Balachandra, and A. Davis. 2018. "The Gender Gap in Venture Capital—Progress, Problems, and Perspectives." *Venture Capital* 20 (2): 115–36.

Business Wire. 2019. "Korn Ferry Analysis of Largest U.S. Companies Shows Percentage of Women in C-Suite Roles Inches Up from Previous Year". https://www.businesswire.com/news/home/20190417005204/en/Korn-Ferry-Analysis-of-Largest-U.S.-Companies-Shows-Percentage-of-Women-in-C-Suite-Roles-Inches-Up-from-Previous-Year.

Castilla, E. J. 2011. "Bringing Managers Back In: Managerial Influences on Workplace Inequality." *American Sociological Review* 76 (5): 667–94.

Cook, L. D. 2019. "Unequal Opportunity: The Innovation Gap in Pink and Black." In *Does America Need More Innovators?* ed. E. Hintz, M. Stettler Kleine, and M. Wisnioski, 221–49. Cambridge, MA: MIT Press.

———. 2020. "Policies to Broaden Participation in the Innovation Process." Hamilton Project, Brookings Institution, Washington, DC.

Cook, L. D., and C. Kongcharoen. 2010. "The Idea Gap in Pink and Black." Working Paper no. 16331, NBER, Cambridge, MA.

David, P. A. 1994. "Positive Feedbacks and Research Productivity in Science: Reopening another Black Box." In *Economics of Technology*, ed. O. Granstrand, 65–89. Amsterdam: Elsevier.

Delgado, M. 2020. "The Co-location of Innovation and Production in Clusters." *Industry and Innovation* 27 (8): 842–70.

Delgado, M., M. Mariani, and F. Murray. 2019. "The Role of Location on the Inventor Gender Gap: Women Are Geographically Constrained." DRUID Conference Paper, Copenhagen Business School, June 19–21.

Delgado, M., and F. Murray. 2020. "Catalysts for Gender Inclusion in Innovation: The Role of Universities and Their Top Inventors." Paper presented at the American Economic Association Conference, San Diego, CA, January 3–5.

Delgado, M., M. E. Porter, and S. Stern. 2014. "Clusters, Convergence, and Economic Performance." *Research Policy* 43 (10): 1785–99.

Ding, W. W., F. Murray, and T. E. Stuart. 2006. "Gender Differences in Patenting in the Academic Life Sciences." *Science* 313:665–67.

———. 2013. "From Bench to Board: Gender Differences in University Scientists' Participation in Corporate Scientific Advisory Boards." *Academy of Management Journal* 56 (5): 1443–64.

DiPrete, T. A., and G. M. Eirich. 2006. "Cumulative Advantage as a Mechanism for Inequality: A Review of Theoretical and Empirical Developments." *Annual Review of Sociology* 32:271–97.

Eaton, S. C. 1999. "Surprising Opportunities: Gender and the Structure of Work in Biotechnology Firms." *Annals of the New York Academy of Sciences* 869:175–88.

Feldman, M. P., and D. Audretsch. 1999. "Innovation in Cities: Science-Based Diversity, Specialization, and Localized Competition." *European Economic Review* 43:409–29.

Florida, R. 2002. *The Rise of the Creative Class*. New York: Basic.

———. 2010. *Who's Your City? How the Creative Economy Is Making Where to Live the Most Important Decision of Your Life*. New York: Basic.

Forman, C., A. Goldfarb, and S. Greenstein. 2016. "Agglomeration of Invention in the Bay Area: Not Just ICT." *American Economic Review* 106 (5): 146–51.

Fox, M. F. 2005. "Gender, Family Characteristics, and Publication Productivity among Scientists." *Social Studies of Science* 35 (1): 131–50.

Freeman, R. B., D. F. Goroff, D. K. Ginther, and S. Kalui. 2009. "Does Science Promote Women? Evidence from Academia 1973–2001." In *Science and Engineering Careers in the United States: An Analysis of Markets and Employment*, ed. R. B. Freeman and D. F. Goroff, 163–94. Chicago: University of Chicago Press.

Gaule, P., and M. Piacentini. 2018. "An Advisor Like Me? Advisor Gender and Post-graduate Careers in Science." *Research Policy* 47:805–13.

Hall, B. H., A. B. Jaffe, and M. Trajtenberg. 2001. "The NBER Patent Citation Data File: Lessons, Insights and Methodological Tools." Working Paper no. 8498, NBER, Cambridge, MA.

Hofstra, B., V. V. Kulkarni, S. Munoz-Najar Galvez, B. He, D. Jurafsky, and D. A. McFarland. 2020. "The Diversity-Innovation Paradox in Science." *PNAS* 117 (17): 9284–91.

Hoisl, K., and M. Mariani. 2017. "It's a Man's Job: Income and the Gender Gap in Industrial Research." *Management Science* 63 (3): 587–900.

Islam, E., and J. Zein. 2020. "Inventor CEOs." *Journal of Financial Economics* 135 (2): 505–27.

Jensen, K., B. Kovács, and O. Sorenson. 2018. "Gender Differences in Obtaining and Maintaining Patent Rights." *Nature Biotechnology* 36:307–309.

Johnson, K. P., and J. R. Kort. 2004. "2004 Redefinition of the BEA Economic Areas." https://apps.bea.gov/scb/pdf/2004/11November/1104Econ-areas.Pdf.

Joshi, A. 2014. "By Whom and When Is Women's Expertise Recognized? The Interactive Effects of Gender and Education in Science and Engineering Teams." *Administrative Science Quarterly* 59 (2): 202–39.

Joshi, A., and A. P. Knight. 2015. "Who Defers to Whom and Why? Dual Pathways Linking Demographic Differences and Dyadic Deference to Team Effectiveness." *Academy of Management Journal* 58:59–84.

Kerr, S. P., W. Kerr, Ç. Özden, and C. Parsons. 2017. "High-Skilled Migration and Agglomeration." *Annual Review of Economics* 9 (1): 201–34.

Kerr, W. 2008. "The Ethnic Composition of US Inventors." Working Paper no. 08-006, Harvard Business School, Cambridge, MA.

Koning, R., S. Samila, and J. P. Ferguson. 2020. "Inventor Gender and the Direction of Invention." *AEA Papers and Proceedings* 110:250–54.

Lax Martínez, G., J. Raffo, and K. Saito. 2016. "Identifying the Gender of PCT Inventors." Economic Research Working Paper no. 33, World Intellectual Property Organization, Geneva.

Li, D., and C. Koedel. 2017. "Representation and Salary Gaps by Race-Ethnicity and Gender at Selective Public Universities." *Educational Researcher* 46 (7): 343–54.

Madsen, S. 2012. "Women and Leadership in Higher Education." *Advances in Developing Human Resources* 14 (2): 131–39.

Mairesse, J., and M. Pezzoni. 2015. "Does Gender Affect Scientific Productivity? A Critical Review of the Empirical Evidence and a Panel Data Econometric Analysis for French Physicists." Revue économique 66:65–113.

McKinsey & Company. 2020. "Diversity Wins: How Inclusion Matters." Report, May 19.

Merton, R. K. 1968. "The Matthew Effect in Science." *Science* 159 (3810): 56–63.

Milli, J., E. Williams-Baron, M. Berlan, J. Xia, and B. Gault. 2016. "Equity in Innovation: Women Inventors and Patents." IWPR Report #C448, Institute for Women's Policy Research, Washington, DC.

Moss-Racusin, C. A., J. F. Dovidio, V. L. Brescoll, M. J. Graham, and J. Handelsman. 2012. "Science Faculty's Subtle Gender Biases Favor Male Students." *Proceedings of the National Academy of Sciences* 109 (41): 16474–79.

NASEM (National Academies of Sciences, Engineering, and Medicine). 2018. "Sexual Harassment of Women: Climate, Culture, and Consequences in Academic Sciences, Engineering, and Medicine." Review, NASEM, Washington, DC.

O'Neale, D. R. J., and S. C. Hendy. 2012. "Power Law Distributions of Patents as Indicators of Innovation." *PLoS ONE* 7 (12): e49501.

Pezzoni, M., J. Mairesse, P. Stephan, and J. Lane. 2016. "Gender and the Publication Output of Graduate Students: A Case Study." *PLOS ONE* 11 (1): 1–12.

Post, C., and K. Byron. 2015. "Women on Boards and Firm Financial Performance: A Meta-Analysis." *Academy of Management Journal* 58 (5): 1546–71.

Roberts, E. B., F. Murray, and J. D. Kim. 2015. "Entrepreneurship and Innovation at MIT: Continuing Global Growth and Impact." Report, Massachusetts Institute of Technology, Cambridge, MA.

Rocha, V., and M. Van Praag. 2020. "Mind the Gap: The Role of Gender in Entrepreneurial Career Choice and Social Influence by Founders." *Strategic Management Journal* 41 (5): 841–66.

Romer, P. 1990. "Endogenous Technological Change." *Journal of Political Economy* 98 (5): 71–102.

Rosenthal, S., and W. Strange. 2012. "Female Entrepreneurship, Agglomeration, and a New Spatial Mismatch." *Review of Economics and Statistics* 94 (3): 764–88.

Saxenian, A. 2002. "Silicon Valley's New Immigrant High-Growth Entrepreneurs." *Economic Development Quarterly* 16 (1): 20–31.

Settles, I. H., L. M. Cortina, J. Malley, and A. J. Stewart. 2006. "The Climate for Women in Academic Science: The Good, the Bad, and the Changeable." *Psychology of Women Quarterly* 30:47–58.

Sheltzer, J. M., and J. C. Smith. 2014. "Elite Male Faculty in the Life Sciences Employ Fewer Women." *Proceedings of the National Academy of Sciences* 111:10107–12.

Sonnert, G., and G. J. Holton. 1995. *Who Succeeds in Science? The Gender Dimension.* New Brunswick, NJ: Rutgers University Press.

Sorenson, O., and M. S. Dahl. 2016. "Geography, Joint Choices, and the Reproduction of Gender Inequality." *American Sociological Review* 81 (5): 900–20.

Stuart, T. S., and W. W. Ding. 2006. "When Do Scientists Become Entrepreneurs? The Social Structural Antecedents of Commercial Activity in the Academic Life Sciences." *American Journal of Sociology* 112 (1): 97–144.

Thursby, J. G., and M. C. Thursby. 2005. "Gender Patterns of Research and Licensing Activity of Science and Engineering Faculty." *Journal of Technology Transfer* 30:343–53.

USPTO (US Patent and Trademark Office). 2017. PatentsView, June. https:// www.uspto.gov/ip-policy/economic-research/patentsview.

———. 2020. "Progress and Potential: 2020 Update on US Women Inventor-Patentees." Office of the Chief Economist, IP Data Highlights, no. 4, USPTO, Alexandria, VA.

Whittington, K. B., and L. Smith-Doer. 2008. "Women Inventors in Context: Disparities in Patenting across Academia and Industry." *Gender and Society* 22 (2): 194–218.

Wolfinger, N. H., M. A. Mason, and M. Goulden. 2008. "Problems in the Pipeline: Gender, Marriage, and Fertility in the Ivory Tower." *Journal of Higher Education* 79 (4): 388–405.

Woolley, A. W., C. F. Chabris, A. Pentland, N. Hashmi, and T. W. Malone. 2010. "Evidence for a Collective Intelligence Factor in the Performance of Human Groups." *Science* 330 (6004): 686–88.

Zuckerman, H., J. R. Cole, and J. T. Bruer. 1991. *The Outer Circle.* New York: Norton.

Funding Risky Research

Chiara Franzoni, *Polytechnic University of Milan*, Italy

Paula Stephan, *Georgia State University and NBER*, United States of America

Reinhilde Veugelers, *KU Leuven*, Belgium, and *Peterson Institute for International Economics*, United States of America

Abstract

The speed with which COVID-19 vaccines were developed and their high performance underlines how much society depends on the pace of scientific research and how effective science can be. This is especially the case for vaccines based on the new designer messenger RNA (mRNA) technology. We draw on this exceptional moment for science to reflect on whether the government funding system is sufficiently supportive of research needed for key breakthroughs, and whether the system of funding encourages sufficient risk-taking to induce scientists to explore transformative research paths. We begin with a discussion of the challenges faced by scientists who did pioneering research related to mRNA-based drugs in getting support for research. We describe measures developed to distinguish risky from nonrisky research and their citation footprint. We review empirical work suggesting that funding is biased against risky research and provide a framework for thinking about why principal investigators, panelists, and funding agencies may eschew risky research. We close with a discussion of interventions that government agencies and universities could follow if they wish to avoid a bias against risk.

JEL Codes: I23, O31, O33, O38

Keywords: research funding, risky research, bias, peer review

I. Introduction

The COVID-19 pandemic has underlined how much society depends on the pace of scientific research and how effective science can be. The

Entrepreneurship and Innovation Policy and the Economy, volume 1, 2022.

speed with which COVID-19 vaccines were developed and their high performance surpassed even the most optimistic expectations. This is especially the case for those based on the new designer messenger RNA (mRNA) technology, which enabled the identification of a vaccine with high efficacy in less than 3 months after sequencing of the virus and holds huge promise for the future of vaccines and medicine more broadly.[1]

We draw on this exceptional moment for science to reflect on an important and pressing theme. Is the government funding system sufficiently supportive of the science needed for key breakthroughs, such as mRNA-based drugs? If the science needed for such breakthroughs requires transformative research, particularly in its early phases, does our system of science funding encourage sufficient risk-taking to induce scientists to explore transformative research paths?

In this contribution, we discuss risk-taking and the funding of risky science. We start in Section II by describing problems faced by Katalin Karikó, a scientist who did pioneering research related to mRNA-based drugs. In Section III, we briefly describe measures developed to distinguish risky from nonrisky research and the extent to which the citation footprint of risky research differs from that of nonrisky research. We then review empirical work concerning the funding of research, which suggests that funding is biased against risky science. Section IV provides a framework for thinking about why funding agencies may eschew funding risky research. We focus first on how factors within the research system, such as pressure to show results in a short time period and the widespread use of bibliometrics, contribute to risk aversion. We then focus on three key players affecting research funding and the role the three play in determining the amount of risky research that is undertaken: (1) principal investigators, (2) panelists, and (3) funding agencies. Section V closes with a discussion of interventions that government agencies and universities could do if they wish to avoid a bias against risk.

II.   Messenger RNA Design: Difficulties Encountered Advancing a Risky Agenda

We begin by describing the development of designer messenger RNA, the breakthrough technology used by Pfizer-BioNTech and Moderna to develop the first two vaccines against COVID-19 to obtain Food and Drug Administration approval in the United States and European Medicines Agency approval in the European Union.

The mRNA is a protein-coding single-stranded molecule, produced by cells during the transcription process, when the genes encoded in DNA are copied into the molecule of RNA. The discovery of mRNA was reported in *Nature* in May 1961, a result of scientists' search concerning the synthesis of proteins coded in DNA. The path to synthesize mRNA in a test tube was made possible in 1984 when Paul Krieg and Doug Melton, scientists at Harvard University, identified that, by using SP6 RNA polymerase, functional mRNA can be produced in vitro. By 1990, a group of scientists demonstrated that injection of synthetic, in vitro–transcribed mRNA into animals led to expression of the encoded protein (Wolff et al. 1990). Soon, the scientific world realized this system could potentially be used to turn human bodies into medicine-making factories and treat a variety of disorders, ranging from infection to cancer to rare diseases, and possibly mend such things as damaged heart tissue (Sahin, Karikó, and Türeci 2014). But, at the time, mRNA was not the only conceivable way to introduce protein expression into cells: other nucleic acid–based technologies were under investigation. Moreover, there remained two critical problems that needed to be addressed. In vitro–transcribed mRNA, when delivered to animals, could be destroyed by the body before reaching its target as the body fielded an immune response, or worse yet, could cause serious side effects (Sahin et al. 2014). No one knew how to make mRNA effective in humans despite years of interest on the part of scientists.

Katalin Karikó was determined, by all accounts, to find a way to make synthetic mRNA applicable to the treatment of human diseases. Born and educated in Hungary, she came to the United States in 1985, first as a postdoctoral fellow at Temple University, then at the Uniformed Services University of the Health Sciences. In 1989, she moved to a faculty position at the Perelman School of Medicine at the University of Pennsylvania (Penn).[2] She submitted more than 20 grants, initially for smaller sums, to Penn and the American Heart Association, then for larger sums to the National Institutes of Health (NIH).[3] Despite her efforts, she repeatedly failed to get funding for her research. "Every night I was working: grant, grant, grant," recounts Karikó. "And it came back always no, no, no."[4] Her inability to support her research on grants eventually resulted in her being taken off her faculty position by the university. In 1995, she accepted a nonfaculty position at Penn, which she describes as "more like a post-doc position," without any prospect of advancement.[5]

Two years later, Drew Weissman, an MD PhD immunologist, moved from NIH (where he had worked with Anthony Fauci) to Penn. The same year, Karikó and Weissman met at one of the school's photocopy machines. While chatting, they recognized a shared interest in developing a synthetic mRNA vaccine against the human immunodeficiency virus (HIV). They realized the potential of combining their biochemistry, molecular biology, and immunology expertise and decided to begin working together. At the time, Karikó was focused on mRNA-based therapy for treating cerebral diseases and strokes. With Weissman, Karikó switched focus to mRNA-based vaccines. Weissman supported the early stage work partly on one of his existing NIH grants, which had no direct connection to mRNA research.[6] Their breakthrough occurred when they recognized that uridine was the nucleoside in the mRNA that provoked the human immune system. They discovered that, when replacing uridine with pseudouridine, another naturally occurring nucleoside in the mRNA, it could enter cells without alerting the RNA sensors. Their research was eventually published in *Immunity* in 2005, after being rejected by several leading journals (Kolata 2021). Karikó was the first author, Weissman the senior author. It eventually became a highly cited paper, receiving to date more than 1,000 Google Scholar citations, although it took until 2015 to reach its first 500. They disclosed their joint work to Penn, which filed and obtained patents. Karikó and Weissman were listed as coinventors. These patents, in line with the Bayh-Dole Act, acknowledge NIH grants, including the grant that had no direct connection to mRNA research. The patents were licensed exclusively to CellScript by Penn. CellScript sublicensed the university's patent to the German-based firm BioNTech, incorporated in 2008, and US-based Moderna, incorporated in 2010. The subsequent development of the mRNA-based drugs was conducted by these companies with both equity investments and a large involvement of public money.[7]

Even after the 2005 discovery, the two found funding for mRNA research difficult to obtain. According to Weissman, "We both started writing grants. We didn't get most of them. People were not interested in mRNA. The people who reviewed the grants said, "mRNA will not be a good therapeutic, so don't bother" (Kolata 2021). Weissman, however, continued to receive funding from NIH; some, but not all, of it was for mRNA research. Karikó continued to have difficulty getting funding.[8] A 2007 application that Karikó submitted to the National Institute of Neurological Disorders and Stroke (NINDS) at NIH, for example, was not discussed at the study section meeting, having been judged by reviewers to be in the lower half of the applications. The proposal focused on the anti-inflammatory effects of neurotropics in ischemia stroke. Two reviewers described the proposed work as "novel," but the third described the proposal as suffering from a "relative lack of novelty." Other comments from reviewers included statements such as "Preliminary data should be provided to support that the proposed experiments can be carried out" and "insufficient preliminary data." The work related to one of the aims was described as "very preliminary and there is high likelihood that these experiments, especially in vivo, will not work."[9] An application submitted in 2012 with Weissman, with the goal of developing "a new therapeutic approach to treat ischemic brain injury by delivering specific mRNAs" was scored, but neither it nor the resubmission received a sufficiently strong score to be funded. Concerns included: "preliminary data presented are insufficient to suggest that this approach is worthy of in-depth evaluation in a stroke model" and that the first aim of the study was "largely descriptive."[10]

In 2006, Karikó and Weissman founded the company RNARx with the intention of using mRNA to treat anemia. Karikó was the CEO of the company from 2006 to 2013. In her role, she applied for and received one Small Business Technology Transfer (STTR) grant from NIH.[11] In 2013, Karikó became senior vice president at BioNTech.

We have no way of knowing what would have played out in terms of research outcomes if Karikó's early applications for funding had not been turned down or if she had gotten research support from Penn in the early period. Perhaps mRNA-based vaccines would have been available for swine flu in 2009. But, without the casual meeting with Weissman at the photocopy machine, she could also have given up researching a way to make designer mRNA technology effective for drug development in humans. What we do know is that her early proposals were not funded and that Penn moved her out of her soft-money faculty position. This could reflect a failure to address the problem of the immune system response, which later on was facilitated by her collaboration with Weissman. It could also reflect risk aversion on the part of review panels that considered the area too risky to be fundable, especially because Karikó had, at that time, few publications and citations, few preliminary results, and no prior record of funding. More generally, the example tells us that the early funding of designer mRNA research, now considered promising in future medicine, was difficult.

Karikó is not the only scientist to hear "no, no, no." Similar anecdotal evidence is not difficult to find. A researcher at a top research institution in the United States, in speaking of the National Aeronautics and Space Administration and the National Science Foundation (NSF), said that "programs are not very adventurous" and "what I experienced was that I couldn't get any new idea or anything I was really excited about funded by NSF. It never worked . . . the feedback is 'well this is too new: we don't know whether it's going to work'" (Franzoni and Stephan 2021). James Rothman, the day after he shared the Nobel Prize in Medicine or Physiology in 2013, told an interviewer that "he was grateful he started work in the early 1970s when the federal government was willing to take much bigger risks in handing out funding to young scientists." Rothman went on to say, "I had five years of failure, really, before I had the first initial sign of success. And I'd like to think that that kind of support existed today, but I think there's less of it. And it's actually becoming a pressing national issue, if not an international issue" (Harris 2013).

III.   Risk Aversion in Science Funding: A Review of Empirical Evidence

Concerns that the selection of grant proposals is overly conservative have been growing in recent years. Commentators on science policy have long lamented that science funders are too conservative and risk averse and skimp on supporting breakthrough research (e.g., Viner, Powell, and Green 2004; Mazzucato 2015; Laudel 2017). Funding agencies are accused of placing too much emphasis on the downside of avoiding failure and too little emphasis on the upside potential of supporting truly courageous ideas (Azoulay, Graff Zivin, and Manso 2012; Nicholson and Ioannidis 2012). But do we have more than anecdotal evidence on risk bias by science funding agencies? Do we have any science of science funding insights on this?

Although research in the area is limited, a handful of recent empirical works have begun to address the topic. The results support the view of risk aversion in funding. Before we review this evidence, it is important to note that risk remains an ill-defined concept (Althaus 2005; Aven 2011; Hansson 2018; Franzoni and Stephan 2021). Moreover, it is difficult to measure. Here we follow Franzoni and Stephan (2021) and use the term "risk" in its "speculative" meaning, in the sense that risk refers to uncertainty concerning the outcomes of research, where the outcomes vary predominantly in the spectrum of gains and potentially lead to exceptional results, but also could lead to no results.[12] We preface the literature review with ways to measure risky research.

A.   Measures of Risky Research

Empirically identifying risky research is challenging (Franzoni and Stephan 2021). Most researchers who study risk depend on partial measures that look at the degree to which research results deviate from past results and/or look at the building blocks upon which the research is based. Foster, Rzhetsky, and Evans (2015) adopt the first approach and distinguish among three types of papers based on the chemical relationships described in the work. Research that makes a "jump" explores previously unexplored chemical relationships—jumping beyond current knowledge. Such research arguably is more likely to "fail" but, if the research succeeds, is more likely to make a breakthrough. Research that explores relationships between previously studied entities is subdivided into research that tests a new relationship not published before, or research that repeats an analysis of a previously studied relationship. Foster et al. (2015) find that "jump" papers (reporting highly innovative chemical combinations) receive 52% more citations on average than "repeat" papers (reporting known combinations), whereas "new" papers (reporting moderately innovative combinations) enjoy 30% more citations than those reporting known combinations. Their findings suggest that taking the risk associated with jump and new research makes it more likely to achieve high impact. But they also find this research is more likely to fail. The authors thus find that the citation distribution associated with jump papers and new papers has a higher mean than that of repeat papers. They also find that the distribution has a higher variance, both characteristics that we expect in risky research, suggesting their measure correlates with risk. The additional rewards associated with jump papers are, however, relatively small and may not compensate sufficiently for the possibility of failing, suggesting higher expected returns of a safer research path.[13]

Wang, Veugelers, and Stephan (2017) view scientific research as a combinatorial process and measure novelty in science by examining whether a published paper makes first-time ever combinations of scientific knowledge components as proxied by referenced journals, accounting for the difficulty of making such combinations. Almost all new combinations made by novel papers cross subject categories. Although they recognize novelty is but one dimension of risk, they show that novel papers have patterns consistent with risky research of a higher mean and higher variance in citation performance. Novel papers also have a higher probability of becoming a highly cited paper but at the same time a higher probability of becoming a no/low cited paper. Wang et al. (2017) also find strong evidence that novel research takes more time to become top-cited (fig. 1) and that it is published in journals having a lower impact as measured by the journal impact factor. These findings suggest that bibliometric indicators based on citation counts and journal impact factors

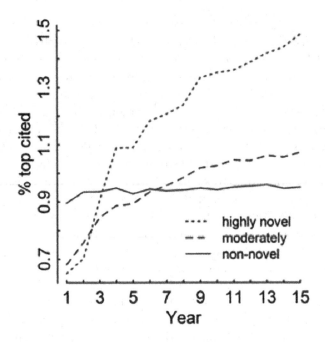

Fig. 1. Delayed recognition: novel papers take more time to be cited. A color version of this figure is available online.

with a short citation window may be biased against risky, novel research. They also show that citations to novel papers are more likely to come from a broader set of disciplines and from disciplines that are more distant from their "home" field (fig. 2), suggesting that novel research has a tendency to both be best appreciated and to spark applications well beyond the disciplinary boundaries.

B. Assessing Bias in Funding Risky Research

Using their novelty measure, Veugelers, Stephan, and Wang (2021) examine whether the European Research Council (ERC)—the most important funding agency of the European Commission, set up in 2007 with the explicit aim to fund "high gain, high risk" research—is biased against novelty. They find that applicants to the ERC Starting Grant program with a history of highly novel publications are significantly less likely to receive funding than those without such a history. The major penalty for novelty comes during the first stage of selection, when panel members screen a large number of applications based on a short summary of the

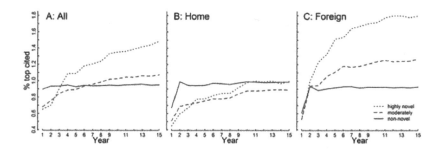

Fig. 2. Transdisciplinary impact over time. A color version of this figure is available online. Source: Wang et al. (2017).

proposed research and a curriculum vitae listing the candidate's main publications, for which they are most likely to use readily available bibliometric indicators. The finding is thus consistent with the use of bibliometric indicators in grant selection as a source of bias against risky research.

In an experiment conducted at Harvard Medical School, Boudreau et al. (2014) find that more novel research proposals, as measured by the percentage of keywords not previously used, receive more negative evaluations during peer review. This result is driven by proposals with particularly high levels of novelty. Their preferred explanation for this finding rests on bounded rationality of reviewers. "Experts extrapolating beyond the knowledge frontier to comprehend novel proposals are prone to systematic errors, misconstruing novel work. This implies that, rather than receiving unbiased assessments (with zero mean errors), novel proposals are discounted relative to their true merit, quality and potential" (Boudreau et al. 2014, 2779). Lanoë (2019), using a measure of novelty, finds evidence that funding decisions made by French National Research Agency are biased against risk-taking. Wagner and Alexander (2013) evaluate the Small Grants for Exploratory Research, an NSF program designed to support high-risk, high-reward research that ran from 1990 to 2006. Funding decisions were made entirely by program officers with no external review. The authors find that program officers routinely used only a small percentage of available funds. The authors interpret the findings as suggesting that either officers were averse to funding risky research, despite the number of funded proposals that had transformative results, or that risk-taking was not rewarded within the NSF. Packalen and Bhattacharya (2018), using the vintage of ideas embodied in a paper as a proxy for novelty, find that NIH's propensity to fund projects that build on the most recent vintage of advances has declined over the past several decades.

Although the evidence discussed above is preliminary, it suggests that risky research is disfavored in the competition for funding. This seems the case not only when the funding is directed to "standard" science, but even when a deliberate goal of the funding agency is to support high-risk, high-gain research, as in the case of the ERC.

Assuming the preliminary evidence is correct, why do funding agencies eschew supporting risky research and thus possibly miss the opportunities of funding breakthroughs? Is this a conscious or unconscious choice, embedded in their modes of operating? And what can be done to encourage risk-taking among funders? These are the questions we explore further in the next sections.

IV.   Why Would Funding Agencies Eschew Supporting Risky Research?

To the best of our knowledge, there is no research that directly addresses why funding agencies may be light on risky research. Moreover, there may be multiple factors that converge to play a role. Given the lack of research that informs on clear causes, we can only formulate a set of hypotheses. In this section, we provide an overview of hypotheses that deserve more scrutiny in the future. We start with hypotheses that arise from outside the funding agencies and relate to the broader research system. We then discuss how these translate into a set of incentives and opportunities that could induce funding agencies to eschew supporting risky research and instead fund "safe" research at different levels of analysis. We consider three such levels: (1) the principal investigators who write and submit grant proposals, (2) the panels in charge of selecting research to fund (composed by panelists and research officers), and (3) the funding agencies. Figure 3 provides a summary of the hypotheses.

A.   Research System

Calls for more accountability when using public funds and the trend toward more and regular evaluations of policy programs put increasing pressure on publicly funded science institutions to show results, especially those aligned with political cycles. Shorter windows for results already bias against basic research programs in general; witness the heated discussions on the share of overall public research and development (R&D) budgets for bottom-up basic research agencies such as ERC, NSF, and NIH,

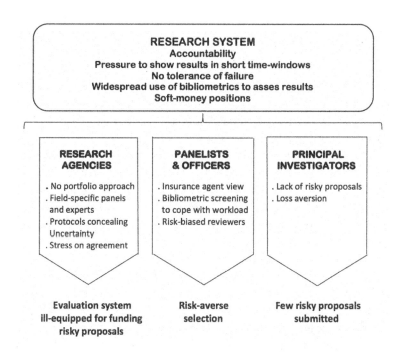

Fig. 3. Incentives and opportunities regarding risky research: a summary

compared with more directed, applied, and closer-to-market programs. But even within basic research programs, the pressure to show results quickly may discourage publicly funded agencies from funding more risky research. A major factor is the length of time it takes risky research to have an impact: novel breakthroughs typically take a long time to materialize. As shown in figure 1, Wang et al. (2017) find that novel research requires a longer time window than nonnovel research to achieve impact. For the first 3 years after publication, the probability that a highly novel paper is among the top 1% of cited papers is below that of nonnovel papers, but beyond these 3 years, highly novel papers start accumulating a lead; 15 years after publication, novel papers are nearly twice as likely to be in the top 1% of highly cited papers. This longer time window for big impact means that it takes the community a longer time to learn about new approaches and switch from established research paths to adopting new ones. Funding agencies, in an effort to maintain or expand funding, may feel they cannot afford to wait for risky research to show its impact and opt instead to fund safer research that has measurable effects in the near term, even if these effects are less likely to become breakthroughs.

An important factor in discouraging risky research may be the general lack of tolerance for failure and the meager rewards for those who take uncertain paths within the science system. As hiring, promotion, and funding decisions are important conditions for engaging in research, and as reputation is a key reward for doing science, a lower inclination of researchers to engage in risky research can be traced back to biases against risk in the science system in general.

Universities routinely make crucial career decisions, such as hiring, midyear review, tenure, and promotion. When these career evaluations are made using bibliometric indicators with relatively short time windows (such as Journal Impact Factors or short windows for calculating citations) to measure research "quality," they can discourage risky research, as these measures appear to be biased against risk-taking (Stephan, Veugelers, and Wang 2017).

Career status and progression is not only an important reward for scientists themselves but also an element that goes into the track record and reputation that funding agencies and their panels consider as part of the applicant's profile. Any bias against risk in career decisions may thus have indirect effects on funding decisions, which may in turn affect career progression negatively when a candidate's productivity in acquiring external funding is a crucial factor in determining career progression, as the story of Karikó illustrated.

The large number of researchers in the United States in "soft-money" positions—that is, positions for which salary is funded from grants that the researcher is responsible for obtaining—encourages the submission of proposals with little risk. If their research is not deemed fundable or comes up empty handed, the university can cut its losses and hire another individual into the position. It is notable that soft-money positions have been on the rise in recent years. In the United States, for example, the majority of basic medical faculty are hired in soft-money positions and are responsible for bringing in most of their own salary (Stephan 2012). Soft-money positions also are common outside of medical institutions. Stephan (2007) documents that during the years in which the NIH budget doubled, the majority of new hires were made into soft-money positions. Soft-money positions not only transfer risk to the faculty, but also discourage risk-taking on the part of the faculty given the importance of continued funding.

Beyond affecting career progression and funding decisions, track record matters more generally as it affects a scientist's reputation and recognition. Although by no means the only reward for doing science, peer recognition and reputation are key drivers of scientists' choices (Merton 1957; Stephan and Levin 1992).[14] With peer recognition and reputation biased against risky research, scientists may be less prone to choose risky research paths. This is, however, not obvious; examples of scientists who have taken a risky course receiving a Nobel Prize, for example, are readily available and there is research suggesting that prestigious prizes can encourage risk-taking (Rzhetsky et al. 2015).[15]

B. Principal Investigators

The "Lack of Risky Proposals" Hypothesis

When Story Landis was director of NINDS at NIH, she noticed that the amount of support the institute provided for what it classified as "basic-basic" research was declining, compared with what it was spending on "basic-disease" and applied research. Finding this disconcerting, the institute set out to investigate why. Somewhat to their surprise, they found that the dollar amount researchers requested to do basic-basic research had declined by 21%. Landis, when asked why she thought the decline was occurring, replied, "My concern is that the decrease in the number of basic-basic applications reflects the perception that NINDS is only interested in disease-oriented research."[16] Basic research is not, of course, the same thing as risky research, but the two are arguably close cousins. The example may suggest that researchers, anticipating that risky proposals have a difficult time at review, may simply refrain from conceiving and submitting risky research proposals. This is difficult to test, given a lack of data on proposals. But it is a plausible hypothesis. Some evidence consistent with a lack in supply of risky proposals is reported in Veugelers et al. (2021). They find that nonfunded junior ERC applicants who fail in the second stage have significantly lower likelihood of producing novel papers after being rejected, compared with the successful ones. The evidence is consistent with rejected applicants learning that risk is not rewarded. Faced with the pressures to apply and reapply for funding, they adjust their research portfolio away from risky research, something the successful applicants are "freed" from doing.

Overall, the reward premium awarded by the science system for doing risky research, compared with that of doing not-so-risky research, appears insufficient to encourage risk-taking. The findings from Foster et al. (2015) discussed previously suggest that taking the risk associated with "jump" and "new" research makes it more likely to achieve high impact.

But the additional rewards in terms of the extra citations they find are relatively small and may not compensate sufficiently for the possibility of failing, in terms of not getting published and its negative impact on the researchers' careers. Their results thus suggest that returns may be higher for following a safer research path. Stephan (2019) has called this the "quad effect," referring to the fact that competitive female figure skaters attempt fewer quadruple jumps, arguably because the incremental score they can earn for completing a quad, compared with successfully completing a triple jump, is insufficient to compensate for the risk of failing to complete the quad jump. For male figure skaters, scoring is different: the incremental score is larger and arguably provides sufficient incentive to attempt the quad. The work of Uzzi et al. (2013) is consistent with the findings of Foster et al. (2015), showing that "[t]he highest-impact science is primarily grounded in exceptional conventional combinations of prior work yet simultaneously features an intrusion of unusual combinations," which suggests that a risky approach, when embedded in a more standard conventional approach, can better escape the citation premium bias. Stated differently, a little bit of risk adds spice to the research, but conventionality is the dominant characteristic of highly cited papers.[17]

The "Loss Aversion by Principal Investigators" Hypothesis

The preferences of scientists for the level of risk involved in the projects they wish to pursue may not only reflect biases against risk in the reward structure of science, as discussed previously, but also loss aversion on the part of scientists. Behavioral psychology has shown that humans are generally loss averse. They overestimate the magnitude of prospective losses and underestimate the magnitude of prospective gains (Kahneman and Tversky 1979; Tversky and Kahneman 1991). It is not implausible to expect that scientists are no exception to the rule.

C. Research Agencies

"Lack of a Portfolio Approach" Hypothesis

A common approach taken by investors to stabilize the volatility of outcomes is to include in the same portfolio stocks that have uncorrelated outcomes, or that have outcomes that are negatively correlated (i.e., when one loses, the other gains). In finance, where investors normally want to maximize the overall return of the portfolio and are risk averse, a portfolio approach enables purchasing more risky stocks than when the investor buys stocks one by one without reference to what is in her portfolio. The "one-by-one" practice is frowned upon in the investment literature, given that the choice of a stock whose outcomes are highly correlated to those already in the portfolio may expose the investor to extreme gains, but also extreme losses, foregoing any advantages from using the portfolio to diversify away the risk.

The same logic holds to some extent for funding agencies. Agencies generally review proposals one by one, rank them in descending order of overall aggregated score, and then distribute funds according to the score until the budget is exhausted.[18] This one-by-one approach may arguably restrict the level of risk agencies take. To the extent they are risk averse, the one-by-one approach only aggravates the risk-taking problem.

The "Interdisciplinary Bias" Hypothesis

Review panels are often designed by funding agencies to be discipline-based. This, for example, is generally the case at NSF and ERC. The latter, for instance, operates with 25 panels, which are mostly discipline-focused. It follows that investigators who want to propose research involving multiple disciplines often must make hard choices concerning the most appropriate panel to consider their proposal. It also means their proposal may face obstacles at review that discipline-focused proposals do not face. Bromham, Dinnage, and Hua (2016) studied more than 18,000 proposals submitted to the Australian Research Council Discovery Program. They found that the probability of receiving funding decreased as the degree of interdisciplinarity of the proposal increased.[19] Banal-Estañol, Macho-Stadler, and Pérez-Castrillo (2019) studied the success rate of teams of coinvestigators that sought funding from the United Kingdom Engineering and Physical Sciences Research Council. They showed that team members with interdisciplinary backgrounds (i.e., who had balanced shares of publications in different fields) were penalized, even if those with an interdisciplinary background who were eventually funded were more successful ex post.

A penalty directed at interdisciplinary research may work against funding risky science, because, as noted previously, papers of high novelty are often interdisciplinary. Moreover, Wang et al. (2017) also find that novel work that is highly cited is more likely to garner citations from outside, not from within, its own field, suggesting that the research is appreciated more by others than by colleagues. Monodisciplinary panels may thus more likely be biased against risks associated with novel interdisciplinary research.

"Peer Review Protocols Conceal Uncertainty" Hypothesis

Peer review opinions, especially for risky proposals, involve forecasting research outcomes in conditions of uncertainty (Knight 1921/1964; Nelson 1959). However, protocols commonly used to elicit experts' opinions arguably provide little room for uncertainty, usually requiring reviewers to provide a single score on a numeric ordinal scale to represent a criterion. For example, the ERC requires a single score to rate the "groundbreaking nature and potential impact of the research project." Given the uncertainty of future outcomes, the request of a single-point estimate score can conceptually be thought of as the median value of the possible outcome distribution envisaged by the reviewer. Whereas in peer review of "standard" science, the provision of a single-point estimate may provide a necessary time-saving compromise, in evaluations of risky research the outcomes of interest can be expected to be in the tails and a single-point estimate may have little meaning. Furthermore, uncertainty regarding the outcomes is the key piece of information in this case (Morgan and Henrion 1990; Morgan 2014). It seems plausible that similar practices that demand experts to express a score that conceals, rather than represents, uncertainty may induce poor judgments.[20]

"Practices that Stress Reviewers' Agreement May Disfavor Risky Science" Hypothesis

It is customary in grant peer review to collect several expert opinions about each proposal before making a decision. The underlying idea is that aggregation of a larger number of opinions improves accuracy (Kaplan, Lacetera, and Kaplan 2008; Snell 2015), because random errors likely cancel each other out when averaging results (Larrick and Soll 2006).[21] This would especially be important for risky proposals, which are more difficult to evaluate, hence more exposed to imprecisions and misjudgments.

The efficacy of this approach relies on two assumptions. First, a large number of independent reviewers are available. Second, the mechanisms for aggregating multiple views are unbiased toward risk. In practice, however, both assumptions are problematic. The costs of the review process (Ismail, Farrands, and Wooding 2008) and the unwillingness of reviewers constrain the number of opinions that can be collected. For example, the NIH advises 4 reviews for each proposal, and ERC panels solicit between 3 and 10 external reviews but only for proposals that are short listed to go to the second stage of evaluation. Moreover, reviewers may not be independent and instead have correlated errors (biases) because they share the same background knowledge or beliefs (Clemen and Winkler 1999).

Another critical point when moving from multiple opinions to a single aggregated opinion and to a final deliberation (i.e., binary choice to fund or not) relates to whether methods and rules used in the decision are unbiased toward risk.[22] Prior studies of peer review have evidenced low levels of agreement among reviewers even in the evaluation of "standard" proposals (Pier et al. 2018). Risky proposals probably spark even greater disagreement, given the larger uncertainty involved. Current practices at NIH and ERC use behavioral aggregation—that is, consensus meetings—during which multiple views are confronted and disagreement resolved with discussion (Lamont 2009). However, behavioral aggregation is exposed to groupthink (Cooke 1991; Lamont 2009) and may lead people to herd away from the truth, following influential opinions (Banerjee 1992; Mengel 2019). Consistent with the findings from DellaVigna and Pope (2018) that academics overestimate the accuracy of beliefs of highly cited scholars, this may lead to herding on their beliefs. Furthermore, the requirement of consensus may arguably induce a bias against risky research. Assuming that risky proposals lead to outcomes in the "tails" of the distribution—that is, either "hits" of "flops" (Azoulay, Graff Zivin, and Manso 2011)—it is plausible that the related opinions would also be polarized. If this is the case, methods of aggregation and deliberation that do imply consensus may be systematically biased against risk-taking (Linton 2016). Alternative methods that do not imply consensus exist or are conceivable, such as gold cards, or lotteries among those above a given threshold (Fang and Casadevall 2016; Gross and Bergstrom 2019; Roumbanis 2019), but their limited use has not to date enabled analyses.

D.   Panelists and Research Officers

The "Insurance Agent" Hypothesis

Many agencies and panels are acutely aware that the future of their program depends upon supporting researchers who do not come up "empty handed." They may look at the opportunity cost of funding more risky research and compare it with benefits of funding safer research. These concerns may be magnified by the size of the grant. It is one thing to place $200,000 on a project that may come up empty handed. It is entirely another to place $2 million.

Such concerns can lead panels to place considerable emphasis on "what can go wrong" rather than "what can go right" during the review process. One of the "what can go wrong" concerns is that the proposed research cannot be accomplished. This concern undoubtedly fuels the heavy emphasis at many funding agencies on strong "preliminary findings" or, at some agencies, contingency plans as part of the proposal. In so doing, the implicit requirement is that research be derisked before it is funded. In this way, the panel supports research with little chance of failure, funding sure bets rather than research that is not a sure bet but may have considerable upside potential.

The "Bibliometric Screening and Workload" Hypothesis

Scientists and agencies collectively invest a huge amount of time in peer review. For example, the NIH evaluates approximately 80,000 applications annually, engaging more than 2,000 reviewers per year, and has more than 150 standing Study Sections.[23] The ERC averages 15 members on each of its 25 separate panels. The average panel member for the Starting Grants looks at 137 proposals per call; for Advanced Grants, 83 proposals.[24]

Given the heavy workload, it is not surprising that reviewers and panel members may seek ways to rapidly screen proposals, especially on a first pass. One of the easiest ways to do so is to focus on the publishing record of the scientist proposing the research by examining readily available measures of citations to papers and other bibliometric indicators on platforms such as Google Scholar and Scopus. Such was not always the case: as late as the early 1990s, the only way to count citations was to laboriously look in the volumes published by the Institute of Scientific Information, usually only available in the panel member's institutional library.

Does a heavy focus on bibliometrics affect the panel's decision when it comes to supporting risky research? The work by Wang et al. (2017) suggests that the answer could be yes: they find that novel research is systematically less likely to be published in high Impact Factor journals.[25] Moreover, as noted above, novel research takes longer to become a top hit than does nonnovel research. Such a bibliometric bias against novel research can lead panels to select against individuals with a history of novel (risky) research, especially when the applicant is young and has a short history of citations. More generally, a focus on bibliometrics shifts the basis of decisions away from the substance of the proposal to an easily accessible metric.

How workload affects the selection of novel R&D projects has not been studied for funding agencies; it has, however, been studied in R&D departments of for-profit firms. The authors of one study find that a high panel workload reduces the panel's preference for novel research (Criscuolo et al. 2017).

"Risk-Biased Panel Members" Hypothesis

Reviewers are often selected based on the excellent expertise of their research profile. Selection of top/senior experts specialized in the exact same niche area of the proposal are typically assumed to be the best choice for reviewers. But are top experts also the best reviewers for assessing risky research proposals? What kind of reviewers are needed for an unbiased assessment of risky research? Does it require experience with risky research to be more willing to take risks in evaluating the proposals of others?

Unfortunately, we lack specific knowledge illuminating what kind of reviewer expertise is best suited at assessing risky research, both in terms of willingness to take risks and in terms of capacity to accurately assess risk. Only a handful of studies have looked at reviewers' characteristics and related preferences for funding research proposals. Looking at the intellectual distance between the background of the reviewers and the research being proposed, Li (2017) finds that NIH proposals that were related to the research of the panelist were scored more favorably than those unrelated; they were also scored more accurately. DellaVigna and Pope (2018), however, studying the accuracy of reviewers when predicting the outcomes of experiments in behavioral social sciences, find that scholars with expertise in an area were not more accurate than scholars who were not experts. They also find that more senior scholars, and academics with more citations, were no more accurate. Looking at assessment of novel proposals specifically, Boudreau et al. (2014) find that novel proposals were evaluated less favorably than nonnovel ones. This was not explained by the degree of intellectual proximity of the evaluator. In conclusion, the limited evidence available suggests that reviewers who are expert in the niche area are not necessarily more accurate in assessing research proposals and may be more prone to fund research in their area.

V. Suggestions for Encouraging Risk-Taking among Science Funders

Society needs scientific breakthroughs to tackle many of the challenges it faces. Because many of the paths to such breakthroughs are risky, its science system, and particularly its public science funding system, needs to ensure that risk-taking is encouraged or, at a minimum, that the system is not biased against risky research. The previous sections have made clear that we cannot take for granted this is the case. The findings and hypotheses that we have explored also suggest possible ways for moving forward.

The Karikó-Weissman mRNA case provides some initial thoughts regarding ways that risky research could be promoted. Their early joint work was partially supported on a grant Weissman obtained that did not directly relate to designer mRNA. Such a "back-burner" strategy is not uncommon in science. Scientists regularly rely on funding obtained to support another research objective, particularly in the very early exploratory stages of the other research, when it is still highly risky and without enough preliminary findings to apply for dedicated funding.

The mRNA example also shows the importance luck plays in pathbreaking research: if they had not met at the copy machine, Karikó and Weissman might never have formed the collaboration that led to mRNA vaccines. The probability that such lucky encounters occur can be at least partly "engineered." A work environment enabling more open, serendipitous encounters has the potential of leading to more risky research built on unprecedented connections of knowledge pieces. The mRNA example also underlines the importance of taking an interdisciplinary approach: Karikó was trained as a biochemist, Weissman as an immunologist, a powerful combination to address the critical bottleneck for mRNA to be effective and safe in humans. An open environment enabling cross-disciplinary connections could thus already remove an important impediment for risky research. Moving the example from the mRNA novel scientific insights supported in part by NIH funding, into the development of mRNA-based vaccines for the market, supported in part by Small Business Innovation Research (SBIR) funding, Defense Advanced Research Projects Agency (DARPA), and eventually Biomedical Advanced Research and Development Authority (BARDA) and Warp Speed, shows the importance of staged funding of new approaches.

We conclude with suggestions of ways to encourage risk-taking (or at a minimum avoid a bias against risk) in science, combining insights from the Karikó-Weissman mRNA research with insights from the admittedly limited evidence and research on risk avoidance as it relates to science funding, which were reviewed in the previous sections. As discussed, the promotion of risk needs to be addressed within the entire science system; it cannot be solved by an individual program or funding agency. It requires a holistic perspective on the science enterprise, activating not only funders and their reviewers but also universities and research centers, journal editors and their reviewers and, last but not least, researchers themselves. Without ignoring the holistic perspective, we focus the discussion on suggestions for science funders if they would like to augment their support for risky research. Where appropriate, we suggest further research and experiments designed with the goal of advancing our knowledge of ways to promote risk-taking in science.

A. Deemphasize Bibliometrics

To advance innovation, funding agencies could insist on multiple ways to assess applicants' research records, avoiding an overly focused use of bibliometrics. They could refrain from asking or implying that grant applicants provide short-term citation counts and indicators based on short-term windows, such as the Journal Impact Factor and top field-cited articles. They could instruct panels to abstain from discussing such indicators in reviews, or at a very minimum instruct panels in the potential biases that using such indicators entails.

B. Diversity in Panel Composition

Funders could balance panel composition with a sufficiently large number of panel members holding diverse and independent perspectives. They could avoid a panel design that is narrowly discipline-focused, and thus runs the danger of underappreciating the out-of-field impact from risky research. This is a more complicated task than selecting panel members based on top expertise in the field as the main panel selection criterion, as is commonly done, which runs the risk of relying too heavily on the assumed superior assessment of experts regarding possible outcomes. More importantly, much could be learned concerning the causal impact of panel composition on risky research selection by using random control design to run experiments on panel composition.

C. Allow for Disagreement

Alternatives to the commonly used consensus or average procedures should be considered. Aggregation/deliberation rules could be adapted to the nature of the science that the grant aims at sponsoring. Because riskier research is more prone to extreme outcomes, it matters not only to have reviewers willing to take risk but also an accurate assessment of these extreme outcomes and their probability of occurrence. This requires a large enough number of sufficiently uncorrelated risk-unbiased opinions. In addition, the evidence that risky research may lead to more polarized views warns against aggregation methods that rely on consensus (e.g., behavioral aggregation) or that assume distributions of opinions according to a bell shape (e.g., arithmetic average). To learn more about alternative methods that do not imply consensus, experiments with such alternative procedures could be conducted, using random trials so that we can properly evaluate their impact on the selection of risky research.

D. Portfolio Approach

The "one-by-one" approach typically used in panels works against selecting risky proposals. At a minimum, panel members need to think about correlation among the proposals they are funding. One sure sign of high correlation in terms of low risk is requiring that all successful proposals have convincing preliminary findings. More generally, a portfolio approach to address risk aversion could require panels to put in different baskets highly risky and moderately risky proposals and provide a way to choose proposals from each. In practice such a portfolio approach could be quite challenging to implement for research projects. First, portfolio theory requires that the research paths be sufficiently uncorrelated. This may not hold within panels that are focused on specific subdisciplines that share risk factors. Correlation between research paths, in and of itself, can be hard to determine, particularly when covering vastly different goals across different fields and with different research approaches. Second, there is the question of fairness: in building a portfolio approach some proposals may have to be eliminated in an effort to balance or derisk the portfolio.

E. Staging

An approach to derisking commonly used for funding entrepreneurial projects in the venture capital industry, where it is referred to as the "spray and pray" strategy (Lerner and Nanda 2020), is to fund in stages, where increasingly larger amounts of funding are allocated depending on whether interim milestones are met. Funding in stages can be combined to include a portfolio approach.[26]

Although a staging strategy is used by DARPA and the SBIR program, and was recently introduced into the European Innovation Council program in the EU, it is rarely used for the funding of basic research.[27] Can such a staging approach also be used by science funding agencies, allowing them to take more risk? Interim evaluation is especially useful when initial estimates are unreliable but can be quickly updated when investments start at small scale and can be later scaled up (Vilkkumaa et al. 2015). It is thus especially suitable for research that can make substantial steps forward in a relatively short period of time and does not require large fixed costs to be started (Ewens, Nanda, and Rhodes-Kropf 2018).[28] Some research fields meet these conditions but the conditions are more the exception than the norm in the natural sciences, where the share of research that requires expensive equipment and substantial effort is large (Stephan 2010).

F.   Loose-Play, Early Stage Ideas

In the mRNA example, it was crucial that Weissman could use some of the funding he had already obtained to support early stage risky joint research with Karikó. Other researchers often do the same. Dedicated loose-play programs have a number of pluses: it decreases the amount of effort that goes into preparation of fully fledged proposals, it is reasonably easy to administer, and it has the potential to derisk a research agenda before it goes up for formal evaluation at a granting agency. But a necessary condition to doing so requires that the principal investigator have existing funding that can be redirected. If these are funds obtained from regular science funding programs, this raises the question of selection bias in terms of who obtains such funding. Researchers with a track record in novel research may experience bias against them. Also, early career researchers do not have access to such funds; others, such as Karikó, have tried to get funding but have not succeeded. And even for those who have such funding, the rules of engagement may not allow using funds for other than the research described in the proposal.

Going beyond the "back-burner" option, could dedicated loose-play funding for early stage risky explorations be operationalized? One approach is to have early stage funding readily and quickly available to researchers at their home institution. The California Institute of Technology, for example, had such a program; faculty could submit a short proposal to the vice provost for research and get a decision in a matter of days. Funds ranged from $25,000 to $250,000 a year for a period of 2 years. The idea was to give faculty the wherewithal to engage in early stage risky research that, given the apparent risk aversion of granting agencies, was deemed not yet ready for submission. If the initial findings looked promising, and produced enough preliminary data, the faculty could then submit a full grant proposal. Other institutions, such as ETH Zurich, provide generous base research funding to all their chairs, which they can deploy for research at their own initiative.

Dedicated programs for early stage risky research and base research funding require resources, which institutions often do not have or may not want to redirect from other programs. One way to provide institutions with the financial means for such funding schemes would be for federal funders to shift a tranche of resources to local institutions, with the goal of encouraging risk-taking. But loose-play funding can also have downsides. It could, for example, promote favoritism at the local level. It requires willingness and capacity to support risky projects at the local level, or at least no bias against risky projects, something which may not be present, as argued previously. It also involves a willingness to provide salary support to applicants, especially applicants in soft-money positions. A primary reason Karikó was turned down for the $10,000 Merck starter grant, administered by Penn, that she applied for in 1991 was a request for salary support. The rejection letter singled this out, citing one reviewer who said that "the most substantial weakness is the use of the entire award for faculty salary support."[29] Politically, shifting funds from federal agencies to universities for such programs also involves granting agencies ceding some control to local institutions.[30]

G.   Funding Researchers Rather than Projects and for Longer Periods of Time

Programs that fund researchers rather than projects for longer periods of time allow researchers to engage in more risky research. It gives the scope and time to researchers to redirect their research in case of failure. The example that readily comes to mind is the Howard Hughes Medical Institute (HHMI), which funds successful applicants for 7 years, rather than for 3–5, as is common for most other funding organizations, and where selection is based more on the applicant and their longer-term research strategy rather than a specific research project. HHMI, moreover, does not demand early results nor does it penalize researchers for early failure. Azoulay et al. (2011) compare the research output of HHMI investigators to a group of similarly accomplished NIH investigators using propensity scoring. They find that HHMI investigators use more novel keywords and produce more hits and more flops, compared with the NIH investigators. Although it is not clear whether these results depend upon the longer duration of grants and the practice of HHMI to not demand early results nor penalize researchers for early failure or for other variables, the results suggest that these practices encourage risk-taking.

H.   Targeting Science Funding to Risky Breakthrough Missions

In the Karikó-Weissman case, the vexing problem of immune response was a well-known scientific challenge, impeding the promising mRNA technology from being used as a modality for treating humans. As such, it could have been turned into a "mission" with dedicated funding. Although the science funding system was either unable or unwilling to identify such a mission in the early research stages of mRNA research, a more mission-oriented approach was followed in later stages, when DARPA awarded Moderna up to $24.6 million in 2013 "to research and develop its messenger RNA therapeutics™" after having already awarded the company a "seedling" grant of $0.7 million to begin work on the project.[31] Subsequently, when the search for coronavirus vaccines became more pressing and BARDA and Warp Speed entered the picture, a more targeted approach for funding their development was used.

DARPA is frequently heralded for its successes in funding mission-oriented, high-risk, high-reward research. Azoulay et al. (2019) identify the organizational flexibility and autonomy given to program directors as key success elements of the DARPA model. A key factor for DARPA's success is attracting program staff who are more like risk-taking, idea-driven entrepreneurs than like administrators. These program staff are given individual discretion to design project calls and select projects from across the distribution of reviewer scores, which is seen as antidote to the risk bias DARPA's reviewers may hold. The autonomy program officers enjoy is combined with clear targets for which they are held accountable.

Can the DARPA model be replicated for avoiding the risk bias in funding basic research? Azoulay et al. (2019) identify as "DARPAble" domain mission-motivated research on nascent technologies within an inefficient innovation system. These missions must be clearly identifiable, associated with quantifiable goals, and have trackable progress metrics. Because a focus on basic research for improving understanding is not a clearly defined mission, the authors deem the DARPA model not appropriate for funding basic research. Although DARPA may not be a general model for funding basic research, it may nevertheless be inspirational for specific scientific challenges for which goals can be clearly defined.

I. Prizes

An alternative to a competitive-grant approach is to create prizes to encourage pathbreaking research (e.g., Williams 2010, 2012). Although such prizes for risky breakthroughs can incentivize research, they shift the risk onto the shoulders of the researchers, given that prizes are only awarded conditional upon succeeding in the endeavor. It may thus only incentivize researchers who are risk lovers, who have high (perhaps overly high) estimates of their probability of success, and who have access to resources.

VI.   Conclusions

To conclude, science funding agencies should be encouraged to pave the way for promoting risk-taking in scientific research, given that breakthrough research is often perceived as risky. The way forward is neither safe nor clearly defined. It is risky in the sense that it is not clear which paths will work and which will not. Perhaps the most important contribution funding agencies can make would be to support research that builds knowledge on the design of funding programs and reviewing practices related to risky proposals that have the potential of delivering breakthroughs. This support could entail not only financing such research but also granting access to data and championing experimental approaches to test alternative designs of research funding.

Endnotes

Author email addresses: Franzoni (chiara.franzoni@polimi.it), Stephan (pstephan@gsu.edu), Veugelers (reinhilde.veugelers@kuleuven.be). This paper was written for the NBER Entrepreneurship and Innovation Policy and the Economy (EIPE) meeting held April 27, 2021. The authors wish to thank the organizers, Josh Lerner and Scott Stern, for thoughtful comments on an earlier version. Comments from participants at the meeting are also highly appreciated. The authors thank Katalin Karikó for helpful responses to our emails and her willingness to review our discussion of mRNA research. For acknowledgments, sources of research support, and disclosure of the authors' material financial

relationships, if any, please see https://www.nber.org/books-and-chapters/entrepreneurship
-and-innovation-policy-and-economy-volume-1/funding-risky-research.

1. https://www.nature.com/articles/d41586-021-00019-w.

2. For a summary of Karikó's early career see https://www.wired.co.uk/article/mrna
-coronavirus-vaccine-pfizer-biontech.

3. Emails from Karikó to coauthors, March 17, 2021, and March 18, 2021.

4. https://www.statnews.com/2020/11/10/the-story-of-mrna-how-a-once-dismissed
-idea-became-a-leading-technology-in-the-covid-vaccine-race.

5. Correspondence with Karikó and https://www.ae-info.org/ae/Member/Karikó
_Katalin for Karikó's CV.

6. The grant was for the Role of gp-340 in HIV Infection and Transmissions.

7. For example, in 2013 DARPA awarded Moderna a grant for up to $25 million for
developing mRNA-based therapeutics. https://investors.modernatx.com/news/news
-details/2013/DARPA-Awards-Moderna-Therapeutics-a-Grant-for-up-to-25-Million-to
-Develop-Messenger-RNA-Therapeutics-10-02-2013/default.aspx.

8. Drew Weissman appears as the principal investigator on a total of 10 projects funded
by NIH between 1998 and 2021 according to data at https://reporter.nih.gov in March
2021.

9. Reviews provided to the authors by Karikó on March 18, 2021

10. The application was for the continuation of an R01 that Karikó "inherited" from
Frank Welsh when he retired.

11. Katalin Karikó was the principal investigator of an STTR award project funded by
the NIH between 2007 and 2011: https://www.sbir.gov/sbirsearch/detail/294077 and
https://grantome.com/grant/NIH/R42-HL087688-02.

12. We do not use the term *risk* in the "preventive" meaning, the possibility of a negative event (e.g., a loss or harm), a use that is common in the risk analysis literature.

13. They also find that papers based on "repeat" strategies were six times more likely to
be published than those that used "new" or "jump" strategies during the period 1983–
2008.

14. Rewards also include the satisfaction derived from puzzle-solving, and financial
gain that often accompanies a successful research career (Stephan and Levin 1992;
Stephan 2012). Cohen, Sauermann, and Stephan (2020) also show that scientists are
strongly motivated by an interest in contributing to society.

15. Jim Allison, who shared the Nobel Prize for immunotherapy for cancer in 2018, is
but one case in point.

16. https://blog.ninds.nih.gov/2014/03/27/back-to-basics.

17. Papers characterized as having high medium conventionality coupled with a high
tail "novelty" have a hit rate in the top 5% 9.2 times out of 100.

18. At some agencies, such as NSF, program officers have some leeway in making decisions, but this is not common.

19. The study uses Interdisciplinary Distance, a measure that takes into account the
fields indicated as pertinent to the proposal by the principal investigator and the distance
between the fields, based on the relative frequency with which the fields co-occur
throughout the entire sample.

20. The scholars of expert elicitation have elaborated and tested a number of techniques, which are commonly used in drug approval, risk analysis, climate-change forecasting, and other areas where uncertainty is key and expert opinions are the only way
to collect information (Morgan and Henrion 1990).

21. The term *aggregation* (List 2012; Bolger and Rowe 2015) means the combination of
multiple opinions. Aggregation can be computed with rules or algorithms (e.g., average,
quantile average) or can be done behaviorally, with a consensus meeting (Hora et al. 2013;
Martini and Sprenger 2018).

22. Deliberation (i.e., the binary choice to fund or not) can be directly dependent on the
aggregation method or involve additional rules (e.g., aggregation with arithmetic average
and deliberation in descending order of aggregated score until budget saturation.)

23. https://grants.nih.gov/grants/peerreview22713webv2.pdf. For Study Sections
see https://public.csr.nih.gov/StudySections/StandingStudySections.

24. Average for 2008–13.

25. The fact that these impact factors are calculated using relatively short citation windows, coupled with the above-mentioned finding of Wang et al. (2017) that it takes a longer time window for novel research to become highly cited, may explain why journal editors, striving for good scores on their impact factor, may be biased against novel research.

26. Veugelers and Zachmann (2020), for example, proposed a combination of a staging and portfolio approach to fund vaccine projects and calculated what such an approach would cost to society to obtain a desired number of vaccines at the end.

27. https://fas.org/sgp/crs/natsec/R45088.pdf.

28. In the venture capital industry, this has largely favored information technology and digital companies.

29. Letter to Karikó dated April 29, 1991.

30. NIH already does this by awarding training grants to institutions to administer. In the early years of NIH, candidates for training awards were selected at NIH.

31. https://investors.modernatx.com/news/news-details/2013/DARPA-Awards -Moderna-Therapeutics-a-Grant-for-up-to-25-Million-to-Develop-Messenger-RNA -Therapeutics-10-02-2013/default.aspx.

References

Althaus, Catherine E. 2005. "A Disciplinary Perspective on the Epistemological Status of Risk." *Risk Analysis* 25 (3): 567–88.

Aven, Terje. 2011. "On Some Recent Definitions and Analysis Frameworks for Risk, Vulnerability, and Resilience." *Risk Analysis* 31 (4): 515–22.

Azoulay, Pierre, Erica Fuchs, Anna P. Goldstein, and Michael Kearney. 2019. "Funding Breakthrough Research: Promises and Challenges of the 'ARPA Model.'" *Innovation Policy and the Economy* 19 (1): 69–96.

Azoulay, Pierre, Joshua Graff Zivin, and Gustavo Manso. 2011. "Incentives and Creativity: Evidence from the Howard Hughes Medical Investigator Program." *Rand Journal of Economics* 42 (3): 527–54.

———. 2012. "NIH Peer Review: Challenges and Avenues for Reform." Working Paper no. 18116, NBER, Cambridge, MA.

Banal-Estañol, Albert, Inés Macho-Stadler, and David Pérez-Castrillo. 2019. "Evaluation in Research Funding Agencies: Are Structurally Diverse Teams Biased Against?" *Research Policy* 48:1823–40.

Banerjee, A. V. 1992. "A Simple Model of Herd Behavior." *Quarterly Journal of Economics* 107 (3): 797–817.

Bolger, Fergus, and Gene Rowe. 2015. "The Aggregation of Expert Judgment: Do Good Things Come to Those Who Weight?" *Risk Analysis* 35 (1): 5–11.

Boudreau, Kevin, Eva Guinan, Karim R. Lakhani, and Christoph Riedl. 2014. "Looking Across and Looking Beyond the Knowledge Frontier: Intellectual Distance and Resource Allocation in Science." *Management Science* 62 (10): 2765–83.

Bromham, Lindell, Russell Dinnage, and Xia Hua. 2016. "Interdisciplinary Research Has Consistently Lower Funding Success." *Nature* 534 (7609): 684–87.

Clemen, Robert T., and Robert L. Winkler. 1999. "Combining Probability Distributions from Experts in Risk Analysis." *Risk Analysis* 19 (2): 187–203.

Cohen, Wesley M., Henry Sauermann, and Paula Stephan. 2020. "Not in the Job Description: The Commercial Activities of Academic Scientists and Engineers." *Management Science* 66 (9): 4108–17.

Cooke, Roger M. 1991. *Experts in Uncertainty: Opinions and Subjective Probabilities in Science.* New York: Oxford University Press.

Criscuolo, Paola, Linus Dahlander, Thorsten Grohsjean, and Ammon Salter. 2017. "Evaluating Novelty: The Role of Panels in the Selection of R&D Projects." *Academy of Management Journal* 60 (2): 433–60.

DellaVigna, Stefano, and Devin Pope. 2018. "Predicting Experimental Results: Who Knows What?" *Journal of Political Economy* 126 (6): 2410–56.

Ewens, Michael, Ramana Nanda, and Matthew Rhodes-Kropf. 2018. "Cost of Experimentation and the Evolution of Venture Capital." *Journal of Financial Economics* 128 (3): 422–42.

Fang, Ferric C., and Arturo Casadevall. 2016. "Research Funding: The Case for a Modified Lottery." *MBio* 7 (2): e00422-16.

Foster, Jacob G., Andrey Rzhetsky, and James A. Evans. 2015. "Tradition and Innovation in Scientists' Research Strategies." *American Sociological Review* 80 (5): 875–908.

Franzoni, Chiara, and Paula Stephan. 2021. "Uncertainty and Risk-Taking in Science: Meaning, Measurement and Management." Working Paper no. 28562, NBER, Cambridge, MA.

Gross, Kevin, and Carl T. Bergstrom. 2019. "Contest Models Highlight Inherent Inefficiencies of Scientific Funding Competitions." *PLoS Biology* 17 (1): e3000065.

Hansson, Sven Ove. 2018. "Risk." In *The Stanford Encyclopedia of Philosophy*, ed. E. N. Zalta. Stanford, CA: Stanford University.

Harris, Richard. 2013. "Scientists Win Nobel for Work on How Cells Communicate." National Public Radio, October 7. https://www.npr.org/templates/story/story.php?storyId=230192033.

Hora, Stephen C., Benjamin R. Fransen, Natasha Hawkins, and Irving Susel. 2013. "Median Aggregation of Distribution Functions." *Decision Analysis* 10 (4): 279–91.

Ismail, Sharif, Alice Farrands, and Steven Wooding. 2008. "Evaluating Grant Peer Review in the Health Sciences: A Review of the Literature." Research Brief, Rand Corporation, Santa Monica, CA.

Kahneman, Daniel, and Amos Tversky. 1979. "Prospect Theory: An Analysis of Decision under Risk." *Econometrica* 47 (2): 263–92.

Kaplan, David, Nicola Lacetera, and Celia Kaplan. 2008. "Sample Size and Precision in NIH Peer Review." *PLoS ONE* 3 (7): e2761.

Knight, Frank. (1921) 1964. *Risk, Uncertainty and Profit*. New York: Sentry.

Kolata, Gina. 2021. "Kati Karikó Helped Shield the World from the Coronavirus." *New York Times*, April 8. https://www.nytimes.com/2021/04/08/health/coronavirus-mrna-kariko.html.

Lamont, Michèle. 2009. *How Professors Think. Inside the Curious World of Academic Judgment*. Cambridge, MA: Harvard University Press.

Lanoë, Marianne. 2019. "The Evaluation of Competitive Research Funding: An Application to French Programs." PhD diss., L'Universite de Bordeaux.

Larrick, Richard P., and Jack B. Soll. 2006. "Intuitions about Combining Opinions: Misappreciation of the Averaging Principle." *Management Science* 52 (1): 111–27.

Laudel, Grit. 2017. "How Do National Career Systems Promote or Hinder the Emergence of New Research Lines?" *Minerva* 55 (3): 341–69.

Lerner, Josh, and Ramana Nanda. 2020. "Venture Capital's Role in Financing Innovation: What We Know and How Much We Still Need to Learn." *Journal of Economic Perspectives* 34 (3): 237–61.

Li, Danielle. 2017. "Expertise versus Bias in Evaluation: Evidence from the NIH." *American Economic Journal: Applied Economics* 9 (2): 60–92.

Linton, Jonathan D. 2016. "Improving the Peer Review Process: Capturing More Information and Enabling High-Risk/High-Return Research." *Research Policy* 45 (9): 1936–38.

List, Christian. 2012. "The Theory of Judgment Aggregation: An Introductory Review." *Synthese* 187:179–207.

Martini, Carlo, and Jan Sprenger. 2018. "Opinion Aggregation and Individual Expertise." In *Scientific Collaboration and Collective Knowledge*, ed. Thomas Boyer-Kassem, Conor Mayo-Wilson, and Michael Weisberg, 180–201. Oxford: Oxford University Press.

Mazzucato, Mariana. 2015. *The Entrepreneurial State: Debunking Public vs. Private Sector Myths*. New York: Anthem.

Mengel, Friederike. 2019. "Gender Biases in Opinion Aggregation." *International Economic Review* 62 (3): 1055–80.

Merton, Robert K. 1957. "Priorities in Scientific Discovery: A Chapter in the Sociology of Science." *American Sociological Review* 22 (6): 635–59.

Morgan, Millett Granger. 2014. "Use (and Abuse) of Expert Elicitation in Support of Decision Making for Public Policy." *Proceedings of the National Academy of Sciences of the United States of America* 111 (20): 7176–84.

Morgan, Millett Granger, and Max Henrion. 1990. *Uncertainty: A Guide to Dealing with Uncertainty in Quantitative Risk and Policy Analysis*. 6th ed. Cambridge: Cambridge University Press.

Nelson, Richard R. 1959. "The Simple Economics of Basic Scientific Research." *Journal of Political Economy* 67 (3): 297–306.

Nicholson, Joshua M., and John P. A. Ioannidis. 2012. "Research Grants: Conform and Be Funded." *Nature* 492 (7427): 34–36.

Packalen, Mikko, and Jay Bhattacharya. 2018. "Does the NIH Fund Edge Science?" Working Paper no. 24860, NBER, Cambridge, MA.

Pier, Elizabeth L., Markus Brauer, Amarette Filut, Anna Kaatz, Joshua Raclaw, Mitchell J. Nathan, Cecilia E. Ford, and Molly Carnes. 2018. "Low Agreement among Reviewers Evaluating the Same NIH Grant Applications." *Proceedings of the National Academy of Sciences of the United States of America* 115 (12): 2952–57.

Roumbanis, Lambros. 2019. "Peer Review or Lottery? A Critical Analysis of Two Different Forms of Decision-Making Mechanisms for Allocation of Research Grants." *Science, Technology, and Human Values* 44 (6): 994–1019.

Rzhetsky, Andrey, Jacob G. Foster, Ian T. Foster, and James A. Evans. 2015. "Choosing Experiments to Accelerate Collective Discovery." *Proceedings of the National Academy of Sciences of the United States of America* 112 (47): 14569–74.

Sahin, Ugur, Katalin Karikó, and Özlem Türeci. 2014. "mRNA-Based Therapeutics: Developing a New Class of Drugs." *Nature Reviews Drug Discovery* 13 (10): 759–80.

Snell, Richard R. 2015. "Menage a Quoi? Optimal Number of Peer Reviewers." *PLoS ONE* 10 (4): e0120838.

Stephan, Paula, Reinhilde Veugelers, and Jian Wang. 2017. "Blinkered by Bibliometrics." *Nature* 544 (7651): 411–12.

Stephan, Paula E. 2007. "Early Careers for Biomedical Scientists: Doubling (and Troubling) Outcomes." Presentation at Harvard University, Cambridge, MA, February 26.

———. 2010. "The Economics of Science." In *Handbook of Economics of Innovation*, ed. Bronwyn H. Hall and Nathan Rosenberg, 217–73. Amsterdam: North-Holland.

————. 2012. *How Economics Shapes Science*. Cambridge, MA: Harvard University Press.

————. 2019. "Practices and Attitudes Regarding Risky Research." Presentation at Metascience Symposium, Stanford University, Stanford, CA, September.

Stephan, Paula E., and Sharon Levin. 1992. *Striking the Mother Lode in Science: The Importance of Age, Place, and Time*. Oxford: Oxford University Press.

Tversky, Amos, and Daniel Kahneman. 1991. "Loss Aversion in Riskless Choice: A Reference-Dependent Model." *Quarterly Journal of Economics* 106 (4): 1039–61.

Uzzi, Brian, Satyam Mukherjee, Michael Stringer, and Ben Jones. 2013. "Atypical Combinations and Scientific Impact." *Science* 342 (6157): 468–72.

Veugelers, Reinhilde, Paula Stephan, and Jian Wang. 2021. "Excess Risk-Aversion at ERC." Photocopy. Working Paper, KULeuven.

Veugelers, Reinhilde, and Georg Zachmann. 2020. "Racing against COVID-19: A Vaccines Strategy for Europe." *Policy Contribution* no. 2020/07 (April).

Vilkkumaa, Eeva, Ahti Salo, Juuso Liesiö, and Afzal Siddiqui. 2015. "Fostering Breakthrough Technologies: How Do Optimal Funding Decisions Depend on Evaluation Accuracy?" *Technological Forecasting and Social Change* 96:173–90.

Viner, Neil, Philip Powell, and Rod Green. 2004. "Institutionalized Biases in the Award of Research Grants: A Preliminary Analysis Revisiting the Principle of Accumulative Advantage." *Research Policy* 33 (3): 443–54.

Wagner, Caroline, and Jeffrey M. Alexander. 2013. "Evaluating Transformative Research Programmes: A Case Study of the NSF Small Grants for Exploratory Research Programme." *Research Evaluation* 22 (3): 187–97.

Wang, Jian, Reinhilde Veugelers, and Paula Stephan. 2017. "Bias against Novelty in Science: A Cautionary Tale for Users of Bibliometric Indicators." *Research Policy* 46 (8): 1416–36.

Williams, Heidi. 2010. *Incentives, Prizes, and Innovation*. Paper prepared for NSF. https://www.nsf.gov/sbe/sosp/tech/williams.pdf.

————. 2012. "Low-Performing Schools Attract and Keep Academically Talented Teachers? Evidence." *Journal of Policy Analysis and Management* 31 (3): 752–76.

Wolff, J. A., R. W. Malone, P. Williams, W. Chong, G. Acsadi, A. Jani, and P. L. Felgner. 1990. "Direct Gene Transfer into Mouse Muscle in Vivo." *Science* 23 (247): 1465–68.

Crisis Innovation Policy from World War II to COVID-19

Daniel P. Gross, *Duke University and NBER,* United States of America

Bhaven N. Sampat, *Columbia University and NBER,* United States of America

Abstract

Innovation policy can be a crucial component of governments' responses to crises. Because speed is a paramount objective, crisis innovation may also require different policy tools than innovation policy in noncrisis times, raising distinct questions and trade-offs. In this paper, we survey the US policy response to two crises in which innovation was crucial to a resolution: World War II and the COVID-19 pandemic. After providing an overview of the main elements of each of these efforts, we discuss how they compare and to what degree their differences reflect the nature of the central innovation policy problems and the maturity of the US innovation system. We then explore four key trade-offs for crisis innovation policy—top-down versus bottom-up priority setting, concentrated versus distributed funding, patent policy, and managing disruptions to the innovation system—and provide a logic for policy choices. Finally, we describe the longer-run impacts of the World War II effort and use these lessons to speculate on the potential long-run effects of the COVID-19 crisis on innovation policy and the innovation system.

JEL Codes: H12, H56, I18, N42, N72, O31, O32, O38

Keywords: crisis innovation, innovation policy, World War II, COVID-19

The COVID-19 pandemic has illustrated that innovation and innovation policy can be crucial components of governments' responses to crises. It has also brought into focus that crisis innovation problems raise different questions for science and technology (S&T) policy, and may require different tools, than noncrisis times. Though crisis innovation policy was not a major feature of the US innovation policy dialogue immediately before COVID-19, it has been a prevailing theme of the past year. It also has a long

Entrepreneurship and Innovation Policy and the Economy, volume 1, 2022.

and storied history: the most famous earlier response—indeed one appealed to by many in the COVID-19 pandemic—was the US World War II research effort. Led by the Office of Scientific Research and Development (OSRD) under the direction of Vannevar Bush, the wartime effort helped develop, test, and get into practice numerous technologies and medical treatments that were essential to the Allied victory, including radar, mass-produced penicillin, the proximity fuze, malaria treatment, and the atomic bomb. The wartime R&D experience also led to long-run changes in the US innovation system and postwar innovation policy.

In this paper, we survey the efforts undertaken in World War II and the COVID-19 pandemic and consider implications for innovation policy in crisis and regular times. We begin with the premise that crises can put unique demands on the innovation system that may require a distinct response (Gross and Sampat 2021). Whether a given problem or situation rises to the level of a "crisis" can often be subjective, but in our view, what makes crisis problems distinctive is that they are urgent, high-stakes, and often unanticipated. In a crisis, losses can accumulate quickly or spiral out of control if a problem is not quickly contained, and once it does, a crisis may require a focused innovation effort to resolve, like developing new weapons or vaccines. We believe the responses to these two crises can offer lessons in method and contrast. Our goal for this chapter is to summarize what each of these efforts comprised, draw comparisons, identify key policy trade-offs, and provide insight on the short- and long-run effects of crisis innovation.

We begin in Section I by examining the World War II response to distill the main elements of the wartime model of crisis innovation policy and the high-level questions it needed to consider. The OSRD model, although specific to its time, was also by most accounts successful, and the experience is cited as precedent for a wide range of crisis innovation activities. In Section II, we discuss the evolution of the postwar innovation system and how policy was shaped by World War II, traversing and summarizing 75 years of science policy from the end of the war to the dawn of the pandemic. This evolution would in turn mean that the COVID-19 crisis confronted a very different innovation system than existed in 1940.

As of the time of this writing, it is challenging to fully evaluate the COVID-19 model, as we are still in midst of the crisis and the crisis response. Moreover, we lack for COVID-19 the types of data, correspondence, and other records available to study the World War II period. In Section III, we nevertheless attempt to describe the COVID-19 innovation response based on currently available information, anticipating that more will be written when the full story can be told. We then discuss how the COVID-19 response seems similar to and different from the World War II model, and how that may reflect broader differences in today's innovation system and the different nature of the central innovation policy problem.

In Section IV, we use the two episodes to identify key trade-offs in crisis innovation policy, discuss how they manifested in each crisis, and suggest what factors may influence policy choices. We focus on four tensions: top-down versus bottom-up priority setting, concentrated versus distributed funding, patent policy, and managing disruptions to the innovation system. Though several of these tensions are endemic to S&T policy even in ordinary times, we argue they can be particularly acute in a crisis.

In Section V, we use the World War II experience to survey the short- and long-run effects of crisis innovation. Beyond impacts on the crisis at hand, these include effects on the rate and direction of innovation, effects on R&D-intensive firms and industries, effects on scientific careers, and effects on science policy. In Section VI, we put the collective evidence into perspective and consider some ways in which the COVID-19 R&D effort might also have long-lived impacts on US innovation and innovation policy. Although we will have to wait for the postpandemic future to unfold, if the past is any guide, more changes may yet be in store for the United States and global innovation system in the years ahead.

I.   The World War II Research Effort

A.   *Historical Background*

World War II began in September 1939 when Germany invaded Poland; the United Kingdom, France, and several other countries declared war on Germany; and Russia counterinvaded Poland 2 weeks later. Two months later, Russia invaded Finland, and 4 months after that, Germany controlled Denmark and Norway. In early May 1940, Germany invaded Belgium, the Netherlands, Luxembourg, and France, and on June 14, Paris fell to Germany, with France formally surrendering on June 22.

Americans could observe this conflagration from a distance, as the United States was not at immediate risk of being invaded. But the fall of France broke the general sense of complacency and made clear to many US leaders that the country would be drawn in: for the United States, the war in Europe was a crisis in the making. It was also on June 14 that a small group of scientists and science administrators, led by Vannevar Bush (president of the Carnegie Institute of Washington and former vice president and dean of engineering at the Massachusetts Institute of Technology [MIT]), met with President Franklin D. Roosevelt to express concerns that the United States was "unprepared to fight a modern war" (Stewart 1948) and propose that he put civilian scientists to work on developing military technology. On June 27, 1940, Roosevelt formally created the National Defense Research Committee (NDRC) for this end. The United States would not formally enter the war until December 8, 1941.

The NDRC was led by Bush as its chair, supported by Karl Compton (president of MIT), James Conant (president of Harvard University), and Frank Jewett (president of the National Academy of Sciences and of Bell Labs), Richard Tolman (California Institute of Technology [Caltech] physicist), Conway Coe (the US patent commissioner), and one representative from each of the army and the navy, who together composed "the Committee." Funded by the president's discretionary budget, NDRC's mandate was to "coordinate, supervise, and conduct scientific research on the problems underlying the development, production, and use of mechanisms and devices of warfare." To do so, it was authorized to perform research directly as well as to contract for extramural research. NDRC's work was to supplement that of other agencies, including the military.

NDRC began with an ambitious mission but only eight staff (the members themselves) and no precedent to follow. At its first meeting, the committee organized into five divisions by subject (table 1) and concurrently began recruiting other top scientists to fill the new agency's ranks. It also decided that it would contract out research rather than perform it directly—a radical move for its time.

Impressed by a string of early accomplishments, on June 28, 1941, President Roosevelt issued Executive Order 8807 creating OSRD. The new

Table 1
National Defense Research Committee (NDRC) Divisions (1940–1941)

NDRC Division	Director
A—Armor and Ordnance	Tolman
B—Bombs, Fuels, Gases, Chemical Problems	Conant
C—Communications and Transportation	Jewett
D—Detection, Controls, Instruments	Compton
E—Patents and Inventions	Coe
Committee on Uranium	Briggs[a]

[a]Lyman Briggs, Director of the National Bureau of Standards.

organization, to be led by Bush, addressed several deficiencies in the original structure (including expanding its scope to medical research) and would be the principal agency organizing civilian science and technology for war. Now funded by congressional appropriations, OSRD subsumed NDRC (now chaired by Conant) and added a Committee on Medical Research (CMR), chaired by A. N. Richards, a pharmacologist at the University of Pennsylvania. The scope of crisis activities that OSRD engaged in was broader than research alone. In addition to NDRC and CMR, the OSRD included an advisory council, which coordinated research activities across the government. It later added an Office of Field Service (to deploy scientists to the field, where they would study field problems and aid in training and use of OSRD devices in combat operations), a liaison office (for sharing and coordinating research with Allied countries, including via foreign branches), a scientific personnel office (to manage personnel shared by the OSRD and other agencies, and to handle draft deferments for technical staff at OSRD and its contractors), and an administrative office (for contract management).

Both NDRC and CMR were organized into divisions by subject matter led by scientific experts. NDRC's structure expanded significantly as the scope of its work grew, and by the end of the war it had grown to 26 divisions (table 2). The largest were Radar and Rocket Ordnance, which primarily funded large, central labs: the MIT Radiation Laboratory ("Rad Lab") and the Caltech Jet Propulsion Lab, which were created or significantly expanded to meet the needs of the war effort.

Despite having just one-tenth of NDRC's budget, CMR was also essential to the wartime effort. Its mandate was to mobilize medical researchers and identify "the need for and character of contracts to be entered into with universities, hospitals, and other agencies conducting medical research activities." Funding of extramural medical research was also new: one of the leaders of the effort (Chester Keefer, the "penicillin czar") later characterized CMR as "a novel experiment in American medicine" noting "planned and coordinated medical research had never been essayed on such a scale" (Keefer 1969).

OSRD's annual budget grew from $6.2 million in 1940–41 to $160–170 million in 1944 and 1945 (table 3). By the end of the war, OSRD had spent more than $536 million on R&D across more than 2,500 contracts, including 1,500 contracts by NDRC, 570 by CMR, and about 100 for research on atomic fission before this work was spun out into the Manhattan Project, as we describe below. It also grew to be a large organization, at its peak employing nearly 1,500 personnel across multiple locations (Stewart 1948).

Table 2
OSRD Divisions, Panels, and Special Sections (1941–1947)

National Defense Research Committee (NDRC)		Contract Authorizations
Division/Section	Name/Description	($, '000s) (1943–1947)
1	Ballistics	5,327.2
2	Effects of impact and explosion	2,701.4
3	Rocket ordnance	85,196.5
4	Ordnance accessories	20,014.3
5	New missiles	12,881.2
6	Subsurface warfare	33,883.5
7	Fire control	7,711.7
8	Explosives	11079.9
9	Chemistry	4,698.2
10	Absorbents and aerosols	3,524.2
11	Chemical engineering	9,216.2
12	Transportation development	2,199.4
13	Electrical communication	2,073.9
14	Radar	104,533.4
15	Radio coordination	26,343.0
16	Optics	5,923.9
17	Physics	7,655.3
18	War metallurgy	3,794.4
19	Miscellaneous weapons	2,416.1[a]
AMP	Advanced mathematics panel	2,522.9
APP	Applied psychology panel	1,542.5[a]
COP	Committee on propagation	453.0[a]
TD	Tropical deterioration	232.4[a]
SD	Sensory devices	272.5[a]
S-1	Atomic fission	18,138.2[a]
T	Proximity fuzes	26,400.0[a]
Total		400,735.1

Committee on Medical Research		Contract Authorizations
Division	Name/Description	($, '000s) (1941–1947)
1	Medicine	3,873.3
2	Surgery	2,847.6
3	Aviation medicine	2,466.5
4	Physiology	3,981.5
5	Chemistry	2,383.9
6	Malaria	5,501.9
	Miscellaneous	3,635.3
Total		24,689.9

Note: OSRD = Office of Scientific Research and Development. NDRC authorizations from January 1, 1943, onward, except where noted below.
[a]Authorizations for Division 19 from April 1, 1943; APP, from September 18, 1943; COP, from January 22, 1944; TD, from May 18, 1944; SD, from November 1, 1945. Authorizations for Sections S-1 and T are from June 27, 1940 onward, with Section S-1 terminating in September 1943.

Table 3
OSRD Expenditures, by Fiscal Year, 1941–1946

Fiscal Year	FY1941	FY1942	FY1943	FY1944	FY1945	FY1946	Total
Obligations ($, MMs)	6.2	39.6	142.5	162.5	167.5	17.9	536.1

Source: Data are from Stewart (1948).
Note: OSRD = Office of Scientific Research and Development. Government fiscal years at
this time ran from July 1 to June 30.

In the space of 5 years, this effort produced major developments in a
wide range of technologies. Figure 1 illustrates the focus of OSRD's work,
using words in the titles of OSRD patents and publications. NDRC was
responsible for many of the most notable technological developments of
the war, including radar, electronic communication (including early computing), underwater detection (sonar), rockets and jet propulsion, and
atomic fission, among others. CMR's work helped support the mass production of penicillin; influenza and other vaccines; new malaria treatments;
new approaches to managing wartime hardships such as sleep and oxy-
gen deprivation, cold temperatures, nutrient deficiencies, and psycholog-
ical stress; and techniques for treating injuries and wounds. Beyond its immediate impacts on the war and on science, the OSRD also created the
template for federal R&D procurement, laid the foundation for postwar
S&T policy, and reshaped the postwar innovation system, as we will discuss below.

B.   The Wartime Model for Crisis Innovation Policy

The war posed a challenge to the budding US innovation system: develop
a range of new technologies, produce them at scale, and get them deployed
quickly enough to deliver an Allied victory. As Conant wrote, "The basic
problem of mobilizing science during World War II was [one] of setting
up rapidly an organization or organizations which would connect effectively the laboratory, the pilot plant, and the factory with each other and
with the battlefront" (Conant 1947, 198–99). Bush likewise wrote, "It was
the function of [OSRD] to channelize and focus an amazing array of var-
iegated activities, to co-ordinate them both with the military necessities
which they were designed to help to meet and with the requirements of
the powerful industrial structure on which their effective application relied" (Bush 1944).

A. Words in patent titles

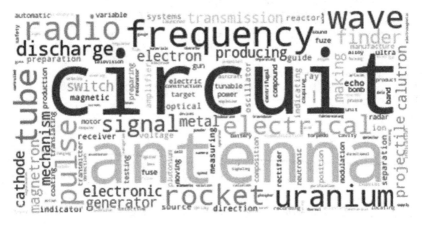

B. Words in publication titles

Fig. 1. Common words in Office of Scientific Research and Development (OSRD) patent and publication titles. Color version available as an online enhancement.

Notes: The most common words appearing in the title of OSRD-supported patents and academic publications. Font size is proportional to number of occurrences, with larger words being more common. Patents primarily resulted from National Defense Research Committee-supported technological research and development, and academic publications from Committee on Medical Research–supported medical research.

How did OSRD meet this challenge? In recent work (Gross and Sampat 2020b), we examine the OSRD model in detail, focusing on six features: (1) priority setting, (2) engaging researchers, (3) the contract mechanism, (4) incentives, (5) coordination, and (6) downstream production and diffusion.

Applied Focus, Top-Down Priority Setting

OSRD led a primarily applied research effort.[1] Executive Order 8807 explicitly tasked it with the following duties, which leave no ambiguity about the purpose of its work:

- Advise the President with regard to . . . scientific and medical research relating to national defense.
- Serve as the center for mobilization of the scientific personnel and resources . . . to defense purposes.
- Co-ordinate, aid, and, where desirable, supplement . . . research activities relating to national defense carried on by the Departments of War and Navy and other . . . agencies of the Federal Government.
- Develop broad and co-ordinated plans for the conduct of scientific research in the defense program.
- Initiate and support scientific research on [instruments] of warfare . . . required for national defense.
- Initiate and support scientific research on medical problems affecting the national defense.
- Initiate and support such scientific and medical research as may be requested by the government of any country whose defense the President deems vital to the defense of the United States.

Its priorities were thus defined by military need, and the urgency of the crisis meant that it mostly had to take basic science as given. As we explain below, this approach is a contrast to many postwar R&D funding institutions, where research is investigator initiated, often fundamental, and scientists have a larger role in shaping the agenda. At NDRC it was ultimately divisions, and within them individual study sections, which identified research priorities, organized proposals, and made arrangements with contractors. CMR, on the other hand, partnered with the National Research Council's Division of Medical Sciences (DMS) in setting priorities and soliciting proposals.

Engaging Top R&D Performers

A second feature of the wartime effort was its focus on funding top institutions and researchers. To support this activity, one of NDRC's first undertakings in 1940 was to build a roster of potential contractors by subject area, which became a standard reference for placing contracts. It prioritized getting results quickly over distributional concerns, favoring contractors "with the facilities and the manpower which promised the best results in the shortest possible time" (Stewart 1948, 13).

Incentives and the Contract Mechanism

The decision to outsource research, rather than perform it directly, was novel. To do so, OSRD invented the federal R&D contract, which balanced specificity with flexibility to explore. The language was standardized but negotiable, and contractors "almost invariably started work under letters of intent which preceded the signing of contracts by weeks or months" (Stewart 1948, 194–95), so as to not delay progress. Though contracts were written for short (e.g., 6-month) periods, there was an "informal understanding that they would be extended if the progress of the work warranted." In the end, OSRD effectively procured research services rather than specific outputs, making its contracts grant-like in nature.

Because results from this work were often patentable, it also developed a novel, contractual patent policy that balanced private incentives with the public interest. OSRD contracts bore either a "short form" or "long form" patent clause, specifying which party retained title to inventions produced under patent (the government and the contractor, respectively), while ensuring that the US government retained a royalty-free license for military use. These terms were standardized but adapted for specific contracts as needed, with the government generally relinquishing patent rights to industrial contractors but retaining them with academic ones and in especially sensitive subject matter such as nuclear energy.

Coordinating Research Efforts

As the principal agency mobilizing research for war, the OSRD was also responsible for coordinating research with the military, other US scientific agencies, and the broader Allied research effort. This was achieved in part through cross appointments, as members of other agencies were appointed to OSRD's advisory council, and Bush was concurrently chairman of the Joint Committee on New Weapons and Equipment at the Joint Chiefs of Staff, which ensured that the scientific perspective would remain close to military strategy. Day-to-day coordination on individual research projects was performed by division-specific military liaisons. In some cases, research programs begun by one division or agency were transferred to another, most notable being the NDRC's atomic fission project being transferred to the US Army Corps of Engineers as the Manhattan Project when it advanced to a weapons development project.

International coordination was also a feature of the OSRD model. American-British collaboration began in the fall of 1940, shortly after NDRC was created, when the British Tizard mission to the United States ended in an exchange of data, plans, and prototypes of a wide range of technologies being developed in each country (most notably the British cavity magnetron, the key input to the US radar program). OSRD later opened a field office in London, which was a conduit for information to flow between American and British researchers, and the British similarly opened an office in Washington, DC. In some cases, individual OSRD research programs also ran foreign branch laboratories near their British counterparts.

Investment in Production and Diffusion

Though it was foremost a research funding and R&D management organization, OSRD also took a role in production and diffusion. The philosophy behind this choice was that fulfilling its mission required, in the previously quoted words of Conant (1947, 198–99), "connect[ing] effectively the laboratory, the pilot plant, and the factory with each other and with the battlefront." This meant that OSRD's work needed to be advanced from laboratory prototypes to reliable, mass-produced units in the field. Because time was of the essence, OSRD was at times aggressive in building capacity at risk. This was particularly true for the atomic fission project, in which it scaled up multiple enrichment sites and methods before knowing which approach would be able to produce enough fissionable uranium to manufacture a bomb.

OSRD also had specific offices focused on getting technology from bench to battlefield, supporting initial production runs, clinical trials and field tests, manufacturing at scale, and deployment. Tight links between researchers and military users facilitated rapid feedback and tweaking. That the military was the main user may have also made it easier to adapt established practices than it would have been otherwise, circumventing common organizational frictions to technology adoption.

C.   The OSRD Model in Action: Atomic Fission

As table 2 shows, OSRD managed a broad portfolio. Here we use the fission program—one of OSRD's larger research endeavors—to illustrate several features of its approach.

The atomic fission project originated in the prewar discovery of nuclear fission in Germany and Denmark in 1938–39. Scientists quickly discovered that the uranium isotope U-235 was fissile, and that because its bombardment with neutrons and subsequent fission released additional neutrons, it could be engineered to create chain reactions that released an immense amount of energy. In 1939, at the urging of Leo Szilard and Albert Einstein, President Roosevelt established a secret committee to study the matter, which was folded into NDRC at its founding in 1940 (the Committee on Uranium, table 1).

Because atomic fission was new, NDRC first contracted with several universities to deepen the basic science of fission—an undertaking that was relatively distinctive for OSRD, which otherwise mostly funded applied research. Among the questions that needed to be answered were what elements and isotopes were fissile and how to separate U-235 from the more common isotope U-238 at scale or produce chain reactions in U-238. As Baxter (1946, 422) explained, "One approach was to place unseparated uranium in a 'pile' with carbon or heavy water as a moderator or 'slower down' of neutrons to increase the chances of a chain reaction"; the other was "to separate the isotopes and accumulate a stock of U-235."

By the fall of 1941, the project was beginning to show promise, despite relatively modest funding, but the bottleneck was the ability to produce enough fissile material for a bomb. The program was scaled up into five parallel efforts: electromagnetic separation at the University of California, Berkeley; gaseous diffusion and centrifugal separation of U-235 at Columbia University; and graphite and heavy-water pile methods of obtaining plutonium from uranium at University of Chicago. The bombing of Pearl Harbor on December 7, 1941, intensified this effort into an "all-out attack on the uranium problem," with Roosevelt urging them to "press as fast as possible on the fundamental physics and on the engineering planning" (Baxter 1946, 428, 439).

Until it became clear which enrichment method would succeed, OSRD invested in them all. In early 1942, OSRD began planning pilot plants for all five methods, with the army taking charge of construction. Baxter (1946, 440) explained, "Fear that the Germans would be the first in the field with atomic bombs led to a telescoping of stages, in which pilot plant work often overlapped research in the laboratory, and the design and construction of the huge production plants were carried out before lessons could be learned and obstacles surmounted in the pilot plant." Throughout 1942, as the OSRD's R&D continued, the army began building reactors and separation plants at Oak Ridge and Hanford (among others) and a weapons manufacturing facility at Los Alamos, under the umbrella of the Manhattan Project. By early 1943, two of the enrichment methods had failed, leaving gaseous diffusion and electromagnetic separation, and the graphite pile, as frontrunners. In May 1943, with the science established and pilot plants running, the fission project was transferred to the army, whose job was then to produce a functioning atomic weapon. The British had been simultaneously advancing a nuclear weapon program, and shortly thereafter agreed to fold its effort into the Manhattan Project. Bush and Conant continued in an advisory capacity until July 16, 1945, when the first nuclear weapon was detonated in the Trinity test.

The fission program illustrates several of OSRD's core features in practice, including coordination, outsourcing research, and a focus on technology diffusion. Other aspects of the program, such as funding parallel R&D and investment in production at risk, were more idiosyncratic, though they illustrate the general principle that in a crisis, getting a solution developed and diffused quickly is a key objective.

Other programs also deviated in ways from the four features highlighted above. Though in many ways the radar program exemplified key OSRD features—including demand-driven priorities, focus on top scientists and engineers, coordination with the military, international coordination, and funding for production and diffusion activities—it was also highly centralized, operating primarily out of a single building on the MIT campus. This reflected the nature of the problem (building a technological system) and the importance of feedback and spillovers across the innovation chain (Gross and Sampat 2020b).

At CMR, several of the major efforts also did more than just outsource research (Bush 1970). The malaria program (aiming to find a better malaria treatment than the drug that was broadly used, atarabine) helped oversee and coordinate private-sector efforts to synthesize and test thousands of candidates, even without formal contracts. Similarly, the large synthetic penicillin effort promoted knowledge and information sharing among private-sector firms. Interestingly, each of these programs were nominally failures during the crisis itself. The major development from the malaria effort, chloroquine, arrived too late to be used in the war. And the costly effort to synthesize penicillin, originally viewed by Bush and others as the best route to the production of large quantities, was unsuccessful during the war (and rendered moot by progress in the natural penicillin production program), though historians have argued it helped pave the way for synthetic penicillins that came to the market in the 1950s (Swann 1983).

D. Criticisms and Difficulties

Overall, policy makers and the public were broadly impressed with the effort, as we will discuss below. However there were strong critics of various aspects of the efforts during the crisis. One line of criticism came from liberal critics of OSRD, led by Senator Harley Kilgore (D-WV), who expressed concerns that OSRD focused exclusively on elite institutions and scientists/engineers known to its leadership, an approach which, in his view, would not only contribute to long-term inequities and concentration but also limit the range of useful ideas brought to its attention and thus delay crisis resolution (Kevles 1977). Associations representing specific scientific disciplines (e.g., mathematics and biology), regions (western states), and small businesses expressed disgruntlement at being overlooked by the OSRD (Kevles 1977; Owens 1994; Appel 2000). Related to the concerns about concentration, Kilgore and others questioned OSRD's patent policy, which often gave rights to contractors, arguing that doing so may create legal bottlenecks hindering the response and monopolies based on taxpayer research after the war (Kevles 1977; Sampat 2020).

Throughout the war there were complaints about the lack of political accountability of the new organization as well, and about stepping on the toes of scientists and engineers in the Navy and War departments (Owens 1994). The flexibility that Bush viewed as important to OSRD's success sometimes also drew scrutiny. Bush (1970, 31–32) wrote in his memoirs, "There were those who protested that the action of setting up NDRC was an end run, a grab by which a small company of scientists and engineers, acting outside established channels, got hold of the authority and money for the program of developing new weapons. That, in fact, is exactly what it was. Moreover, it was the only way in which a broad program could be launched rapidly and on an adequate scale." Other decisions made in the name of speed, including CMR "challenge trials" of therapies on prisoners, raised ethical concerns even at the time (Rothman 1991).

Though after the fact the effort was widely celebrated, it certainly had struggles along the way, unsurprisingly for a new agency operating under tremendous pressure with little precedent. OSRD made numerous policy changes and realignments during the course of the war to adapt to new information from the field or feedback from contractors on what was and was not working (Stewart 1948). One example of the challenges it faced was in liaison with the military. We suggested above that close relations with the military were important, and the evidence suggests that they helped facilitate priority setting and diffusion, but this process was by no means seamless. The military was a complex, bureaucratic organization, and liaison was complicated by frequent turnover of military attachés. This challenge was partially relieved by having points of contact with the military at multiple levels of the OSRD hierarchy, though it was never fully resolved; the relevant knowledge was more embodied in these individual people than the organization.

II. The Evolution of the Postwar Innovation System: Science and Technology Policy in "Normal" Times

Despite these difficulties, the wartime R&D effort advanced scores of technologies crucial to the resolution of the crisis. These included radar, the atomic bomb, the mass production of penicillin, and a number of other technologies and medical treatments (Baxter 1946). Near the end of the war, President Roosevelt asked Bush to reflect on lessons from OSRD—"a unique experiment of team-work and cooperation in coordinating scientific research and in applying existing scientific knowledge to the solution of the technical problems paramount in war"—for postwar innovation policy. Roosevelt wrote, "There is, however, no reason why the lessons to be found in this experiment cannot be profitably employed in times of peace. The information, the techniques, and the research experience developed by the OSRD and by the thousands of scientists in the universities and in private industry, should be used in the days of peace ahead for the improvement of the national health, the creation of new enterprises bringing new jobs, and the betterment of the national standard of living."

In July 1945, Bush responded with *Science, The Endless Frontier*, sometimes considered the blueprint for postwar US innovation policy (Bush 1945). The "Bush Report," as it came to be known, did not explicitly discuss crisis innovation much, beyond noting that most of the applications of technology during the war relied on preexisting basic knowledge. Instead, it mainly focused on the need for government support of basic research in peacetime (anticipating aspects of the Nelson-Arrow "market failure" theory of innovation policy), the importance of basic research for technological progress, the need for scientific autonomy in setting priorities, and the role of universities in performing basic research.[2] Some economists (Nelson 1997; Romer 2020) have argued that the Bush ideology has fixated US innovation policy on science and blinded it to possibilities of technology policy, including the kinds of applied endeavors that were essential to the wartime effort (and later would be in the COVID-19 crisis).

While Bush, Kilgore, and their allies introduced and debated a slew of competing bills embodying the different visions, OSRD research was spun off to existing agencies rather than the single foundation both Bush and Kilgore wanted. The Office of Naval Research absorbed military contracts, the Atomic Energy Commission (AEC) nuclear work, and the National Institutes of Health (NIH) medical research (Kleinman 1995; Brooks 1996). By the time the National Science Foundation (NSF) Act was signed by President Truman in 1950, the agency it created had become a "puny partner" in the overall enterprise (Kevles 1978, 358). The US system was instead fragmented and pluralistic, as different agencies had different responsibilities and modi operandi. In the Cold War and expansion of federal R&D over the ensuing decades, "mission-oriented" R&D funders would come to dominate the funding landscape (Smith 2011).

Of particular relevance for the COVID-19 era is the NIH. The National Institute of Health (then singular) was created in 1930. Though it had its roots in the Marine Hygienic Laboratory, a bacteriology lab created in 1887 that made significant contributions to vaccine development against infectious diseases in the early twentieth century, the institute focused on basic studies on chronic diseases like cancer. Before the war, it did not have a broad research funding program (Swain 1962).

We previously described how during World War II the OSRD's CMR coordinated and funded medical research activities. After the war was over, and as Bush's proposed National Research Foundation faced legislative delays, CMR's open contracts were transferred to NIH and became the foundation of its extramural grants program (Swain 1962; Fox 1987). Buoyed by the wartime demonstration of the value of medical innovation and the returns to government research funding, the NIH grew rapidly in the decades that followed, adding myriad new institutes focused on specific diseases, organs, professions, and fields of research. It inherited not only CMR funds but also its peer review system and administrative personnel.[3] Unlike CMR, the NIH focused primarily on basic research. Though Congress made allocations to individual institutes, by and large priority setting at NIH has been investigator initiated. Disease advocates (and Congress) have at times questioned the wisdom of this, especially in years of tight budgets and in the context of specific health crises (e.g., cancer or AIDS; see Sampat 2012).

With some exceptions, the postwar division of labor in medicine was that the public and academic sectors focused upstream, and the private sector was responsible for more "applied" activities, including development, costly clinical trials, and diffusion. The "integrated research model"

(Hoyt 2006) that characterized wartime medical research was largely abandoned at NIH for a more "linear" approach to innovation like that advocated by Bush (Balconi, Brusoni, and Orsenigo 2010). Since the late 1990s, the NIH has begun to emphasize "translational research" as well, partly in response to criticisms of the linear model (Butler 2008).[4]

The NSF focused on fundamental research activities, also driven by investigator-initiated research, and also faced tensions historically (Brooks 1996). Both agencies have emphasized funding top scientists, mainly though grants rather than contracts. However, aspects of the wartime approach were present in other fields, particularly military research funded through the Department of Defense (DOD) and space research at the National Aeronautics and Space Administration (NASA). Within DOD, the Defense Advanced Projects Research Agency (DARPA, initially known as ARPA) has a focused approach to technology development (Azoulay et al. 2019) that in many ways resembled OSRD, and there have long been calls for bringing aspects of that approach to biomedical research (Cook-Deegan 1996). As we will describe below, one such experiment, the Biomedical Advanced Research and Development Authority (BARDA), would have an outsize role during the COVID-19 response.

Three other aspects of the postwar biomedical innovation system help frame the COVID-19 response. We noted above that the postwar system involved the public sector supporting fundamental research, and private firms supporting clinical testing, development, manufacturing, and sales and marketing. A long history of empirical research in economics suggests that patents are important for incentivizing private-sector R&D activities, especially in the life sciences (Levin et al. 1987). However, frustrations that patents restrict access and diffusion (some of which became prominent in a previous global health crisis, HIV-AIDS) and that they may not work effectively for some types of research (including vaccines without large rich-country markets) has led to proposals for alternative "pull" mechanisms, including prizes and advance market commitments (Kremer and Williams 2010).[5]

Second, in response to concerns about a lack of commercialization of publicly funded research, the 1980 Bayh-Dole Act created a uniform patent policy allowing universities and small businesses to retain rights to patents resulting from publicly funded research, and to license these patents exclusively at their discretion.[6] Bayh-Dole was a culmination of decades of debate about whether the government or contractors should retain patent rights. These debates had their roots in criticisms by Harley Kilgore that OSRD's "long form" patent policy effectively gave ownership of the results of publicly funded research to private firms (Sampat 2020)—an issue we return to in Section IV. These debates have since continued in pharmaceuticals (e.g., in debates about prices of/access to HIV-AIDS drugs during this crisis) and, as we will discuss, have resurfaced in the context of COVID-19 vaccines and treatments.

Finally, the innovation system grew massively over the postwar era. OSRD's budget was about $2.5 billion annually at its height, and $7.5 billion total (both in 2020 dollars). In FY2019, the federal R&D budget was more than $130 billion (of which $40 billion went to the NIH), about a 50-fold increase.[7] Although Bush wrote that only a handful of universities had adequate resources for research in 1940, 75 years later hundreds of universities and thousands of firms and researchers in the United States and globally were actively involved in research and innovation (Moses et al. 2015). Globally, scores of agencies and philanthropies now fund research, with their own missions, procedures, and idiosyncrasies. For all these reasons, when the COVID-19 crisis hit in early 2020, it encountered a much larger, mature, and established innovation system than what existed during World War II, including large and sophisticated government research bureaucracies with established procedures, norms, and missions, as well as a wider set of research-performing firms and institutions that could be mobilized in a crisis. The crisis has illuminated both strengths and weaknesses of this system, one that had changed considerably since it emerged in the aftermath of World War II. We will return to these issues in later sections of this paper.

III. The COVID-19 Innovation System

Seventy-five years later, COVID-19 presented a new crisis in which science, technology, and innovation were crucial to an effective response. From early on, scientists and policy makers focused on developing a safe and effective vaccine. Drugs to treat the disease were also required. Diagnostic tests and contact tracing technologies were needed to reduce spread, as were models to understand the epidemiology of the disease and design the needed public health interventions. Because fighting the virus also necessitated suppression, and thus social distancing, masking, and lockdowns, there was also value in innovation to mitigate the economic and social costs of these interventions. There was a need for new business models at schools, restaurants, medical practices, and other organizations that could accommodate social distancing, often enabled by the rapid adoption and improvement of digital conferencing tools. Firms needed risk-mitigating technologies to protect employees and customers. In the absence of vaccines and treatments, frontline doctors and nurses required nonpharmacological interventions to manage COVID-19 patients, including patient management techniques (e.g., proning), hospital workflows, and others. To be effective, not only did innovations need to be generated quickly, but it was also essential that they diffuse broadly to the relevant users, another important aspect of crisis innovation policy (Gross and Sampat 2021).

This breadth may be informative about the different nature of the innovation challenge, and the innovation system, relative to the 1940s. Unlike the US World War II research effort, where there was essentially one major user that helped articulate a specific set of priorities, in the pandemic the demand was widespread and diffuse, and in some cases the needed innovations were quite specific to particular actors. There were no generals in the field reporting back key problems and bottlenecks.

Innovations to combat COVID-19 had high potential social value. Cutler and Summers (2020) estimate the cumulative US economic and health costs of COVID-19 through 2021 to be $16 trillion, or about 90% of US annual gross domestic product. Reflecting the high social value, and the importance of time in addressing a spreading pandemic, policy makers worldwide mobilized. As we have argued previously (Gross and Sampat 2021), the urgency of a crisis may magnify traditional market failures, increasing the scope for productive government intervention beyond what a decentralized market can achieve on its own.

Vaccine innovation, the "silver bullet" many sought since early 2020, is particularly prone to a range of supply- and demand-side market failures beyond those present for other types of technologies (Xue and Ouellette forthcoming).[8] Beyond incentives, scholars and policy makers had also expressed concerns about the current lack of US capacity for targeted vaccine development and failure of existing policy models for vaccines (Hoyt 2006, 2012). Partly reflecting these market failures, the US response appears heavily focused on vaccines. It is interesting that, at least in financial terms, much of the response would be not through the crown jewel of the biomedical research enterprise—the NIH—but instead the previously small agency BARDA. Despite the vaccine focus of the US policy response, a range of decentralized innovative efforts appear to have been active in many of the other types of innovation described above, collectively resulting in a massive pivoting of the innovation system to working on COVID-19-related research.

A.   The US Federal Policy Response

As of the beginning of March 2021, the US government had appropriated $4 trillion to COVID-19 recovery and spent nearly $3 trillion. Of this, less than 1% was allocated to vaccine and treatment R&D (Whoriskey, MacMillan, and O'Connell 2020). This was small relative to what some economists had recommended given the high social value of such interventions (Athey et al. 2020; Tabarrok 2020). Some R&D funding for treatment and vaccine research came from agencies' existing budgets, but most funding was provided by special appropriations via the Coronavirus Preparedness and Response Supplemental Appropriations Act, or CARES Act, and the Paycheck Protection Program and Health Care Enhancement Act. Beyond funding earmarked for R&D, some of the broader funds in these packages may have been rerouted to R&D, especially through Operation Warp Speed (OWS), which we describe below (Cohrs 2021).

The NIH and NSF

Given that the NIH is the biggest single funder of biomedical research in the world, it is not surprising that it has been part of the US innovation response. By late April 2020, through a series of emergency supplemental appropriations, NIH had received an additional $3.5 billion for COVID-19 research. Unlike previous instances of emergency funding (e.g., the American Recovery and Reinvestment Act in 2009), which had to be spent quickly, the COVID-19 appropriations do not need to be spent for several years. Facing the need to respond more quickly than its normal peer review process would allow, and a large number of applications for funding, the NIH decided to prioritize 1-year supplements to existing grants, which do not require peer review, and it accelerated peer review for new applications (Kaiser 2020). Nonetheless, the crisis did reveal some of the difficulties of crisis response through standard peer review approaches, which may be better suited to other goals, such as promoting basic science (Azoulay and Li 2020).

NIH has helped fund a number of the important trials of COVID-19 vaccines—including the messenger RNA (mRNA) vaccine developed by Moderna, where prepandemic NIH-funded research also contributed to the basic platform technology, and the Johnson & Johnson/Janssen vaccine—and treatments including remdesivir and convalescent plasma. Funding of late-stage trials is atypical for the agency, and also illustrates the uniqueness of the crisis. As of April 1, 2021, NIH has funded 2,126 COVID-19 grants, totaling $3.9 billion.[9] Figure 2, panel *A* shows a word cloud illustrating topics NIH has supported.

In addition to funding research, NIH has also taken a coordinating role, including through its ACTIV program (Accelerating COVID-19 Therapeutic Interventions and Vaccines), which promotes information sharing, coordination, and standardized trial protocols among public and private actors. Its Rapid Acceleration of Diagnostics initiative (RADx) aims to accelerate diagnostic innovation and engages in a range of downstream development activities beyond the agency's traditional ambit.

The NSF also pivoted to COVID-19. In April 2020, it invited researchers to propose nonmedical, nonclinical research on COVID-19 epidemiological modeling, transmission, and prevention. It expanded its Rapid Response Research program (RAPID) to advance research quickly, recognizing the need for speed and the slow pace of traditional peer review mechanisms. As of April 1, 2021, it has funded 1,339 grants, totaling $278 million.[10] The word cloud in figure 2, panel *B* illustrates topics NSF has funded.

OWS and BARDA

In a February 9, 2020, memo to the newly created White House Coronavirus Task Force, 3 weeks after the country's first confirmed COVID-19 case and 3 days after the first death, economic advisor Peter Navarro called for an immediate "Manhattan Project" for vaccines (Navarro 2020). Mimicking the original Manhattan Project, Navarro called for "multiple shots on goal" and "flexible funding" that could be redirected to more promising candidates "as the science develops." Though NIH had early plans to coordinate the vaccine and therapeutics research efforts (Cohen 2020), these were superseded in April 2020 by the announcement of OWS, which took the lead on these problems. Warp Speed was an "America First" approach to vaccine development, with the bold goal of developing, approving, and delivering hundreds of millions of doses of safe and effective COVID-19 vaccine doses by the end of 2020. Its name alone conveys that in this crisis, like World War II, speed was a paramount objective.

OWS has been notoriously opaque (Cohen 2020), making it difficult to provide a comprehensive assessment at this time. As was true with World War II, we expect the records of this effort and a much more complete picture of its work will be available to future scholars. Based on the data currently available, we can nevertheless describe the broad contours of the effort.

A. Words in NIH awards

B. Words in NSF awards

Fig. 2. Common words in National Institutes of Health (NIH) and National Science Foundation (NSF) COVID-related award titles (through April 1, 2021). Color version available as an online enhancement.

Notes: The most common words appearing in the title of NIH and NSF COVID-related research grants, weighted by frequency and contract value. COVID-related contracts were identified with Boolean searches for COVID (as in COVID-19), CoV (as in SARS-CoV-2), and nCoV (as in 2019-nCoV) in the title, abstract, or keywords of research grants from 2020 and 2021. Data as of April 1, 2021.

Warp Speed was organized as an interagency collaboration that brought together organizational elements, funding vehicles, and staff from several government agencies—including BARDA, NIH, the Federal Drug Administration (FDA), the Centers for Disease Control and Prevention, and the military—with private-sector firms in a public-private partnership. Its leadership reflected all three constituencies (public health officials, military officers, and executives), though a leaked organizational chart reveals heavy DOD staffing (Florko 2020). The extensive military involvement is in part a reflection of the needs and ambitions of the effort, which were as much the logistics of production and distribution as they were R&D—activities that the military may have comparative advantage in. Paul Mango, the Department of Health and Human Services (HHS) deputy chief of staff, explained, "There's really not a need for anyone to place scores of scientists inside HHS or DOD to get this done," as Warp Speed was not itself performing research directly (Florko 2020).

Warp Speed routed most of its funding not through NIH but through BARDA. BARDA was created through the 2006 Pandemic and All-Hazards Preparedness Act as part of a broader effort "to improve the Nation's public health and medical preparedness and response capabilities for emergencies, whether deliberate, accidental, or natural." This was a response to perceived market failures and risks in medical countermeasures that were limiting private investment in such technologies. The act tasked BARDA with funding "advanced development" activities (product development, clinical trials, manufacturing scale-up, and getting FDA approval) on medical countermeasures including drugs and vaccines (Matheny, Mair, and Smith 2008; Tucker 2009).[11]

Before the COVID-19 crisis, BARDA was a minor actor; in dollar terms, authorized to spend less than $3 billion over the 2014–18 period (Larsen and Disbrow 2017). With Warp Speed, however, BARDA took center stage. Compared with the roughly $4 billion spent by NIH during the pandemic, BARDA's COVID-19 contracts now total $26.5 billion. Based on available data, about 75% is on vaccines. Though there are no comprehensive public data on BARDA contracts, information from contracts published on its website illustrate the heavy vaccine focus in dollar terms (fig. 3).[12]

Its exact priority-setting process is unclear. According to former director of Warp Speed Moncef Slaoui, the effort focused on vaccine candidates that, based on evidence from preclinical and early-stage data, would have a chance at entering trials by the end of 2020 and had the potential to be manufactured at scale quickly (Slaoui and Hepburn 2020). It chose candidates across four different platforms (mRNA and three others) it believed

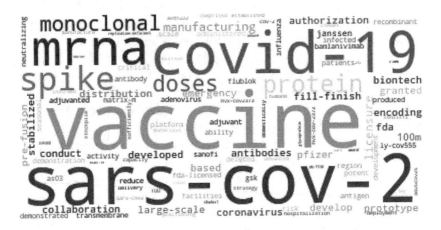

Fig. 3. Common words in Biomedical Advanced Research and Development Authority (BARDA) contract titles (through April 1, 2021). Color version available as an online enhancement.

Notes: The most common words appearing in the title of BARDA COVID-19-related research contracts, weighted by frequency and contract value. Data as of April 1, 2021.

held the most promise. Reflecting the "Manhattan Project" approach, one of its guiding principles was portfolio diversification and advancing candidates in parallel. It also funded clinical trials, manufacturing capacity at risk, and production of doses before trials were complete. This represented a sharp departure from the types of activities public-sector research supported before COVID-19—though as noted, several of these were always part of the BARDA playbook (Sampat and Shadlen 2021).

In addition to "push" funding, BARDA's contracts typically included "pull" incentives via large advanced procurements. These contracts include options to prepurchase doses if successful, at set prices. This differed from theoretical advanced market commitments in that they were producer-specific, which seemingly misses out on one attractive benefit of prize-based approaches: avoiding the need to "pick winners" in advance (Kremer and Williams 2010). Nonetheless, the commitments de-risked the process for participating firms.[13]

The specific instruments varied by contract (see Sampat and Shadlen 2021) but through these push and pull approaches, Warp Speed/BARDA supported eight vaccines. The six that are publicly announced include mRNA approaches (Moderna, Pfizer/BioNTech), live-vector approaches (AstraZeneca, J&J/Janssen), and recombinant-subunit-adjuvanted protein approaches (Novavax, Sanofi/GSK).

This appears to have been extremely successful. On April 30, 2020, early in Warp Speed's effort, an editorial in *The New York Times* predicted "The grim truth . . . is that a vaccine probably won't arrive any time soon," noting high failure rates in vaccine development and that the previous record time was 4 years. As of this writing, the Pfizer/BioNTech, Moderna, and J&J/Janssen vaccines have been approved in the United States (through emergency use authorizations) and are being administered across the country, and two others (AstraZeneca and Novavax) are in late-stage trials. As was true of the penicillin, radar, and fission efforts during World War II, and as Bush later emphasized in *Science, The Endless Frontier*, the fact that we had invested in some of the key platform technologies before this crisis seems to have been crucial to the success of COVID-19 vaccine development efforts in 2020 (Kiszewski et al. 2020).

B. International and Other Efforts

Beyond the United States, other governments also contributed to funding COVID-19 therapies and vaccines, including the European Union, individual EU member states, and the United Kingdom, albeit at levels much lower than the United States, based on available data (Sampat and Shadlen 2021). The Chinese and Russian governments also funded vaccines that are now approved and being administered in multiple countries (CoronaVac, Sputnik V). Another major set of actors are internationally funded nongovernmental organizations, including the Coalition for Epidemic Preparedness Innovations, which has also been funding vaccine candidates—at much lower levels than national governments—and its partner global purchaser COVAX, which has entered advanced purchase commitments and postapproval purchases with vaccine manufacturers for distribution to low-income countries (Sampat and Shadlen 2021).

Researchers globally have pivoted to working on COVID-19 related research, often crossing field, geographic, and institutional boundaries to do so. Like World War II, the crisis has (at least anecdotally) spurred new collaborations. Some observers believe the pandemic response ushered in a new era of "open science." *The New York Times* has asserted "COVID-19 Changed How the World Does Science, Together." Reflecting the need for speed, much of the dissemination has been through scientific preprints, which now number in the hundreds of thousands for COVID-19-related research. Many journals have also expanded their capacity and accelerated review. The speed and openness have been accompanied by concern about the quality of the research (Yong 2021), reflecting the challenge facing journals and the public of screening this flood of papers on a new disease. The open science approach has also enabled real-time public critiques and debates of specific findings, at times leading to retractions (Kupferschmidt 2020)—though these retractions have in many cases gone unseen or ignored by subsequent work (Piller 2021).

C.   *How Does the Response to COVID-19 Compare with World War II?*

Parallels and contrasts between the World War II and COVID-19 efforts are already becoming apparent. In some respects—such as parallel funding, manufacturing at risk, the government's role in applied activities, and an emphasis on speed—Warp Speed has similarities to OSRD programs. But there are several important differences. One is that OSRD identified and contracted out work on dozens of problems, whereas the COVID-19 response seems to have been more focused, especially on drug development. The COVID-19 effort has also involved firms as key performers of government-funded research to a greater degree than in World War II, in part reflecting the nature of the problem it was solving and where the R&D capabilities to address it reside in the modern innovation system. Moreover, whereas OSRD had one customer, the military, which could have a voice in setting priorities and could diffuse technologies, COVID-19 problems had many customers—up to the complete population, in the case of vaccines. The initial difficulties in distributing the vaccines may illustrate the differences between military officers diffusing technologies by fiat and decentralized diffusion by states and through the fragmented US health care system.

The public posting of the SARS-CoV-2 gene sequence by Chinese researchers in January 2020 was perhaps the COVID-19 equivalent of the World War II Tizard Mission (through which the British shared key military technologies with US researchers in 1940) and set off the international sprint to produce a vaccine. Although vaccine innovation appears to have been a success, vaccines are only one of many public health innovations recognized as valuable at the start of the pandemic, which included rapid, scaled-up testing, contact tracing, therapeutics and other treatments, strategies for protecting health care workers, changes in social behaviors, changes to the organization of work, and other public health interventions. Economists and others have raised concerns about the lack of coordinated investments: as far as we know there was no CMR-like entity looking for holes in the portfolio or preventing duplication, as illustrated by the large number of trials on just one therapy (hydroxychloroquine).[14] Lack of coordination is particularly problematic for clinical trials competing to enroll sick patients, who are limited in number. It is notable that during the war, CMR was active in this problem, allocating patients and scarce penicillin stock across investigators and across the natural/synthetic penicillin programs. Conti et al. (2020) have argued that better coordination in repurposing off-patent drugs in particular could yield high returns, given that they can be deployed more rapidly than new molecules and that private firms may lack adequate incentives to conduct the needed trials.

Similar to the lack of coordination for drugs, another difference is the seeming lack of any real priority-setting mechanisms for nonpharmaceutical COVID-19 research. During the war, research priorities were decided in coordination with the military. OSRD then distributed research questions to competent researchers, collected progress reports, synthesized evidence, and made recommendations for practice. To our knowledge, there was no such apparatus in the United States during the COVID-19 pandemic to take stock of the key questions where research was needed (e.g., transmissibility, school and business reopenings, mask design, the effectiveness of lockdowns), farm out the research, and synthesize the often imperfect evidence, distilling insights for practice. The "science for policy" interface was much more decentralized, fragmented across agencies, and sometimes chaotic. Even though the set of users for COVID-19 research results is more heterogeneous than during the war, an OSRD-type approach may have been useful, especially in the early days of the pandemic when there was considerable uncertainty about risk and protective measures.

That the major R&D response, Warp Speed, ran through BARDA suggests that more entrenched agencies with embedded routines (such as peer review) may have a harder time pivoting quickly to new problems or activities. However, we do not currently know the precise logic for the specific institutional choices that were made—including the role of politics and other factors—so we also caution against premature conclusions. International coordination is a second area where the US federally organized effort has been weak, almost by design. Although Warp Speed coordinated among the firms it funded, the US vaccine effort in particular has not collaborated with Chinese and Russian vaccine development efforts, which stands in contrast to the strong Allied cooperation during a global war against a common enemy.

One more way in which the COVID-19 innovation response differs from the World War II era is in the broad, decentralized mobilization of researchers worldwide. Overall, a large share of the innovative effort was based on "bottom-up" efforts by individual organizations and academics, rather than through top-down planning. Since the COVID-19 pandemic began, more than 130,000 academic articles on the disease have been written (more than 100,000 in the biomedical literature alone), attacking questions on the science of COVID-19 from transmission to therapeutics, on social phenomena from social distancing to mask-wearing, and on engineering problems from sanitation to ventilation.[15] This is in some ways similar to what happened during World War II vis-à-vis distributed invention, when independent inventors around the country were creating and volunteering their inventions to OSRD (Stewart 1948), albeit on a much smaller scale. It is striking that much of this pivoting came without specific federal policy direction, at least if we define innovation broadly. However, it is almost certainly the case that the infrastructure created by decades of previous federal funding helped create the capacity for this broad, decentralized response.

IV. Policy Trade-Offs for Crisis R&D Efforts

Public officials must make a number of choices in a crisis, which the World War II and COVID-19 experience can inform. One high-level choice is how involved (versus laissez-faire) an approach to take to crisis innovation. Organizers of centralized crisis R&D efforts, in turn, have to set research priorities, select R&D contractors, allocate intellectual property rights, and make plans for production and distribution at scale. Individually, these questions present complex trade-offs, but collectively the challenge is even greater, because an effective strategy has to thread all of these needles at once.

In this section, we explore four specific trade-offs in crisis R&D policy:

1. Priority setting: top-down versus bottom-up
2. R&D performance: elite versus distributed
3. Appropriability: promoting innovation versus diffusion
4. Managing disruptions to the innovation system

This set is by no means exhaustive, and we consider a wider range of questions and considerations in other recent writing (Gross and Sampat 2020b). Our focus here is on those we see as likely to be either the most contentious or consequential. There is another category of issues that may be policy goals in ordinary times, but which could potentially impede a crisis response, such as distributional considerations or reporting requirements. Forgoing some noncrisis policy goals can be justified by the extraordinary returns to resolving a crisis (Gross and Sampat 2021), and they are not our focus here. A third set of issues for crisis R&D policy is related not to what to do in a crisis, but what can be done in advance to prepare for one. We defer discussion of this question to Section V.

A.   Top-Down versus Bottom-Up Priority Setting

A basic question for crisis R&D is how to set research priorities—including who should decide. When time is short, directing funding and labor to top-priority projects is a first-order problem for leaders of crisis R&D efforts. The approach to priority setting can thus be consequential.

Modern US S&T policy takes a range of approaches. The primary "pull" mechanism, patent policy, is largely bottom-up. In principle, patents reward any invention that is novel, nonobvious, and useful, without ex ante delineation of priorities. The theoretical benefit is that the private sector may have better information on the costs and benefits of different approaches to solving problems than policy makers. However, the downsides of pull approaches, such as excess correlation of portfolios, a lack of idea sharing, and competition for scarce resources (e.g., patients in clinical studies), may be particularly problematic during a crisis, suggesting a role for government funding and coordination. As we discuss below, using patents to incentivize innovation may have other drawbacks in a crisis, including high prices and restricted diffusion.

"Push" mechanisms are more mixed in their approach. Science funding agencies like NSF and NIH are also largely bottom-up: although they at times announce broad categories they plan to support (like nanotechnology or climate science), most funding is distributed through disciplinary programs, and scientists do the proposing. The rationale for the "investigator-initiated" model is that scientists have better knowledge of feasibility and scientific importance than policy makers do. Though review panels screen these proposals, the research ideas begin with the research performers, who get funded to do the work they propose. The DOD, in contrast, funds more applied research and engineering than basic science, often for specific uses related to its mission, and more often top-down.[16] The Department of Energy supports both, including substantial intramural work.

Like DOD today, in World War II OSRD largely defined R&D priorities and contracted for specific research such as "gyroscopic director" or "cholera vaccine," reflecting the applied nature of wartime problems. The proposing process at NDRC is illustrative. Research ideas could originate with internal scientific staff, the military services, or an Allied government, but generally did not come from the scientific community at large. NDRC's study sections—which included staff scientists and military liaisons—workshopped these ideas into formal proposals that included an action plan, candidate contractors, and the anticipated cost and duration, which were forwarded up the chain of command and voted on by OSRD leadership. This approach fused scientific expertise with user insight into the nature of a problem and its military importance (Bush 1970). CMR took a somewhat different approach, setting priorities jointly with the National Research Council's DMS, which a year earlier had organized a set of committees around "problems with which the Services expected to be confronted" (Richards 1946, 576). CMR then solicited proposals from investigators on problems of importance. These proposals were reviewed by elite medical researchers on the DMS committees and graded, and high-scoring proposals were funded. CMR's approach thus mixed centralized priority setting with investigator proposing, mediated by peer review.

The COVID-19 effort has been more difficult to pierce, and details on any internal deliberations over priorities may only become known over time. What we do know is that agencies involved in the effort had to choose both the scope of what they would support (e.g., vaccines, therapeutics, or nonpharmaceutical measures) and specific projects and performers. As far as we can tell, OWS has taken a top-down approach to vaccine development, focused on known firms with capabilities to deliver them quickly.

Why would a top-down approach be appropriate in a crisis? From an economic perspective, decision rights are best delegated to the party with the most information. A central agency may have a clearer view of what the important problems are and the means to coordinate efforts. It can also take a broader perspective that goes beyond R&D to manufacturing and distribution, and consider how constraints in these downstream activities should influence R&D (e.g., quality control in the production of radar sets and engineering tolerances, or the availability of cold storage for COVID-19 vaccines and storage temperatures). User needs and supply constraints are issues that scientists are not always positioned to evaluate or perhaps even recognize—whereas central organizations like OSRD or OWS are more likely to be able to.

B. Concentrated versus Distributed R&D Funding

Another question—especially for government sponsors of crisis R&D efforts—is whether to concentrate crisis R&D funding in elite scientists, firms, and institutions or to solicit efforts from a wider group. In short, who should do the work? Answering this question may require weighing competing objectives, like maximizing the return on the public investment in R&D versus the (at times) political necessity of attracting broad-based political support. But even when the principal goal is to achieve "the best results in the shortest possible time" (Stewart 1948), the optimal distribution of funding is less than clear. We see this tension as boiling down to a mean-variance trade-off: relative to engaging a broad population, concentrating R&D efforts with top scientists raises expected quality but may sacrifice tail innovation.

In World War II, the OSRD primarily contracted with top firms and institutions. It had multiple criteria for selecting contractors, with the first being the ability to deliver outstanding results as fast as possible, and secondary criteria including spreading the work and reducing cost. As we noted in Section I, it placed more than one-third of all funding with just two institutions—MIT and Caltech—and spent more than 90% of its obligations in 10 states. This concentration exposed it to criticism from some contemporaries that it was not employing the nation's full scientific talent in the war effort (Kilgore 1943).

But this was partly driven by necessity. Work on large, complex systems engineering problems like radar or rockets was less divisible and generally benefited from centralization.[17] Centralization also characterized the atomic fission research effort, which was based at UC Berkeley, Chicago, and Columbia. Yet where research problems were divisible—as in the hunt for antimalarials, or more generally for most medical research—OSRD permitted a decentralized effort. Stewart (1948, 23) explained:

[For] problems which . . . had a lower order of urgency, a wider distribution of contracts was possible. This was also the case where problems were of such a nature as to permit their division into a number of unrelated parts upon each of which a few men at a number of different institutions might be engaged. In the field of chemical warfare, for instance, there were cases where a competent chemist with a small number of assistants could attack a discrete problem. On the other hand, concentration was demanded by many problems in the field of physics where each part had an intimate connection with all other parts of an over-all system.

OWS's focus on vaccines over other technologies left relatively less room for decentralization: with only a handful of vaccine candidates, there is need for only a handful of R&D performers, though some observers have argued that given the ex ante uncertainty as well as intrinsic market failures due to racing, it should have funded more vaccine candidates than it did (e.g., Athey et al. 2020; Bryan, Lemus, and Marshall 2020).

The choice between concentrating R&D efforts with elite scientists versus a more distributed approach thus comes down to a handful of considerations: how capable is the wider pool of scientists, firms, and institutions; how divisible is the work; and how easy is it to screen results. When any of these conditions fails, concentration may be a more attractive strategy.

C. Patent Policy for Innovation and Diffusion

The traditional trade-off of patent policy is between dynamic and static efficiency, balancing incentives for innovation against the benefits of broad access (including diffusion and low prices). The urgency of a crisis only heightens this tension, as the willingness to pay for a quick solution is high, but patents can also delay a resolution if they impede diffusion, production, and implementation.

Reflecting this concern, in both World War II and the COVID-19 crisis there were early calls for compulsory licensing, patent pooling, and other approaches to relaxing intellectual property rights to promote diffusion (see Contreras [2020] for an overview). There are two potential limits to these approaches. One is feasibility: for many important technologies, like penicillin, synthetic rubber, and vaccines, the scale-up problem requires costly know-how transfer as well, which may limit the impact of relaxing patents alone. A second is desirability; proposals to relax patent rights in crises must consider not only the effects on innovation during the crisis but also the dynamic effects on precrisis incentives to do research on potential solutions.[18]

In the context of government-funded research, there is also the narrower question of who should bear title to resulting inventions. This issue was contentious during World War II and is again today. Private actors bring advanced R&D capabilities and must be assured return on investment to incentivize their participation. At the same time, the government may wish to guard against profiteering and promote broad diffusion.

Highlighting this tension is that although OSRD initially sought the right to decide whether to file patents on inventions it funded, and the disposition of title and licenses, a number of leading firms refused to sign contracts under these terms. Stewart (1948, 222) summarized the problem:

[The] NDRC was asking America's leading companies to take their best men off their own problems and put them (at cost) on problems selected by NDRC, and then leave it to NDRC to determine what rights, if any, the companies would get out of inventions made by their staff members. . . . These companies had acquired a great deal of "know-how" as a result of years of effort and the expenditure of their own funds, often in large amounts. The research they were being asked to undertake was in many cases in line with their regular work . . . and might result in some cases in inventions they might be expected to make at some future date at the appropriate place in their own programs. In some cases the Government contract involved minor adaptations of past inventions made by the contractors, and in such cases the contribution to the final product attributable to the work financed by the Government was relatively insignificant. But under the patent clause thus far offered by NDRC a company might be excluded from using its inventions under an NDRC contract in its own business, and might even find its competitors licensed by the Government while licenses were refused to it.

These concerns are representative of the challenge facing crisis R&D efforts, and Stewart points to many reasons why ceding patent rights may be a smart policy choice. Many of these concerns could be compensated by cash, but one requires assigning rights: firms that retain title are incentivized not only to participate in crisis R&D but also to put top talent and other resources into the crisis problem. Facing this imperative, the OSRD developed contract language giving contractors right of first refusal in patenting inventions produced under contract, plus title, subject to a royalty-free license for military use.[19]

This policy led to one of the main criticisms of OSRD by Kilgore and its other liberal critics, who objected to giving away publicly funded technologies to private firms, contributing to concentration of economic power and effectively forcing taxpayers to pay twice for technologies—first by funding them, then through monopoly prices (Sampat 2020). Bush acknowledged these concerns but feared that asserting government ownership would throw a "monkey wrench" into the public-private partnership that had developed during the war and dissuade participation by firms with the requisite capabilities (Bush 1943).

These issues resurfaced in the pandemic. There have been calls by state attorneys general to invoke the never-used "march in" provisions of the Bayh-Dole Act to promote broader access to Gilead's antiviral remdesivir, which—according to several legal scholars—the NIH helped develop. Scholars, activists, and others have also pointed to NIH and BARDA funding of, and potential government patent rights in, Moderna's mRNA platform, and some have proposed leveraging these rights to promote broader access as well (Stone 2020). Activists also called on the government to build access and diffusion provisions into Warp Speed contracts as a condition of public funding (e.g., Kashyap and Wurth 2020). Others have argued that firms are putting in much of the funding and taking most of the risk, and they would not have participated in Warp Speed absent patent rights (Brown 2021). A spokesperson for the HHS, the parent agency of BARDA and NIH, reflected a similar position with regard to waiving government ownership in the vaccine contracts with Pfizer (which did not include push funding, unlike the contracts with other firms), arguing "When the US government does not fund creation of any of the intellectual property, as is the case in our agreement with Pfizer, the government is not entitled to any rights to a company's intellectual property," adding that "the most critical factor was the need to obtain as quickly as possible sufficient doses of safe and effective vaccines against COVID-19 to save lives" (Lupkin 2020).

The key trade-off for crisis patent policy is between incentivizing innovation and diffusing the results rapidly and broadly, each of which can contribute to timely resolution of a crisis. The relative importance of these factors can guide policies concerning the allocation of property rights—though in practice this can be difficult to calibrate, and more evidence on striking this balance would be useful.

D.   Managing Disruptions to the Innovation System

A fourth tension we want to highlight is a result of reallocating inventive activity from regular R&D to crisis R&D. By diverting funding and human capital to new problems, crisis R&D efforts disrupt the regular functioning of the innovation system. This diversion can interrupt ongoing research—some of which might depreciate quickly (e.g., if specimens spoil) or get abandoned entirely (e.g., if crises breathe life into new fields [Sec. V] or reduce costs of switching fields). It might also crowd out new projects. For example, the race for COVID-19 vaccines and therapies required organizational pivoting and may have displaced other research or trials in the R&D pipeline (e.g., Agarwal and Gaule 2021).[20] This may have likewise been the case for academic research, as investigators pivoted to COVID-19-inspired work (e.g., Pai 2020).

When university faculty or students are involved, these disruptions can extend beyond research to education and scientific training. Crisis R&D organizers can nevertheless take steps to limit interference. For example, to avoid disrupting universities by relocating their staff, much of the OSRD's work was done using university facilities, sometimes in investigators' own labs. Disruptions to the normal functioning of the innovation system can also arise by other means. In recent work, one of us has studied compulsory secrecy policy in World War II, which enabled the patent office to suspend patent examination on inventions whose disclosure was considered a security risk and order the inventor to "in nowise publish or disclose the invention or any hitherto unpublished details" (Gross 2022). The US Patent and Trademark Office's secrecy program effectively suspended the normal functioning of the patent system for a subset of technologies.

Though crisis R&D can create collateral damage, this of course does not imply inefficiency: the large social returns can significantly outweigh its costs. Moreover, insofar as there are consequences to scientific disruptions, they are borne in the future, in the form of innovation that has gone missing. Whether this is a favorable trade-off ultimately depends on the urgency of the crisis problem. In the most extreme cases, the intertemporal elasticity of substitution is infinite: without short-run impact there may not be a long run. In these cases, the only option is an all-out attack. More generally, the level of urgency in a crisis implies the degree of acceptable interruption to business as usual.

V.   Long-Run Effects of Crisis R&D

The effects of crisis R&D can also outlive the crisis itself. The impacts of the OSRD's work were significant and far ranging, influencing not only the war's outcome but also postwar entrepreneurship and innovation, innovation policy, and the postwar US economy. Might the same be the case for COVID-19? The book has yet to be written, but there are already signs of lasting effects, from durable shifts to remote work (e.g., Barrero, Bloom, and Davis 2020) to a surge of vaccine R&D (Regalado 2021). Here we review what some of these impacts were in the World War II crisis. If the past is an indication, the COVID-19 pandemic could have lasting effects on what innovation is produced, by whom, and how for years to come.

A.   Contemporary Impacts

Contemporaries and historians view OSRD as having had a major impact on the Allied war effort (Bush 1945; Baxter 1946). Yet the OSRD's work also set the agenda for military R&D in the Cold War era, when missiles, missile detection, and nuclear weapons were focus points, among others—technologies that built directly on the work of the OSRD's Rad Lab, Jet Propulsion Lab, and nuclear fission project. Much of its work also led to development of dual-use technologies like microwave communications and computing, and drugs and medical therapies like penicillin that transformed civilian medical care. Stewart (1948, 298) wrote of the dual-use nature of OSRD's work, noting that "its part in the winning of the war was its greatest contribution," but its full impact would be realized when "the civilian counterparts of its military developments begin to exert their influence upon life in the United States and in the world at large."

Yet the war also interrupted research pipelines and careers, causing some research inputs to be rationed, diverting resources and attention to problems of military importance, and even drafting scientists into the military (much like COVID-19 temporarily forced labs to shut down and severed ongoing experiments, led many researchers to reorient their work to COVID-19-related problems, and saw some scientists redeployed to hands-on pandemic response). Though OSRD's work yielded numerous high-impact dual-use technologies, this may not have come free if it crowded out research in other fields—especially if these directional shifts outlived the war itself. Although it is difficult to know what would have been invented absent the war, some research streams were likely abandoned as wartime demands took over the agenda.

B. Long-Run Effects on Innovation, Entrepreneurship, and Economic Growth

Though the war ended in 1945, OSRD's impact reverberated for decades after. Anecdotally, it did more than simply advance the state of the art: it opened up entire new fields of research. Stewart (1948, 102) wrote of the CMR: "The shift in emphasis and even in direction was enormous. Many subjects of minor importance in peacetime become of controlling importance in war," with some even "born of war." This was in part because some problems were introduced by the conditions of war, but in other cases a result of new technologies opening up new frontiers for research, like penicillin and infectious disease, or preexisting science advancing to a stage where more applications could be explored, such as with nuclear energy.

In Gross and Sampat (2020a), we show that OSRD had long-lasting effects on the direction and domestic geography of US technological innovation, catalyzing fields and locations that were a locus of OSRD activity, and leading innovation in the treated fields to be increasingly concentrating in a handful of technology hubs, including regions like Boston/Route-128 and Silicon Valley. Notably, this innovation appears to have translated into entrepreneurship and ultimately job growth: counties with more OSRD funding in the 1940s saw faster start-up growth in high-tech industries like communications and electronics over the next 30 years, as well as higher manufacturing employment in these industries. Broadly, it appears that entire local innovation ecosystems sprung up in these regions, supported by universities, federally funded research centers, and private invention. An important residual question that we are continuing to study is to what degree the "OSRD shock" was self-sustaining or fed by continued federal R&D spending in the Cold War era, to the extent it mirrored the distribution of OSRD spending.

CMR may have had similar effects on medical research, pharmaceutical innovation, and the life sciences—a topic we are currently exploring in ongoing work. The above quote from Stewart claims this is so, to say the least. Anecdotally, the wartime effort also endowed participant firms with intellectual property, tacit knowledge, and other advantages that persisted in the postwar era. For example, this is thought to be true for firms that participated in penicillin research and production, among others.

Pfizer is a case in point. Prior to World War II, Pfizer was a chemical manufacturer that in the 1910s and 1920s developed a method of fermenting citric acid. Because of its expertise in fermentation, in the 1940s it was contracted into the effort to scale up production of penicillin, which succeeded and led to its discovery of one of the first tetracycline antibiotics in 1950 (oxytetracycline). These discoveries, combined with a shift in strategic focus, transformed the firm into a pharmaceutical company. Between 1930 and 1945, Pfizer filed on average 3.4 patents per year. By the 1950s, it was filing 42.8 patents per year. Today it is the second-largest global pharmaceutical company, with more than $50 billion in revenue.

C. Impacts on S&T Policy

As we described in Section II, OSRD laid a foundation for postwar S&T policy, which was led in peacetime by a constellation of federal agencies, including DOD, AEC, NASA, NSF, and NIH. The Bush Report (Bush 1945) was itself a product of World War II, and one of the channels through which OSRD had a lasting impact on science policy—though it focused on peacetime and did not offer a framework for crisis innovation policy per se. Several institutional innovations developed or refined during the war remained features of the postwar era. The federal R&D contract itself was one. A. Hunter Dupree (1970, 457–58) has called it "one of the great inventions of the NDRC-OSRD" and "the glue which held the whole system together," and its use continues today. Modern indirect cost recovery and government patent rights also trace back to OSRD (Rosenzweig 2001). In medicine, the NIH "dual" peer review model that emerged in the postwar era was based on the CMR/DMS approach we described above (Mandel 1996).

D.   Impacts on the Organization of Science

Finally, it also seems the scale and intensity of the wartime effort left a lasting impact on the organization of science. This in part took shape in the birth, and growth, of federally funded research centers and the rise of the research university (Geiger 1993). But wartime experience also trained a generation of researchers and R&D managers and established new partnerships (1) among researchers and (2) between firms, institutions, and the federal government, which persisted into the postwar era.

In more ongoing work, we are also evaluating these impacts. World War II research labs employed thousands of recent college graduates, PhD students, and recent PhDs, providing hands-on experience and serving as a feeder to graduate study, faculty positions, and industry jobs. Managing a sprawling research organization was itself a distinctive talent, and many of OSRD's senior scientists and lab directors went on to become university presidents, provosts, and deans after the war. Moreover, the collaboration of researchers involved in the crisis effort may have forged new productive relationships among scientists. The war effort drew established academics from around the country to major research labs and research hubs, where they often worked together before dispersing at the end of the war, with most returning to their home institutions. Examples include the scientists who relocated to Los Alamos, or Fred Terman (colloquially, "the father of Silicon Valley"), who was drawn to Harvard to direct research on radar countermeasures, brought colleagues, and later returned to Stanford, bringing new students with him.

These partnerships are not limited to the academy. World War II effectively gave birth to the defense R&D contractor: firms such as Western Electric and General Electric were top OSRD contractors in the 1940s and remained top defense R&D contractors 25 years later (Office of the Secretary of Defense 1966–75). Not surprisingly, major aircraft suppliers to the War Department such as Boeing, Lockheed, and Douglas could also be found at the top of this list in the 1960s, as they remain today.

VI.   Insights for the Post-COVID-19 Era

Looking forward, one of the major lessons from World War II and COVID-19 alike is that crisis innovation problems are different from those in ordinary times, presenting distinct pressures, challenges, and opportunities (Gross and Sampat 2021). Urgency is a paramount feature of crisis problems, and with it the large social returns to a successful response. Crises raise difficult tensions around appropriability, but may also in some cases inspire a kind of altruism as those who can contribute their efforts to the cause. Crisis innovation may also benefit from top-down coordination, parallel efforts (e.g., multiple vaccine candidates, approaches to penicillin production, or uranium enrichment techniques) until one succeeds, and manufacturing capacity at risk—approaches that may be infeasible or inefficient in regular times.

In what kinds of situations might these lessons apply? To a first order—per our notion of what a crisis is—it is any situation where urgent problems present and innovation can contribute to their resolution. War, pandemics, and man-made or natural disasters and environmental catastrophes might fit this definition: getting a COVID-19 vaccine or large stocks of penicillin a week sooner had the potential to save lives. Slower-moving calamities like climate change, or long-standing problems like poverty or degenerative diseases (e.g., Alzheimer's disease), we might consider grand challenges for humanity rather than immediate crises per se. Whether the World War II or COVID-19 models could be adapted to grand challenge-type problems is a question that merits further exploration, but the possibility is intriguing. Urgency, however, can be a galvanizing force that is difficult to reproduce in grand challenge settings.

It is notable that both crisis R&D efforts were built on the available stock of basic knowledge. In World War II, this included advances in electrical engineering and microwave communications, the recent discovery and purification of penicillin, and initial results on nuclear fission, among others. Similarly, the first two FDA-approved COVID-19 vaccines built on decades of basic research on mRNA—work that science funding agencies had in fact initially declined to support, but which experienced breakthroughs in the mid-2000s (Garde 2020). Numerous other COVID-19 treatments and countermeasures, from the antiviral drug remdesivir to indoor ventilation, have also benefited from basic research or basic understanding. The ability of the scientific community to pivot to crisis problems, even when funding agencies were slower to do so, points to the value of a highly trained research corps. A second lesson, or perhaps reminder (echoing Bush), is thus the importance of investing in basic science, scientific training, and scientific institutions in regular times: these are the resources that crisis innovation efforts will draw from.

Returning to the World War II context, economists have argued that wartime medical research pointed to new technological opportunities that were pursued in the pharmaceutical industry after the war (Temin 1980; Malerba and Orsenigo 2015). There is considerable enthusiasm among both the scientific community and the public that many of the scientific and technological advances made in the present crisis, especially surrounding mRNA vaccine development approaches, may do the same. As in the aftermath of World War II, the COVID-19 crisis may usher in new forms of R&D management and collaboration, such as new models of public-private partnerships or increasingly open and collaborative science, as materialized in the early days of the pandemic (Kupferschmidt 2020). Norms around scientific communication might also change with the use of preprints and crowdsourced peer review as means of scientific dissemination. Reflecting on the ACTIV program, NIH director Francis Collins has stated, "I can't imagine we'll go back to doing clinical research in the future the way we did in the past" (Yong 2021).

If past is prologue, we may yet see a rethinking of US science and technology policy frameworks as well. Beyond more funding for basic research, it seems plausible that aspects of the COVID-19 model, including more downstream government funding in applied activities, and the use of large procurement agreements as R&D incentives, could outlive the pandemic. The pandemic may also prompt a reassessment of the extent to which government-funded biomedical research should be targeted at specific outcomes (including planning for future crises) and how to set priorities across them, issues that the Bush framework and the institutions built around it sidestepped (Nelson and Romer 1996; Nelson 1997; Stokes 1997). Aspects of the response, in particular difficulties large funders had in pivoting to crisis problems, also raise questions about whether the existing institutional setup is sufficiently flexible, or whether we need to invest in new agencies to respond quickly and nimbly in a coordinated way (à la OSRD) to activate in future crises. The trade-offs here are delicate, and as we have emphasized throughout, we still need much more systematic evidence on what worked and what did not during the pandemic, or in other crises where innovation was key to the response. Notwithstanding, it is a fair bet that like World War II, the pandemic is poised to have lasting effects not only on the direction of innovation but also on innovation policy.[21]

Endnotes

Author email addresses: Gross (daniel.gross@duke.edu), Sampat (bns3@cumc.columbia .edu). We thank Josh Lerner, Scott Stern, Ken Shadlen, Sherry Glied, and participants at the 2021 NBER EIPE workshop for helpful comments. We also thank Harvard Business School and the NBER Innovation Policy grant (2016) for financial support. This material is based upon work supported by the National Science Foundation under Grant No. 1951470. All errors are our own. For acknowledgments, sources of research support, and disclosure of

the authors' material financial relationships, if any, please see https://www.nber.org/books
-and-chapters/entrepreneurship-and-innovation-policy-and-economy-volume-1/crisis
-innovation-policy-world-war-ii-covid-19.

1. Conant (1947, 202–203) wrote, "Time set a limit on what could be done: the basic knowledge at hand had to be turned to good account" and "For the duration of the war further advances in pure science for the most part were suspended."

2. As Mowery (1997) has argued, the Bush Report had a strong imprint on the ideology of S&T policy, including on the importance of basic research and the appropriate division of labor between the government, firms, and universities. Its actual policy recommendations had less of an impact. Its flagship recommendation was a single major foundation supporting basic research, the National Research Foundation. The idea that a single major agency should support research was uncontroversial. But critics of the Bush approach, most prominently Senator Harley Kilgore (D-WV), objected to the limited public accountability of the proposed foundation, geographic and institutional inequity in funding, and lack of attention to applied research guided by specific socioeconomic priorities. Kevles (1977, 16) summarizes: "The differences between Bush and Kilgore boiled down to a basic issue: Kilgore wanted a foundation responsive to lay control and prepared to support research for the advancement of the general welfare; Bush and his colleagues wanted an agency run by scientists mainly for the purpose of advancing science."

3. For example, James Shannon, the NIH head who presided over its postwar expansion during the 1950s and 1960s, was a central part of the CMR malaria research program. Similarly, when the NSF was eventually enacted, its first director was Alan T. Waterman, who had been OSRD's director of field operations.

4. Gittelman (2016) and others have argued, however, the translational approach largely adheres to the linear paradigm.

5. Notably, these mechanisms featured much more prominently in the US COVID-19 effort than they have in regular times.

6. The act was later extended to large businesses as well, through executive order.

7. By comparison, real gross domestic product grew about 10-fold over this period.

8. Reflecting these issues, well before the pandemic economists and others had called for new policy instruments (e.g., advanced market commitments and prizes) beyond the standard biomedical innovation policy tools to stimulate vaccine innovation and development for tropical infectious diseases (Kremer and Williams 2010). Though there were some notable successes (Kremer, Levin, and Snyder 2020), previously these did not attract broad policy support in the United States and other developed countries, perhaps because many of the needed vaccines were for diseases that did not affect rich-country taxpayers.

9. Source: NIH RePORTER keyword search for COVID (as in COVID-19), CoV (as in SARS-CoV-2), and nCoV (as in 2019-nCoV) in the title, abstract, or keywords of research grants from 2020 and 2021. Data as of April 1, 2021.

10. Source: NSF Advanced Search tool, keyword search for COVID (as in COVID-19), CoV (as in SARS-CoV-2), and nCoV (as in 2019-nCoV) in the title or abstract of research grants from 2020 and 2021. Data as of April 1, 2021.

11. BARDA was explicitly intended to bridge the "valley of death" where NIH research failed to enter development and commercialization. BARDA's funding mechanisms included various flexibilities that NIH lacked, including the ability to provide large advanced payments to companies before delivery of products, and the ability to circumvent some antitrust rules to facilitate cooperation among firms. It funded research with an eye toward procurement by the National Strategic Stockpile of medical countermeasures and at least initially had a heavy biodefense focus—though more recently that has expanded to include other subjects, such as research on new antibiotics. It used both "push" funding (including late-stage R&D contracts) and "pull" incentives (market commitments) to support innovation (Larsen and Disbrow 2017).

12. Source: https://www.medicalcountermeasures.gov. Accessed April 1, 2021.

13. Another way in which these commitments differed from standard ones is that they put the United States near the front of the queue for purchasing the vaccines once developed. That is, they may also have been an instrument of so-called vaccine nationalism (Price et al. 2020; Sampat and Shadlen 2021).

14. The lack of coordination may in part reflect the much broader scale and finer division of labor in the innovation system today, which might make coordination more challenging than it was in past crises.

15. Article counts obtained by searching Google Scholar and the National Library of Medicine's PubMed database for articles with the phrase "COVID-19." Results as of April 1, 2021.

16. Individual DOD branches, namely the Air Force, have also recently experimented with bottom-up approaches to Small Business Innovation Research awards (Howell et al. 2021).

17. In some cases, these agglomeration benefits were very explicit. For example, MIT Rad Lab spun out a radar countermeasures research group that set up shop 2 miles away at Harvard—and the two could test new radar sets, radar-jamming, and antijamming technology on each other from the rooftops.

18. It is notable, however, that at least two firms, AstraZeneca and Moderna, have committed to not enforce their patents during the pandemic. Although there is some uncertainty about these pledges—including who decides when the pandemic is over—we have not yet seen broad "generic" entry into the fields, suggesting that either patents may not be the binding constraint on competition or diffusion, or profitable generic entry requires longer horizons.

19. This language became known as the "long form" clause, reflecting its length, and it was used with most industrial contractors. OSRD continued using a variant of its original patent clause—the "short form" clause—in specific categories of contracts, giving the government presumption of title where it supplied significant equipment, personnel, or training to support the work. The short form clause was standard for major OSRD-funded laboratories at academic institutions. CMR contracts were also subject to the short form clause, and atomic energy contracts were converted to short form to ensure that the government controlled intellectual property rights in this field.

20. Interestingly, recent evidence suggests the effect on clinical trial launches for drugs targeting non-COVID-19 diseases was limited to a fairly modest, but statistically significant, 5% decline (Agarwal and Gaule 2021). Note that distortions can arise even within a crisis R&D portfolio: as Bryan et al. (2020) argue, racing behavior can result in too much investment in quicker-to-develop partial solutions (e.g., COVID-19 therapies or repurposed treatments), which undermine incentives for longer-horizon, higher-value innovation (e.g., vaccines) by reducing the size of the remaining market. This intuition is similar to that of Hill and Stein (2021).

21. Recent guidance from the White House suggests that change may indeed be in the offing. In a letter to the incoming White House science advisor Eric Lander in January 2021, echoing President Roosevelt's request of Bush in 1944, then President-elect Biden asked Lander to make recommendations for science policy in relation to public health, climate change, broader technological leadership, and shared prosperity (see Biden 2021).

References

Agarwal, Ruchir, and Patrick Gaule. 2021. "What Drives Innovation? Lessons from COVID-19 R&D." Discussion Paper no. 14079, IZA Institute of Labor Economics, Bonn.

Appel, Toby A. 2000. *Shaping Biology: The National Science Foundation and American Biological Research, 1945–1975*. Baltimore: Johns Hopkins University Press.

Athey, Susan, Michael Kremer, Christopher Snyder, and Alex Tabarrok. 2020. "In the Race for a Coronavirus Vaccine, We Must Go Big. Really, Really Big." https://www.nytimes.com/2020/05/04/opinion/coronavirus-vaccine.html.

Azoulay, Pierre, Erica Fuchs, Anna P. Goldstein, and Michael Kearney. 2019. "Funding Breakthrough Research: Promises and Challenges of the 'ARPA Model.'" *Innovation Policy and the Economy* 19 (1): 69–96.

Azoulay, Pierre, and Danielle Li. 2020. "Scientific Grant Funding." In *Innovation and Public Policy*, ed. Austan Goolsbee and Benjamin Jones. Chicago: University of Chicago Press.

Balconi, Margherita, Stefano Brusoni, and Luigi Orsenigo. 2010. "In Defence of the Linear Model: An Essay." *Research Policy* 39 (1): 1–13.

Barrero, Jose Maria, Nicholas Bloom, and Steven J. Davis. 2020. "Why Working from Home Will Stick." Working Paper no. 28731, NBER, Cambridge, MA.

Baxter, James Phinney. 1946. *Scientists Against Time*. Boston: Little, Brown.

Biden, Joseph R., Jr. 2021. "A Letter to Dr. Eric S. Lander, the President's Science Advisor and Nominee As Director of the Office of Science and Technology Policy." https://www.whitehouse.gov/briefing-room/statements-releases /2021/01/20/a-letter-to-dr-eric-s-lander-the-presidents-science-advisor-and -nominee-as-director-of-the-office-of-science-and-technology-policy

Brooks, Harvey. 1996. "The Evolution of US Science Policy." In *Technology, R&D, and the Economy*, ed. Bruce L. R. Smith and Claude E. Barfield. Washington, DC: Brookings Institution.

Brown, Alex. 2021. "Bayh-Dole Act Marks 40 Years of Innovation." https:// www.insideindianabusiness.com/story/43142910/bayhdole-act-marks-40 -years-of-innovation.

Bryan, Kevin A., Jorge Lemus, and Guillermo Marshall. 2020. "R&D Competition and the Direction of Innovation." Working paper.

Bush, Vannevar. 1943. "The Kilgore Bill." *Science* 98 (2557): 571–77.

———. 1944. *Preface to Organizing Scientific Research for War: The Administrative History of the Office of Scientific Research and Development*. Boston: Little, Brown.

———. 1945. *Science, the Endless Frontier: A Report to the President*. Washington, DC: Government Printing Office.

———. 1970. *Pieces of the Action*. New York: William Morrow.

Butler, Declan. 2008. "Translational Research: Crossing the Valley of Death." *Nature News* 453 (7197): 840–42.

Cohen, Jon. 2020. "Operation Warp Speed's Opaque Choices of COVID-19 Vaccines Draw Senate Scrutiny." https://www.sciencemag.org/news/2020/07 /operation-warp-speed-s-opaque-choices-covid-19-vaccines-draw-senate -scrutiny.

Cohrs, Rachel. 2021. "The Trump Administration Quietly Spent Billions in Hospital Funds on Operation Warp Speed." https://www.statnews.com/2021 /03/02/trump-administration-quietly-spent-billions-in-hospital-funds-on -operation-warp-speed.

Conant, James B. 1947. "The Mobilization of Science for the War Effort." *American Scientist* 35 (2): 195–210.

Conti, Rena M., Susan Athey, Richard G. Frank, and Jonathan Gruber. 2020. "Generic Drug Repurposing for Public Health and National Security: COVID-19 and Beyond." https://www.healthaffairs.org/do/10.1377/hblog20201204 .541050/full.

Contreras, Jorge L. 2020. "Expanding Access to Patents for COVID-19." In *Assessing Legal Responses to COVID-19*, ed. Scott Burris, Sara de Guia, Lance Gable, Donna E. Levin, Wendy E. Parmet, and Nicolas P. Terry. Boston: Public Health Law Watch.

Cook-Deegan, Robert Mullan. 1996. "Does NIH Need a DARPA?" *Issues in Science and Technology* 13 (2): 25–28.

Cutler, David M., and Lawrence H. Summers. 2020. "The COVID-19 Pandemic and the $16 Trillion Virus." *Journal of the American Medical Association* 324 (15): 1495–96.

Dupree, A. Hunter. 1970. "The Great Instauration of 1940: The Organization of Scientific Research for War." In *The Twentieth-Century Sciences: Studies in the Biography of Ideas*, ed. Gerald Holton. New York: Norton.

Florko, Nicholas. 2020. "New Document Reveals Scope and Structure of Operation Warp Speed and Underscores Vast Military Involvement." https://www.stat news.com/2020/09/28/operation-warp-speed-vast-military-involvement.

Fox, Daniel M. 1987. "The Politics of the NIH Extramural Program, 1937–1950." *Journal of the History of Medicine and Allied Sciences* 42 (4): 447–66.

Garde, Damian. 2020. "The Story of mRNA: How a Once-Dismissed Idea Became a Leading Technology in the COVID Vaccine Race." https://www.statnews .com/2020/11/10/the-story-of-mrna-how-a-once-dismissed-idea-became-a -leading-technology-in-the-covid-vaccine-race.

Geiger, Roger L. 1993. *Research and Relevant Knowledge: American Research Universities since World War II*. Oxford: Oxford University Press.

Gittelman, Michelle. 2016. "The Revolution Re-visited: Clinical and Genetics Research Paradigms and the Productivity Paradox in Drug Discovery." *Research Policy* 45 (8): 1570–85.

Gross, Daniel P. 2022. "The Hidden Costs of Securing Innovation: The Manifold Impacts of Compulsory Invention Secrecy." *Management Science*, forthcoming.

Gross, Daniel P., and Bhaven N. Sampat. 2020a. "Inventing the Endless Frontier: The Effects of the World War II Research Effort on Post-war Innovation." Working Paper no. 27375, NBER, Cambridge, MA.

———. 2020b. "Organizing Crisis Innovation: Lessons from World War II." Working Paper no. 27909, NBER, Cambridge, MA.

———. 2021. "The Economics of Crisis Innovation Policy: A Historical Perspective." Working Paper no. w28335, NBER, Cambridge, MA.

Hill, Ryan and Carolyn Stein. 2021. "Race to the Bottom: Competition and Quality in Science." Working Paper.

Howell, Sabrina T., Jason Rathje, John Van Reenen, and Jun Wong. 2021. "Opening Up Military Innovation: Causal Effects of 'Bottom-Up' Reforms to US Defense Research." Working Paper no. 28700, NBER, Cambridge, MA.

Hoyt, Kendall. 2006. "Vaccine Innovation: Lessons from World War II." *Journal of Public Health Policy* 27 (1): 38–57.

———. 2012. *Long Shot: Vaccines for National Defense*. Cambridge, MA: Harvard University Press.

Kaiser, Jocelyn. 2020. "NIH Organizes Hunt for Drugs." *Science* 368 (6489): 351.

Kashyap, Aruna, and Margaret Wurth. 2020. "Whoever Finds the Vaccine Must Share It." https://www.hrw.org/report/2020/10/29/whoever-finds-vaccine -must-share-it/strengthening-human-rights-and-transparency.

Keefer, Chester S. 1969. "Dr. Richards as Chairman of the Committee on Medical Research." *Annals of Internal Medicine* 71 (8): 61–70.

Kevles, Daniel J. 1977. "The National Science Foundation and the Debate over Postwar Research Policy, 1942–1945: A Political Interpretation of Science— The Endless Frontier." *Isis* 68 (1): 5–26.

———. 1978. *The Physicists: The History of a Scientific Community in Modern America*. New York, NY: Knopf.

Kilgore, Harley M. 1943. "The Science Mobilization Bill." *Science* 98 (2537): 151–52.

Kiszewski, Anthony E., Ekaterina Galkina Cleary, Matthew J. Jackson, and Fred D. Ledley. 2020. "The Role of NIH Funding in Vaccine Readiness: Foundational Research and NIH Funding Underlying Candidate SARS-CoV-2 Vaccines." *Vaccine* 39 (17): 2458–66.

Kleinman, Daniel Lee. 1995. *Politics on the Endless Frontier: Postwar Research Policy in the United States*. Durham, NC: Duke University Press.

Kremer, Michael, Jonathan Levin, and Christopher M. Snyder. 2020. "Advance Market Commitments: Insights from Theory and Experience." *AEA Papers and Proceedings* 110:269–73.

Kremer, Michael, and Heidi Williams. 2010. "Incentivizing Innovation: Adding to the Tool Kit." *Innovation Policy and the Economy* 10 (1): 1–17.

Kupferschmidt, Kai. 2020. "'A Completely New Culture of Doing Research.' Coronavirus Outbreak Changes How Scientists Communicate." https://www.sciencemag.org/news/2020/02/completely-new-culture-doing-research-coronavirus-outbreak-changes-how-scientists.

Larsen, Joseph C., and Gary L. Disbrow. 2017. "Project BioShield and the Biomedical Advanced Research Development Authority: A 10-Year Progress Report on Meeting US Preparedness Objectives for Threat Agents." *Clinical Infectious Diseases* 64 (10): 1430–34.

Levin, Richard C., Alvin K. Klevorick, Richard R. Nelson, Sidney G. Winter, Richard Gilbert, and Zvi Griliches. 1987. "Appropriating the Returns from Industrial Research and Development." *Brookings Papers on Economic Activity* 1987 (3): 783–831.

Lupkin, Sydney. 2020. "How Operation Warp Speed's Big Vaccine Contracts Could Stay Secret." https://www.npr.org/sections/health-shots/2020/09/29/917899357/how-operation-warp-speeds-big-vaccine-contracts-could-stay-secret.

Malerba, Franco, and Luigi Orsenigo. 2015. "The Evolution of the Pharmaceutical Industry." *Business History* 57 (5–6): 664–87.

Mandel, Richard. 1996. *A Half Century of Peer Review, 1946–1996*. Bethesda, MD: National Institutes of Health.

Matheny, Jason, Michael Mair, and Bradley Smith. 2008. "Cost/Success Projections for US Biodefense Countermeasure Development." *Nature Biotechnology* 26 (9): 981–83.

Moses, Hamilton, David H. M. Matheson, Sarah Cairns-Smith, Benjamin P. George, Chase Palisch, and E. Ray Dorsey. 2015. "The Anatomy of Medical Research: US and International Comparisons." *Journal of the American Medical Association* 313 (2): 174–89.

Mowery, David C. 1997. "The Bush Report after 50 Years: Blueprint or Relic?" In *Science for the 21st Century: The Bush Report Revisited*, ed. Claude E. Barfield. Washington, DC: American Enterprise Institute.

Navarro, Peter. 2020. "Memorandum to the Coronavirus Task Force." https://coronavirus.house.gov/sites/democrats.coronavirus.house.gov/files/PHLOW_SSCC_0017388_Redacted.pdf.

Nelson, Richard R. 1997. "Why the Bush Report has Hindered an Effective Civilian Technology Policy." In *Science for the 21st Century: The Bush Report Revisited*, ed. Claude E. Barfield. Washington, DC: American Enterprise Institute.

Nelson, Richard R., and Paul M. Romer. 1996. "Science, Economic Growth, and Public Policy." *Challenge* 39 (1): 9–21.

Office of the Secretary of Defense. 1966–75. "Military Prime Contract File." Record Group 330 (Records of the Office of the Secretary of Defense), US National Archives and Records Administration, Washington, DC.

Owens, Larry. 1994. "The Counterproductive Management of Science in the Second World War: Vannevar Bush and the Office of Scientific Research and Development." *Business History Review* 68 (4): 515–76.

Pai, Madhukar. 2020. "Covidization of Research: What Are the Risks?" *Nature Medicine* 26 (8): 1159.

Piller, Charles. 2021. "Many Scientists Citing Two Scandalous COVID-19 Papers Ignore their Retractions." https://www.sciencemag.org/news/2021/01/many -scientists-citing-two-scandalous-covid-19-papers-ignore-their-retractions.

Price, Nicholson, Rachel Sachs, Jacob S. Sherkow, and Lisa Larrimore Ouellette. 2020. "Are COVID-19 Vaccine Advance Purchases a Form of Vaccine Nationalism, an Effective Spur to Innovation, or Something in Between?" https:// writtendescription.blogspot.com/2020/08/are-covid-19-vaccine-advance -purchases.html.

Regalado, Antonio. 2021. "The Next Act for Messenger RNA Could Be Bigger than COVID Vaccines." https://www.technologyreview.com/2021/02/05/1017366 /messenger-rna-vaccines-covid-hiv.

Richards, A. N. 1946. "The Impact of the War on Medicine." *Science* 103 (2680): 575–78.

Romer, Paul. 2020. "What It Takes to Be a Leader in Both Basic Science and Technological Progress." https://paulromer.net/statement-for-house-budget-comittee.

Rosenzweig, Robert M. 2001. *The Political University: Policy, Politics, and Presidential Leadership in the American Research University.* Baltimore: Johns Hopkins University Press.

Rothman, David J. 1991. *Strangers at the Bedside: A History of How Law and Bioethics Transformed Medical Decision Making.* New York: Basic.

Sampat, Bhaven N. 2012. "Mission-oriented Biomedical Research at the NIH." *Research Policy* 41 (10): 1729–41.

———. 2020. "Whose Drugs Are These?" *Issues in Science and Technology* 36 (4): 42–48.

Sampat, Bhaven N., and Kenneth C. Shadlen. 2021. "The COVID-19 Innovation System." *Health Affairs* 40 (3): 400–409.

Slaoui, Moncef, and Matthew Hepburn. 2020. "Developing Safe and Effective COVID Vaccines—Operation Warp Speed's Strategy and Approach." *New England Journal of Medicine* 383 (18): 1701–1703.

Smith, Bruce L. R. 2011. *American Science Policy since World War II.* Washington, DC: Brookings Institution Press.

Stewart, Irvin. 1948. *Organizing Scientific Research for War: The Administrative History of the Office of Scientific Research and Development.* Boston: Little, Brown.

Stokes, Donald E. 1997. *Pasteur's Quadrant: Basic Science and Technological Innovation.* Washington, DC: Brookings Institution.

Stone, Judy. 2020. "The People's Vaccine: Moderna's Coronavirus Vaccine Was Largely Funded by Taxpayer Dollars." https://www.forbes.com/sites/judy stone/2020/12/03/the-peoples-vaccine-modernas-coronavirus-vaccine-was -largely-funded-by-taxpayer-dollars.

Swain, Donald C. 1962. "The Rise of a Research Empire: NIH, 1930 to 1950." *Science* 138 (3546): 1233–37.

Swann, John Patrick. 1983. "The Search for Synthetic Penicillin during World War II." *British Journal for the History of Science* 16 (2): 154–90.

Tabarrok, Alex. 2020. "The Case for Going Big Is Still Strong." https://margin alrevolution.com/marginalrevolution/2020/12/buy-capacity-not-doses.html.

Temin, Peter. 1980. *Taking Your Medicine: Drug Regulation in the United States.* Cambridge, MA: Harvard University Press.

Tucker, Jonathan B. 2009. "Developing Medical Countermeasures: From BioShield to BARDA." *Drug Development Research* 70 (4): 224–33.

Whoriskey, Peter, Douglas MacMillan, and Jonathan O'Connell. 2020. " 'Doomed to Fail': Why a \$4 trillion Bailout Couldn't Revive the American Economy." https://www.washingtonpost.com/graphics/2020/business/coronavirus -bailout-spending/.

Xue, Qiwei Claire, and Lisa Larrimore Ouellette. Forthcoming. "Innovation Policy and the Market for Vaccines." *Journal of Law and the Biosciences*.

Yong, Ed. 2021. "How Science Beat the Virus, and What It Lost in the Process." https://www.theatlantic.com/magazine/archive/2021/01/science-covid -19-manhattan-project/617262.